Company Analysis

Company Analysis

Determining Strategic Capability

Per Jenster and David Hussey

JOHN WILEY & SONS, LTD
Chichester • New York • Weinheim • Brisbane • Singapore • Toronto

Other Wiley Editorial Offices

John Wiley & Sons, Inc., 605 Third Avenue,
New York, NY 10158-0012, USA

WILEY-VCH GmbH, Pappelallee 3,
D-69469 Weinheim, Germany

John Wiley & Sons Australia Ltd, 33 Park Road, Milton
Queensland 4064, Australia

John Wiley & Sons (Asia) Pte Ltd, 2 Clementi Loop #02-01,
Jin Xing Distripark, Singapore 129809

John Wiley & Sons (Canada) Ltd, 22 Worcester Road,
Rexdale, Ontario M9W 1L1, Canada

British Library Cataloguing in Publication Data

A catalogue record for this book is available from the British Library

ISBN 0-471-49454-2

Typeset in 11/13 Times by Dorwyn Ltd, Rowlands Castle, Hampshire.
Printed and bound in Great Britain by Biddles Ltd, Guildford and King's Lynn.
This book is printed on acid-free paper responsibly manufactured from sustainable
forestry, in which at least two trees are planted for each one used for paper production.

Contents

Introduction

We decided to write this book for two reasons. The first is that for many organisations the task of assessing strengths and weaknesses has become an annual charade of little meaning, so much so that some organisations give little thought to this basic step in strategic thinking.

The second reason is that we could not find any book that covered this subject in the way that we felt it should be covered. This does not mean that there are not books which deal with aspects of it, but on the whole the strategy books give it little more than a page or two, or a chapter if you are lucky. Books on marketing, finance and other functional areas of management will often cover methods of analysis that are relevant, but not positioned in the context of an overall appraisal.

What has also happened is that some concepts that are still popular, like the value chain and core competencies, are positioned in a way that makes them seem remote from the task of assessing the overall position of the organisation, and few writers on strategy try to integrate them into the overall task.

Corporate strengths and weaknesses do not of themselves make good strategies, but they are an essential foundation. If you want a tree to grow, you ensure that its roots are sound and that it is planted in a carefully prepared hole. Then it may need a bit of nurturing. It might grow and do well even if you ignored these things, but the chances of success are reduced.

Many of the methods described here are also of value in

corporate turn-around situations, or in the due diligence process during acquisitions.

How organisations currently tackle the task of the corporate appraisal – the process of identifying strengths and weaknesses – is amazingly variable. Rather than produce endless lists, we have written some of these into an imaginary situation. To the best of our knowledge the Strategic Planning Society of the UK (and David Hussey was one of the founder members and a signatory of the original incorporation documents) has never had the sort of meeting we describe here, nor do any of the people or companies exist. But the methods our characters discuss are very real.

"THERE'S ONLY ONE WAY TO DO THE CORPORATE APPRAISAL"

There were nine people at the meeting of the Strategic Planning Society. They were a small group that had been working through the various stages in the preparation of a strategy, with a view to producing a booklet on best practice. The chairman of the meeting, Bill Symes, said 'This should be a short meeting. There is really only one way to undertake the internal appraisal, so it's just a question of working out a form of words to describe it clearly."

Nine heads nodded approval.

"Perhaps you would start the ball rolling, Jim," continued the chairman, 'By saying what you do in your organisation. The rest of us can add the bells and whistles to this.'

Jim Turner, Director of Strategic Management, of a Medium-Sized Engineering Company, with Operations in Several Countries

"Our method is pretty much the same as for the rest of you," Jim began, "We actually combine the internal strengths and weaknesses with the external appraisal which establishes the opportunities and threats, into a SWOT list. I think you will find an example of a SWOT analysis in most text books. We find it useful to be able to boil it all down to one large sheet of paper at the centre, and of course each of our businesses has its own list.'

He went on to explain the process, an example of which can be found, among other places, in Argenti (1980). All the assessments were made by the managers in the company, in a four-stage process:

1. Strengths and weaknesses are identified, defined and agreed in meetings of managers in one master list.
2. The planning team examines each item on the list in some detail, so that it can be more fully defined.
3. The carefully defined strengths and weaknesses are boiled down to a few pithy sentences in another meeting of the team.
4. Finally, it is sometimes found useful to rank them in order of importance.

"This way," he continued, "we tap into the greatest source of knowledge of our own organisation that exists. And the process helps to keep the strategic decisions connected to the grass roots of our management."

John Williams, Managing Director of a Firm of Consulting Engineers

John Williams vigorously voiced his support for this approach, but added refinements. "The mechanism of our process is slightly different, in that we involve all of our professional staff in the process, but otherwise it is much the same, except that we follow something we picked up in Thompson (1997). Our extra step is to relate our strengths and weakness to competitors and the needs of the wider business environment. We really try to get to our *relative* strengths and weaknesses, the things we do better or worse than our competitors."

Tom Ball, Planning Manager of the UK Operation of a US-Owned Bank

"I'm amazed," he said, "because that method may not get to the things that really matter. We use critical success factors (CSFs) the standards we should be achieving, and expect our general managers to evaluate their strengths and weaknesses against these. I was reading an article in *Strategic Change* (Pickton and Wright, 1998), where the authors argue that SWOT is often used uncritically, and is a naïve tool which may lead to strategic errors.

"Our management agrees with this, so what we do is to take about a dozen key success factors, assess objectively where we are in comparison with these and define the gap. Part of our appraisal process is to define the actions we will take to close the gap."

The chairman interrupted, asking how the CSFs were defined. Tom replied that they had been set for the whole world by the head office in the USA, which had employed a firm of management consultants to identify and define them for the global business.

"I am glad we do not have to work them out ourselves. One of the readings head office sent us was by a guy called Per Jenster. It looked a hell of a lot of work." (Jenster, 1987)

Jane Egan, Planning Director at the Head Office of a Food Manufacturing Company

"What I've heard so far worries me a bit. It seems as much about opinion as analysis. There may be value in knowing what managers think is important, but is this the same as turning the stones over to see what is underneath? Our approach is unashamedly analytical. The managers can debate the facts, but we do not let them obscure them.

"We try to establish where we are, how our resources are used, where we have vulnerabilities, and what our flexibility is. Nothing goes on our SWOT analysis that does not have a basis of objective evidence. Yes, of course we make a careful financial analysis of the company, at head office, SBU and country levels. Our main inspiration for how to relate our sources of earnings to our use of resources came from an old book by Peter Drucker. We've built on his ideas, and added quite a number of new areas." (Drucker, 1964)

Drucker's approach started at the product level, with an analysis of the revenue, market shares and profit contribution of each. He suggested a number of headings under which to classify the products, using terms such as "today's breadwinners", "yesterday's breadwinners" and "investments in management ego", and to follow these means that there is an element of looking outwards as well as internally. He had a lot to say about judging the value of each product, cautioning against taking accounting cost figures without first checking that they are relevant to the decisions that may be taken: he has a particular concern about apportioned costs, which enable a full cost to be calculated but which do not always reflect the true economic contribution. He then moves on to analyse resource utilisation (all aspects, including management), so that it is possible to see both the sources of profits, and the resources consumed by each. To all this he adds a marketing analysis and a "knowledge analysis", the latter having some relationship with the "distinctive competence" concept of a group of Harvard professors around the same time (Learned et al, 1965).

Roger McCall, a General Manager with the UK Petrol Retailing Division of an International Oil Giant

"I don't say that anything any of you do is wrong, and we somehow manage to get every one of the approaches you use into our corporate planning process, perhaps on the grounds that if you look at something from enough angles, you will find things you might otherwise have missed. We have found that the bottom-up SWOT approach can turn into a do-it-yourself hangman's kit, with managers identifying numerous corrective projects, which they cannot possibly undertake in the promised time. But that is a question of how the approach is managed, not the method itself.

"But what you have all missed out is the customer. Our internal appraisal has to be against how we provide value to the customer, and we have found that the most useful tool for this is Porter's value chain". (Porter, 1985)

Jim interjected, "We tried that, but all we got out of it was our organisation chart written out in his famous arrow diagram, instead of the normal pyramid. What was the use of that?'

"Nothing, if that's all you did." Roger went on to describe the way in which the processes under each of the generic headings were analysed, and attempts made to assess the value each delivered to the customer, and the costs of each. His team had to look outwards and find out what the customers valued, as well as virtually turning the management accounting system upside down to extract information in the way they needed it. The result was a very different way of thinking about internal strengths and weaknesses.

Samantha Brown, Analyst at a Diversified Conglomerate

"I thought when we started that we all meant the same thing by the corporate appraisal. I've now heard five different methods, none of which have much to do with what my management needs at head office level. Some of the methods may be relevant for our businesses, but I don't get involved with this.

" What we need is three things: careful financial analysis of the results at corporate and business level, so that we can take actions to continue to offer earnings growth, and know our financial strengths and weaknesses; a way of seeing all of our businesses in relation to each other, to get a handle on the distribution of our assets, profits and cash generation; and an analysis of how we create value for our shareholders.

"Financial analysis is fairly standard. For the way of seeing our businesses in relation to each other we use portfolio analysis. Our method is a nine-cell matrix, using scoring rules based on those in Hussey (1998). Also, we use portfolio analysis in a dynamic way, to see how the positions of our businesses are changing, so that we can take the necessary strategic decisions. We do not take much notice of the indicative strategy labels that some people attach to each cell of the matrix.

"Shareholder value thinking was influenced by several authors. Porter (1987) gave a useful listing of how a diversified company may create value, and we look at our overall activities against this. Goold, Campbell and Alexander (1994) provide another way of comparing what we do with what perhaps we should do, and we have found other useful areas to include in our appraisal in Buzzell and Gale (1987) in their work derived from the PIMs database.

J. K. Patel, Strategic Planning Manager at a Diversified Electronics Company

"I think all of your approaches miss the main point. The only way we can succeed is to define our core competencies, those we have and those we need to take us to where we want to go. Assessing these from our internal appraisal is what it's all about. Of course this means relating the internal appraisal to the external needs of the industry and our customers, and the way we hope to change the industry (and I'm not going to talk about that!). The first internal step is to identify what competencies we possess: at a later stage we determine what is important or missing.

"Hamel and Prahalad (1994) say that 'a competence is a bundle of constituent skills and technologies'. A core competence gives access to a wide variety of markets, delivers benefits to the customer, and is hard for competitors to copy. The definitions are engraved on my heart."

Dick Wade, Managing Director of a Medical Equipment Company

"J.K.'s approach to appraisal has a broad similarity with ours, but we believe that the core competence emphasis is inadequate. Our appraisal is largely based on establishing our capabilities, which are individual attributes rather than the clusters that make up a competence. In their *Harvard Business Review* article, Stalk, Evans and Shulman (1992) argue that core competencies emphasise 'technological and production expertise at specific points along the value chain, capabilities are more broadly based, encompassing the entire value chain. In this way capabilities are visible to the customer in a way that core competencies rarely are.'

"Capabilities are processes, rather than functions, and the appraisal has to dig deep to find them. They usually amount to a small part of a lot of people's individual jobs. Our strategic capabilities include the speedy development and introduction of new products, and dealer management, and the service support that we give to customers.

"What we do is audit the capabilities we have as the main plank of our appraisal. At a later stage we relate these to customer needs, and then select what needs to be done to sustain those which are critical to the strategy, and to acquire new capabilities which we see as critical, but which we are deficient in. Our philosophy is that the building blocks of strategy are not products or their markets, but the business processes of the company."

Bill Symes, Management Consultant

"As I said, there is only one way to do the corporate appraisal!" Everyone laughed. "I must say that I am glad that there are only nine of us here, as there seems to be no end to the different ways this task can be tackled.

"Despite all you have said, I think that what we do with our clients goes closer to the heart of what is wanted from the appraisal than some of the things that have been mentioned. We also use an analytical approach, and part of our method is very similar to what Jane described. We identify a platform of hard fact, which helps us see the success and failure areas, profit sources and resource analysis. We put more emphasis on leadership, management and structure than anyone has so far mentioned, and as outsiders it is easier for us to offer unwelcome news than it might be if we were employees. We use a number of pro forma analysis sheets. As a matter of interest, I came across a number of examples of very similar things in McNamee (1998). Of course, ours are even better!

"Where we deviate from Jane, and indeed from all of you, is in the way we audit various functions, such as HRM, to ensure that the main things they do, such as training, directly support the organisation's vision and strategies. Obviously, if the vision or strategies change, there may be a need to reassess these findings. We have another audit process to analyse technologies the organisation possesses."

He paused. "I think we are going to have to go back to the Society to ask them to think again about a booklet. What is really needed is a handbook, which sets out a number of methods with their advantages and disadvantages. Few methods are mutually exclusive, so it is possible that using a combination might enable issues arising from the proposal."

Note: The *Blackwell Encyclopedic Dictionary of Strategic Management* (Channon, 1997) has only one entry about the appraisal of strengths and weaknesses under SWOT analysis, which it describes as "a simple but powerful tool for evaluating the strategic position of the firm. . . . The requirements for undertaking such an analysis are relatively simple". The entry neglects to explain to the reader how to identify the various components of the sample SWOT list which is provided.

SOME THINGS TO THINK ABOUT

Here are a few questions that you may like to think about before moving on to the rest of this book:

- What do you think are the main merits and demerits of each of the approaches described?
- Do you think it might be useful to use more than one approach in the appraisal? Why?
- Does everyone at the meeting appear to be using the approaches competently?

SOMETHING ABOUT OUR EXPERIENCE

Both of us have undertaken consultancy exercises in which the appraisal was a key part. Per Jenster introduced the idea of a live appraisal as part of the executive MBA programme at Copenhagen Business School, and through this gains insight into some 30 to 50 different business situations every year, and has seen how in many cases the strategies of the companies have changed as a result. David Hussey spent the first part of his strategic management career doing the job in industry, and so gained first-hand experience of how to handle the appraisal process. He spent nearly 20 years in the European operations of a US-based consultancy, most of it as managing director, and not only worked with many clients, but also applied the concepts to his own business. Most of the questionnaires which we have included at the end of several of the chapters were collected and developed over the years by Per Jenster, and have been used by him in many consulting and teaching situations. The exceptions, which were developed by David Hussey, are the questionnaires in the chapters on HRM and industry analysis. These two have been used in many practical situations.

Our own experiences have made us see how important the corporate appraisal is, and our unique inside views of many organisations, where the appraisal has not been part of our brief, have helped us to see how so much of what goes on could be improved. This book is the result.

REFERENCES

Argenti, J. 1980. *Practical Corporate Planning*, London, Allen & Unwin.

Buzzell, R. D. and Gale, B. T. 1987. *The PIMS Principles*, New York, Free Press.

Channon, D. ed. 1997. *The Blackwell Encyclopedic Dictionary of Strategic Management*, Oxford, Blackwell.

Drucker, P. 1964. *Managing for Results*, London, Heinemann.

Goold, M., Campbell, A. and Alexander, M. 1994. *Corporate Level Strategy,* New York, Wiley.

Hamel, G. and Prahalad, C. K. 1994. *Competing for the Future*, Boston, MA, Harvard Business School Press.

Hussey, D. 1998. *Strategic Management: from Theory to Implementation*, 4th edn, Oxford, Butterworth-Heinemann.

Jenster, P. 1987. Using critical success factors in planning, *Long Range Planning,* **20** (4).

Learned, E. P., Christensen, C. R., Andrews, K. R. and Guth, W. D. 1965. *Business Policy: Text and Cases, Homewood,* Il, Irwin.

McNamee, P. 1998. *Strategic Market Planning: A Blueprint for Success,* Chichester, Wiley.

Pickton, D. W. and Wright, S. 1998. What's SWOT in strategic analysis?, *Strategic Change*, March/April.

Porter, M. E. 1985. *Competitive Advantage*, New York, Free Press.

Porter, M. E. 1987. From competitive advantage to corporate strategy, *Harvard Business Review*, May/June.

Stalk, G., Evans, P. and Shulman, L. 1992. Competing on capabilities: the new rules of corporate strategy, *Harvard Business Review*, March/April.

Thompson, J. 1997. *Strategic Management: Awareness and Change*, 3rd edn, London, Thomson.

1

The Purposes and Nature of the Appraisal

BACKGROUND

Any strategy for any organisation has to build from what that organisation is, which means that the first task is to understand the present strengths, weaknesses, capabilities, resources and vulnerabilities, in relation to the external environment in which it operates. Neglect of this basic step can result in strategies which appear well founded in relation to the market and the assessments of the future environment, but which cannot be implemented because of ill-founded implicit assumptions about the organisation itself.

The early books on strategy stressed the importance of what, depending on the whims of the author, was called the corporate appraisal, the position audit, the situation audit, or the assessment of strengths and weaknesses, opportunities and threats. All divided the task into two: the internal appraisal and the external appraisal. However, although there are different elements to be addressed, these two sub-tasks are not totally independent of each other. The internal aspects have to be interpreted with one eye on what is going on outside, and the external have to be related to what is happening inside.

Some authorities tried to put their own stamp on the concept of strengths, weaknesses, opportunities and threats, developing mnemonics around various combinations of the initials, or sometimes around the initials of synonyms. Thus we had SOFT (strength, opportunity, fault, threat), TOWS, WOTS UP (weakness, opportunity, threat, strength, underlying planning) and SWOT. The only combination we did not seem to be offered was TWOS! For some reason SWOT has been the winner and is the term in most common use today. There can be few managers who have never been involved in a SWOT analysis.

However, there has also been a change in what is meant by SWOT. The analytical foundation that was the intention of the early writing has disappeared in many modern books, and, more importantly, from what managers actually do in many organisations. SWOT has become a process of asking managers what they believe are the strengths, weaknesses, opportunities and threats for their part of the organisation, either as individuals or in discussion groups, when strategies are under consideration. Managers do have insights that can be important, but they do not always have accurate factual knowledge, so if they are unaware of the importance of various matters, or of what is actually going on in the organisation, they will ignore these things. So the results of the common approach to SWOT may contain nuggets of gold, but are often so mixed up with iron pyrites, fool's gold, that they can be misleading and unhelpful. This is not an inevitable outcome, but is one which is highly likely.

We have seen many SWOT analyses developed in this way, and have seen numerous occasions when they have missed the critical issues, or totally misinterpreted the strategic situation. Frequently, managers find it hard to identify true strengths, and we have seen statements that show only two: one praises the skills of the chief executive, and the other refers to the competence and dedication of the management team. Weaknesses listed often encompass minor operating issues, rather than the main strategic matters, and result in numerous action plans, few of which are relevant to the long-term strategy of the firm, and most of which are never implemented.

We have also observed the opposite, when an organisation has undertaken a comprehensive appraisal, and as a result has completely changed its strategy. Sometimes this has been a result of a management consulting assignment, but it also happens when managers themselves are given the opportunity to make a full assessment. The executive MBA programme of Copenhagen

Business School has as its main final assignment the completion of a full strategic appraisal of the students' own organisations, incorporating various analytical approaches which will be discussed later in this book. As the students are usually senior managers, they are in a position to use the results of their work, and there have been many situations where this exercise has caused a total rethink of the strategy. Despite good management information systems, and a deep knowledge of their business and its markets, many have found critical information from approaching the task in a thorough and holistic way.

Why the Corporate Appraisal Concept has been Corrupted

There may be several reasons why the corporate appraisal has become corrupted to an "ask the managers" approach. They include:

- *Lack of guidance on how to do it.* Despite the emphasis on the appraisal in the earlier literature, there are very few books which attempt to explain how to undertake an appraisal. It is also true to say that many MBA programmes spend very little time on this. Being told that something is important, but not the detail of how to do it, certainly makes it harder to do the job well.
- *Better management information systems.* Managers today have access to better, more comprehensive and more up-to-date management information systems than was the case in the past. This can greatly facilitate the corporate appraisal, provided the right information has been collected in the first place, which does not always happen. Regular access to information can mean that managers really are informed about every important aspect of their business, and therefore do not need special exercises: it can also lead to complacency and a situation where critical factors are not related to each other, or thoroughly understood.
- *Pressure on managers.* The pressure on managers for immediate results has always been high, but is now greater than ever. It is certainly much quicker to ask managers to define the corporate strengths and weaknesses than to spend precious time on special analyses. Therefore, managers have to be

convinced that the extra time is justified. The pressure for a quick fix means that managers will often be tempted to reach for a technique, instead of going back to basic principles, although this is rarely the most effective way to deal with a strategic problem.

* *The complexity of many companies.* Many companies are very large and complex, which can make the task of carrying out a comprehensive appraisal seem rather daunting, and, with the decline of large strategic staff departments, the task of organising such a study is devolved to busy line managers. We hope that this book will show that it is a task which lies within the competence of most managers, and that if approached in a sensible way it need not be overwhelming.

WHO NEEDS AN APPRAISAL ANYWAY?

This is a question which has a number of answers, because an appraisal may be needed in several different situations. They are discussed here in order of probable frequency of occurrence. The importance of various aspects of the appraisal may vary with the purpose, but the overall concepts are applicable to all.

Preparation of a Strategic Plan

We do not assume that all organisations will want to produce a written plan, either as a one-off event or as part of a formal procedure within the overall group. However, we *know* that all organisations have to think about strategy, and that effective strategy is unlikely if divorced from the realities of the present situation.

We can draw a parallel with a personal decision. Let us assume that you want to take an energetic holiday with a group of very fit people exploring remote high mountain country in South America. You may not have taken very much exercise in the last ten years, and may never have walked in mountains before. The penalty of being considerably weaker than the group would vary from embarrassment at causing delays to others if you could not walk as fast as they could, to putting other people in danger if you collapsed or caused such delays that you and others had to walk in rugged country after nightfall.

Faced with that sort of holiday, and knowing what you know about your state of health, you would review your fitness. If you were pretty healthy generally, you might decide to do some training before leaving, to get fit enough for the trip, and indeed you might leave the decision on whether to join the party until you had seen how well you could cope walking long distances on day trips to smaller mountains which are closer to you. You might also want to have a medical examination, to confirm that you had no underlying problems which you did not know about, and which might be exacerbated by strenuous activity and altitude.

If you were irresponsible, you could just sign up and go, without doing any appraisal or taking any remedial action. But to do so would increase the risks of failure, and could even become a disaster. The sensible person would do a self-appraisal, add expert opinion where needed, and take remedial action as necessary. The risks of failure would be much reduced.

In one sense the corporate appraisal has a similar purpose to this personal appraisal. It checks out the organisation's fitness for specific strategies, by testing the things you think you know already, and by taking steps to uncover things which could be critical, but which are currently hidden from you. But the corporate appraisal does more than this, in that it may help the identification of opportunities.

We are not arguing that the corporate appraisal will deliver a total strategy to you. We are emphatic that it is an essential first step to such a strategy. Figure 1.1 shows that analysis (and the corporate appraisal is but one of many essential analytical tasks) is only one of five critical factors that are essential in attaining an effective strategy. It is not a sequential model, in that it does not argue for any particular order for these factors, nor that one has to be completed before another can begin. But strategic success depends on all of them.

At the heart of the diagram is the calibre of senior managers, for weak management can defeat the best strategy, and may prevent you even finding a good strategy. Around the outside of the model are analysis, creative strategic thinking, the way strategic decisions are taken, and implementation. A more detailed description of this model is given in Hussey (1999).

The model implies that a failure to undertake the corporate appraisal could have an adverse impact on the strategic decisions

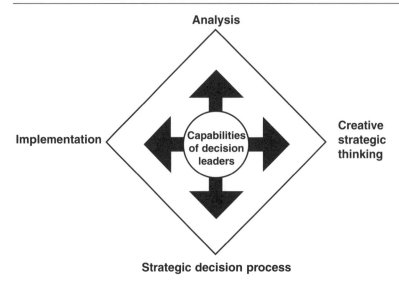

Figure 1.1 Critical factors for strategic success. (Source: D. E. Hussey, Strategic management: past experiences and future direction, *Strategic Change*, **6**(5), 1997. © John Wiley & Sons, Limited. Reproduced with permission)

that are ultimately taken. In addition, it could affect the ability of the organisation to implement those decisions: if – for example – assumptions were made about corporate competencies which were erroneous.

Review of a Strategic Situation

A similar situation arises when a manager takes over a new responsibility. We use a new chief executive as an example, but the same sort of situation can apply with managers at lower levels than this. One of the first tasks of a new CEO is to review the strategies of the organisation, and this includes a need for a detailed corporate appraisal. Sometimes consultants are used for this task, which may be to preserve objectivity, or because of a shortage of resources which makes it sensible to use outsiders. Speed is often very important, particularly if the company is failing.

Although any newly appointed CEO, particularly if brought in from outside, would be well advised to undertake such a strategic review, the task becomes unavoidable in the failing or under-performing company. The order in which the elements of the appraisal are tackled may not be the same as the order in this book, since attention should be focused on the obvious problem areas first, but the approaches discussed are all relevant. The main difference lies in the speed with which decisions have to be made, partly because of external pressures, and partly because a company that is losing cash has an immediate need to do something about it. Not surprisingly, in such situations, the now traditional SWOT approach by asking the managers is unlikely to achieve the results: if they knew where the problem was, they would presumably have done something about it before.

Acquisition or Merger

There have been numerous surveys, stretching back to the early 1970s, which show that there is a high failure rate for acquisitions and mergers. Until recently, if anyone had asked us the chances of success, we should have said it is the same as if you toss a coin. In most surveys success was judged in one of two ways: the organisations' own assessments against the original objectives, or whether the acquisition was subsequently closed or sold off when this was not the original intention. The reason we have not referenced these surveys is because of a more recent study which measured shareholder value (KPMG, 1999). On this criterion only 17% of acquisitions could be called a success, in that they increased value, 30% left the value unchanged, and the rest reduced value. This is a far higher failure rate than had been indicated by the previous less-objective criteria, and comes dangerously near calling tails when the other person is using a double-headed coin. Interestingly, 82% of the companies in the sample believed that the acquisition had been a success, which was almost a mirror image of the true position.

This research identified a number of keys to success, only two of which are of concern here: detailed synergy evaluation and due diligence.

Synergy evaluation requires a detailed knowledge of your own operations as well as those of the potential acquisition, and the KPMG report argues that the evaluation should be undertaken before the deal is struck. The emphasis should be on what can be delivered, not what is theoretically possible. The detailed knowledge that comes from a corporate appraisal is essential for synergy evaluation.

Due diligence, as KPMG (1998) found, is widely undertaken, but is not always comprehensive. For example, 54% of cases did not cover management culture, 35% excluded HRM, and slightly under half included IT (these were aspects specifically covered in the survey questions, and the results do not mean that all other areas were comprehensively included). KPMG (1999) states:

> Sophisticated and forward looking recipients use a "springboard" approach to due diligence which often encompasses a range of investigative tools designed to systematically assess all the facts impacting on value. This can include market reviews, risk assessments, and the assessment of management competencies, as well as areas to concentrate on for synergies or operational impact.

Ideally, similar information should be obtained to that described in this book. When the due diligence is undertaken from outside the target company, as in a hostile bid situation, it is unlikely that such comprehensive information can be obtained, and standards have to be lowered. However, in a friendly acquisition the situation may be different and there may be access, possibly via a consultant, to internal data.

Divestment

Although we do not wish to labour the point, sometimes a corporate appraisal is very helpful in getting a good price for an activity which is to be divested. One company we are aware of undertook a synergy evaluation in reverse to determine which potential buyer could gain the most value from buying the subsidiary it wished to sell. This could not have been done without a detailed knowledge of their own organisation and those of competitors.

OVERVIEW OF A CORPORATE APPRAISAL

The following chapters will examine various aspects of the internal appraisal in some detail. But before we move on to these it is useful to put the whole appraisal process into perspective. Figure 1.2 gives a generalised view of the internal appraisal.

Figure 1.2 Aspects of the internal appraisal

First, the fact that we are reviewing the internal aspects of the organisation does not mean that all the information will come from internal sources. So when we look at performance trends, we will be concerned not just with our own growth and profitability, but also with such matters as market share and customer satisfaction measures. We may need to take stock of our policies in various areas, to confirm, for example, that our HRM policies and resulting procedures are contributing to what we are trying to achieve. We will also want to examine our activities, in terms of products, plant locations and geographical spheres of operation. All these things are included in the words in the centre of the star in Figure 1.2.

The five areas outside the star are assessments drawn out of our study of the facts. Performance trends are interesting, but do not provide much information on which to build strategy. There are other things which need to be known.

- *Vulnerabilities* are the risks to which the organisation is exposed. Although some risks come from the external environment, there are also many areas that can be identified from the internal appraisal. Examples are over-dependence on one customer for most of the sales, a high proportion of profits coming from an unstable country, or problems with management succession.

- *Flexibility* is the ability of the organisation to adapt quickly to external changes. A simple example is that an oil refinery is very inflexible. Although it is possible to make some adjustments to the mix of products, basically it is a very high investment that will only do one thing. On the other hand tableting machines in a pharmaceutical company can make a whole variety of products, so long as tablets are required. Flexibility, of course, is much more than the choice of industry, and can be achieved through means such as outsourcing and attention to employment contracts.

- *Effectiveness* is whether the organisation is doing the right things well. So it might be that the organisation is very effective in gaining distribution for its products, but is not very effective in innovation to secure a flow of future products. A publisher may be very effective in gaining distribution to academic buyers, but even if its products are appropriate may be ineffective in getting books into high-street book shops.

- *Resources* are the factors of economic activity which the organisation can control. Money might be put first, since if there are adequate financial resources, it is often (but not always) possible to solve resource problems of people, machines and materials. The resources the organisation owns or has access to may be an enabling factor to allow it to do more than it is currently doing, or may put a ceiling on what can be achieved.

- *Capabilities*, in this context, is a catch-all term for all the competencies, knowledge and skills the organisation can apply to a situation. Although the underlying resources of two firms in the same industry may be very similar, one may have developed capabilities which the other cannot match. The word capabilities is also used in a narrower context, and this different usage will be explored later.

The final element in Figure 1.2 is the reminder that comparative assessments may be more valuable than the absolute figures. There may be an impressive list of capabilities, but if these do not match the requirements of the strategy being followed, they may be inadequate for the tasks.

Internally a company may believe that it offers excellent customer service and value, but these conclusions should be tested against the expectations of customers. The British motor cycle industry was convinced that it made the best motor cycles in the world, but did not bother with unnecessary things like self-starters. The customers idea of quality was related to the utility and image of the product, rather than just the engineering, and they deserted to the Japanese firms which offered not just a cheaper product, but one which came closer to meeting their requirements. So the British industry went into terminal decline.

Profitability may be judged very good when the company looks at its long-run history, but it is only very good if the shareholders believe it to be. If it falls below the expectations which shareholders have of this type of company, a totally different picture may emerge. Similarly, profitability may be compared to that of competitors, and, again, perceptions of what is good or bad may change.

The organisation may be well satisfied with its internal ways of operating, but these may not meet the expectations of the community at large. For example, in the UK in 1999 it became public knowledge that certain hospitals had removed from dead babies organs which were preserved for future research, without either the knowledge or permission of the parents, and that they had been operating in this way for many years. What appeared to be a logical course of action inside these hospitals looked very different when compared against the values and expectations of the parents, and the community at large.

The term "world class performers" appears in Figure 1.2, again making the point that in many areas it is not enough to be good, as the future profitability may depend on being among the best.

Obviously it is not expected that everything found in the appraisal will be compared to everything listed in Figure 1.2, but it is stressed that there is a value in making such comparisons on a selective basis, instead of relying on an internal feeling that something is good, or excellent, when this may be a blinkered interpretation.

Figure 1.3 puts the elements of Figure 1.2 into the context of the full corporate appraisal. The elements added are industry analysis, which relates the organisation to the power structure of the entire industry ("power" meaning who holds the power to influence the

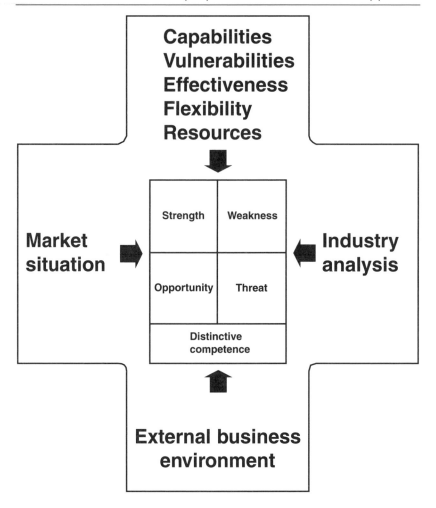

Figure 1.3   The internal appraisal and external appraisal. (Source: D. E. Hussey, Strategy and Planning: *A Manager's Guide.* Wiley, Chichester, 1999. © John Wiley & Sons, Limited. Reproduced with permission)

profitability of one's own organisation, competitors, suppliers and buyers). This is described in Chapter 10. It is not normally written about in the context of the corporate appraisal, but we feel that it belongs to it, and that the appraisal would be incomplete without it. Hussey and Jenster (1999), which might be seen as a companion volume to this book, take industry analysis into the deeper waters of competitor analysis.

The external business environment is also part of the broader context. This is not discussed in depth in this book as a separate topic, and if further guidance is needed, we recommend Hussey (1998, Chapters 4–7). What you will find here is some treatment of the external environment in the context of individual chapter topics

The market situation is a blend of internal and external facts. What happens in a market is influenced by the customers themselves, by competitors and by factors in the external environment, such as legislation. The firm too has an influence through the products it offers, the way it does this and the image it creates. This is an area which is covered in this book.

The centre of Figure 1.3 has a matrix representing our old friend SWOT. However, although the final picture will be leavened by the insight of managers, this SWOT statement is derived from careful analysis. The conventional wisdom is that one builds on strengths, corrects weaknesses (or mitigates their effect by avoiding situations which put stress on the weak areas), exploits opportunities and tries to take action to modify threats, or change strategy so that they are avoided. In fact this is a somewhat simplistic view, as strategies arise in more complex ways than this implies, and, as Figure 1.1 stressed, creativity should play a key role. However, what should arise from the internal analysis is an awareness of what the organisation is currently able or unable to do effectively, which can then be contrasted with what it needs to do in order to achieve its vision and objectives. This may lead to a range of actions which seek to modify the pattern found through the analysis. On the way a number of operational issues might be uncovered which can be dealt with, and there may be opportunities for immediate profit improvement. These are bonuses, by-products of what the exercise is really about, which is strategy and the future of the organisation.

It is something of this overall flavour which is summarised in the term "distinctive competence" in Figure 1.3. Although this might be thought by modern readers to be borrowed from Prahalad and Hamel (1990), in fact it comes from a much earlier book. We took it from Christensen, Andrews and Bower (1978, p. 258), but it also appears in the first edition published in 1965. Thus, it is not just strengths and weaknesses which we should be seeking, but the overall combination of competencies which enable the

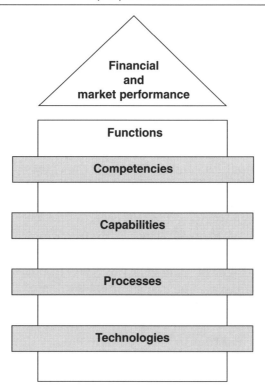

Figure 1.4 Ways of looking at organisations. (Source: D. E. Hussey, *Strategy and Planning: A Manager's Guide.* Wiley, Chichester, 1999. © John Wiley & Sons, Limited. Reproduced with permission)

organisation to occupy a particular strategic position. At this stage, the task is to understand what exists in the present: the strategy formulation task might well include developing an understanding of what will be needed to succeed in the future, and developing the means of filling the gap between the two assessments.

WAYS OF LOOKING AT AN ORGANISATION

There are many different ways of looking at an organisation, each of which can yield different insights. Figure 1.4 explores this statement. The triangle and the underlying box represent what might be termed the traditional view, although it is no less valuable for this, and much of the book describes it. The triangle looks at total performance of the organisation under study, which could be an overall group, a strategic business unit (SBU) within the group, or any self-contained business within the SBU. So in this study we would include items like the overall profitability, shareholder value measures and growth. The box looks at functional activities, building up an analysis which gives depth to the broader corporate-wide figures.

The horizontal bars which overlap the white box on the diagram illustrate other ways in which an organisation might be examined, and we cover these in more detail in three chapters of the book. Using one or more of these integrative concepts does not invalidate the functional view, but may add additional strategic insights which might otherwise be lost in the gaps between the functional chimneys. The diagram shows an integrated organisation, but we could have positioned a number of SBUs side by side, with the bars overlapping all or several of these. Technologies, for example, may stretch across several SBUs within the organisation, and this may be part of its strength.

Competencies are shown by the first bar on the figure. Hamel and Prahalad (1994, p. 35) stress their belief that top managers should view the organisation as a portfolio of competencies. They see a competence as a "bundle of skills and technologies", and add the phrase "that enables a company to provide a particular benefit to customers" (p. 219) when describing a core competence.

Every year since 1993 management consultants Bain & Co. have undertaken an international survey into the use of tools and techniques in companies. The survey covers the top 25 topical tools and techniques which are of value to top management. Core competencies were used by 63% of companies which took part in the 1998 survey, and were ninth in order of popularity (Rigby, 1999). However, no one should view the core competence approach as a stand-alone technique which is not part of a wider corporate appraisal. The development of new core competencies is s strategic activity that should follow a careful appraisal of the current competencies, whether core or non-core. And the appraisal of the competencies requires a careful study to decompose the firm's "economic engine" (see Hamel and Prahalad, 1994, p. 98).

Capabilities, represented by the second bar, are a concept which appears to have been derived from the core competencies method. Stalk, Evans and Shulman (1992) argued that the really important thing was not competencies, but capabilities, defined as "a set of business processes strategically understood". The authors use many of the examples given by Hamel and Prahalad in their works, arguing that it is capabilities rather than competencies that has led to their success. The main thrust of the argument is that it is not just the individual processes but how they are bundled that really matters.

Processes have long been seen as offering a different way of looking at an organisation, and approaches like total quality management (TQM) and business process reengineering (BPR) in their different ways are dependent on identifying and understanding the current processes. We have included the value chain approach (Porter, 1985) under the process heading, although it is different from merely identifying what the processes are, and its focus is on what delivers value to customers.

Technologies are a part of the core competence approach, but also need to be looked at in their own right. It is easy to see how a critical aspect of the technologies owned by an organisation could be overlooked unless an organisation-wide examination were made. Although this may be less likely in a small organisation, it would be a real danger in a large multinational operating with several SBUs.

SOME FOUNDATION QUESTIONS

Although each element of the appraisal has to be looked at individually, and in relation to the purpose of the appraisal, there are some basic questions to be answered which, with common-sense variations, can be applied to every element of the appraisal process. They provide a mindset which is helpful, whether we are looking at overall performance, undertaking a functional analysis, or taking one of the other ways of looking at the organisation which were discussed above. The following list is quoted from Hussey (1999, pp. 35–6).

1. What are we doing now?
2. What are we achieving by doing this?
3. Why are we doing this?
4. Does what we do fit the customers' requirements?

5. How do we know this?
6. How does what we do compare with competitors, in so far as we are able to deduce this?
7. Are there other ways in which we could achieve the same benefit?
8. Should we be doing these instead?
9. How does this contribute to our corporate success?
10. How does it help the corporate vision?

GETTING MORE OUT OF THE "INSIGHT" APPROACHES

Earlier in this chapter we pointed to the deficiencies of approaches which relied on management insight and opinion, but nevertheless said that there could be some value in the "ask the managers" approach. Although the focus of the book is on analytical methods, we are ending this chapter with some ideas on how to get more out of approaches that tap into what the managers know or believe are the strengths and weaknesses.

Results are likely to be more useful if attention is focused on a specific issue or problem, rather than asking managers to identify all the strengths and weaknesses of the firm, which often leads to superficial answers. For example, if a probable strategy of the firm is to expand the geographical operations of the organisation, managers might be asked to define those things about the company which could be used as building blocks for this strategy, the things that act as constraints that would have to be dealt with, and the new skills and competencies which would be needed. Another approach might be to take the two or three major competitors and ask in which areas they are better than us, where they are thought to be worse, and where we are all about the same. The problems and issues chosen must be believed to be relevant to the managers involved, if they are to put their minds to the task.

Another tip is to do some work first, so that key findings from the management information system are provided as part of the process of discussing strengths and weaknesses.

There is a very simple, but useful, tool called the equilibrium approach, which is based on force field analysis, and is intended to aid discussion with groups of managers. The following extract is taken from Hussey (1999, pp. 57–60).

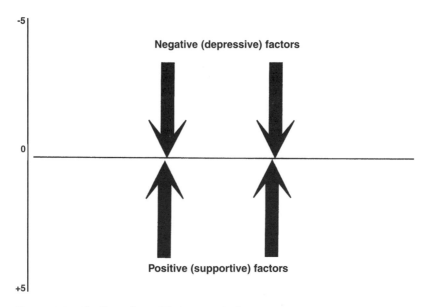

Figure 1.5   Outline of equilibrium analysis

The objectives of equilibrium analysis are:

* To achieve a common understanding of strengths and weaknesses.
* To identify strengths as well as weaknesses.
* To decide priorities for corrective action.
* To identify corrective action.

The basic framework of the approach is shown in Figure 1.5. It is a very simple concept which can be taught to any group in a matter of minutes. The horizontal line represents the present state of anything that is to be studied: labour turnover rates, market position, cost structures, profitability, etc.

Focus should be given by posing a question such as: "Why is our market share 15%?" The base line then represents the current state – a market share of 15%.

It is as high as 15% because certain positive features support it. It is as low as 15% because certain negative features hold it down.

The trick is to get the meeting to identify these two groups of factors, writing them in heading form at the top and bottom of the diagram, across the page. If too many weaknesses are identified attention can be changed to strengths with a remark such as "Now I can't understand why you have any market share at all." If too many strengths come up one can ask why market share has not risen to 50%.

Criteria for successful use of the approach include a group of people

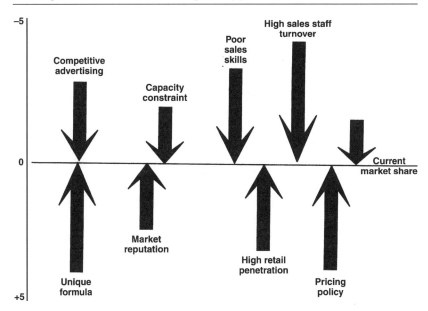

Figure 1.6 Example of equilibrium analysis of market share

who know the situation, and preparation for the meeting by an analyst who has looked at the factual base available. The analyst should be prepared to challenge (e.g. if the group insists that a plus factor is the firm's reputation, whereas market research shows that it is almost unknown, the factual position should over-ride the impression).

The next step in the use of the technique is to rate the relative significance of the various factors identified. This is the reason for the scaling on the vertical line.

Figure 1.6 illustrates what the completed diagram might look like at the end of the meeting.

Once the information is displayed it is possible to use it:

- Would the position best be improved by strengthening a positive factor or removing a negative one?
- Are there any factors which cannot be altered by the firm, and which should not receive more attention?
- What can be done about the really important factors?

The equilibrium approach could be used again if it was decided to tackle the high sales force turnover, and used to try to identify the factors which attract sales people to the firm, and those that cause them to leave. If the assessments move from the known base of fact, it may be useful to accept them for the time being, but to check them out after the meeting.

REFLECTION

This chapter has begun a journey of exploration, and the following chapters will provide a comprehensive guide for the travellers who make this journey with us. Certainly a well-run modern organisation will be able to obtain much of the required information from the management information system, but our experience is that there are always critical aspects, in even the best run organisations, which are not covered in the optimum way for a strategic appraisal, and there are always critical areas which are overlooked. Because organisations are changing fast, their capabilities, resources, strengths and weaknesses also change rapidly, and even well-informed managers can base strategies on out-of-date understanding: a problem which we hope will be avoided by those who follow the advice of this book.

REFERENCES

Christensen, C. R., Andrews, K. R. and Bower, J. L. 1978. *Business Policy: Text and Cases*, 4th edn, Homewood, Il, Irwin.

Hamel, G. and Prahalad, C. K. 1994. *Competing for the Future*, Boston, MA, Harvard Business School Press (page references are to the 1996 paperback version).

Hussey, D. 1998. *Strategic Management: From Theory to Implementation*, 4th edn, Oxford, Butterworth–Heinemann.

Hussey, D. 1999. *Strategy and Planning: a Manager's Guide*, Chichester, Wiley.

Hussey, D. and Jenster, P. 1999. *Competitor Intelligence: Turning Analysis into Success*, Chichester, Wiley.

KPMG 1998. *Colouring in the Map*, Mergers and acquisitions in Europe research report, London, KPMG.

KPMG 1999. *Unlocking Shareholder Value: the Keys to Success*, Mergers and acquisitions global report, London, KPMG.

Porter, M. E. 1985. *Competitive Advantage*, New York, Free Press.

Prahalad, C. K. and Hamel, G. 1990. The core competence of the corporation, *Harvard Business Review*, May/June, **90**(3).

Rigby, D. 1999. *Management Tools and Techniques*, Presentation of the 1998 survey, Boston, MA, Bain & Co.

Stalk, G., Evans, P. and Shulman, L. 1992. Competing on capabilities: the new rules of corporate strategy, *Harvard Business Review*, March/April, **92**(2).

2
Assessing Financial Performance

OVERALL FINANCIAL PERFORMANCE

Initial Thoughts

Any appraisal of a business should start with the overall financial performance. Whether the organisation is large or small, financial performance gives an indication of overall success or failure. How success is judged will vary between different types of organisation. The public quoted company may see its market value as the most important dynamic; the small business may interpret success as the provision of acceptable salaries to its owner-managers; the not-for-profit organisation may be more concerned to ensure that it is able to continue to meet the needs for which it was established.

There are various standard ways of doing this. Many readers will be familiar with the common methods and ratios, and because most organisations will regularly use at least some of them, we have left a description of them to Appendix 2.1. This makes it easier for those who do not wish to read the definitions to skip them.

The value of any ratio is much reduced unless it can be compared to something. The comparator may be internal (e.g. performance for prior periods, or performance of the various units of the group, or the target), but we would argue that more often it should be external (e.g. competitors or companies which the stock market sees as similar). Without the comparison any ratio loses much of its power, as it is harder to judge whether it is good or bad.

However, there is a note of caution, in that there are organisational differences in acceptable accounting treatment within any one particular country, and variations in generally accepted accounting practice between countries. So if comparing a return on investment ratio, for example, with that of a competitor, it is prudent to read the notes to the annual report, and to try to identify as many of the differences as possible. Later we will see how differences in costing methods can change the perception of profitability of business units and products within the company.

What Approach Does the Organisation Currently Use?

Earlier we mentioned that we expected that most organisations would, as a matter of routine, keep tabs on the overall measures of financial performance. Behind this truism lies the fact that not all organisations will do this in the same way. For example, a company that has growth in earnings per share as its driving force is likely to take different actions, and to judge its own performance differently, than if it were using one of the value-based methods.

In the first case there would be emphasis on growth in earnings, with a tendency to choose debt rather than raising funds by an issue of new shares. In the latter, the emphasis would be on cash flow, the market value of the company, and the rate of return earned compared with the overall cost of capital. Both these methods will have different implications on how business units within the group are managed and their performances judged.

It follows that one early question to determine is which of the methods the organisation uses as its main driver. Logically, the next step is to assess the advantages and disadvantages of the chosen method, and to consider the implications of a change in thinking. So there is value in assessing overall financial performance by several different methods, to see what additional insight can be gained.

In addition to gaining a picture of the overall performance, the overall financial appraisal can provide a first idea of where the profit is coming from. Initially this will be at the level of SBUs or operating companies; later we will suggest how the analysis should be taken to a lower level of resolution. Again, we recommend that a number of measures be used, and the figures displayed for each. As a minimum we recommend growth in revenue and profits, return on assets, and a measure of cash flow. In this case too, ratios make more sense when compared with various comparators, one of which should be the weighted cost of capital.

Market Valuation

The organisation's performance in the stock market should be tracked, and the variations in market value calculated. It is easy to argue that, as so much of what affects the share price is outside the control of the organisation, managers should have little concern with it. True, the stock market does sometimes appear to be irrational, but we have to remember that it is driven not just by past performance but by expectations of the future. In all companies, management is to a large degree shaping those expectations, and in companies that follow a value-based approach the choice of strategies is made in a deliberate way with shareholder value as the main determinant.

When the British supermarket chain Somerfield acquired a rival firm Kwik-Save in 1998, the market capitalisation was reported as £1.26 billion. It had soared to £2.2 billion by the end of that year. In November 1999 it had dropped to £409 million, and at this point Somerfield hoped to raise some £400 million by selling some of the stores in the group. By March 2000, when it was announced that the chief executive was leaving the company, the market value had fallen to £283 million.

It looks as if this acquisition was one of the more than 50% which destroy shareholder value. Undoubtedly there were performance problems, which meant that the deal did not deliver its promises, and performance problems frequently lead to cash flow difficulties. Unexpectedly high levels of debt always mean that there are additional costs before any earnings are available as dividends. Share prices, which rose dramatically on expectations of high profits from the merger, fell equally dramatically as the actual results of the merger became clear, putting more pressure by shareholders on the management.

What might come from an examination of market value in the financial appraisal is an appreciation of whether the shares are over- or under-valued, and the vulnerability of the organisation to a hostile takeover bid. In a multi-business organisation, it is also worth trying to establish whether the whole is worth less than the sum of its parts, which could lead to actions such as divesting or floating off certain activities.

Financial Resources

The appraisal is not just about performance and expectations, but should also establish the financial resources the organisation can muster. As a first step the conventional gearing and liquidity ratios should be calculated, to give an indication of the flexibility the organisation has to raise further debt financing if required. When looking at these ratios, it is sensible to look at seasonal patterns, as what is an adequate level of finance for most of the year may be inadequate for the peak periods.

A higher level of liquid capital than is needed for operations may be a strength, in that it gives strategic flexibility, but it can also be a serious weakness, making the organisation a target for corporate raiders and depressing the overall rate of profitability of the whole organisation.

The next task is to assess the flexibility the organisation has to raise additional equity. There may be several strategies available. At this stage the aim is not to make choices, but to understand the limitations of the organisation, in relation to the likely capital requirements of the near future.

Clearly an organisation's ability to grow is affected by its capacity to finance its strategies. In the appraisal the aim is to understand the degree to which the organisation's financial strength (or lack of it) is a help or a hindrance.

This understanding is even more useful if it is placed in the context of the organisation's current pattern of needs. One useful method is portfolio analysis. This of course is not just a financial tool, and can be one of the bases of a corporate strategy. In the financial context here, it is a way of looking at all the units of an organisation in relation to each other to see which are expected to consume cash and which to generate it. Figure 2.1 gives an example of a chart based on the Shell Directional Policy Matrix. For full scoring rules for such a chart, see Hussey (1998).

Although we do not believe that portfolio analysis should be used in quite the way suggested by its early exponents as the main

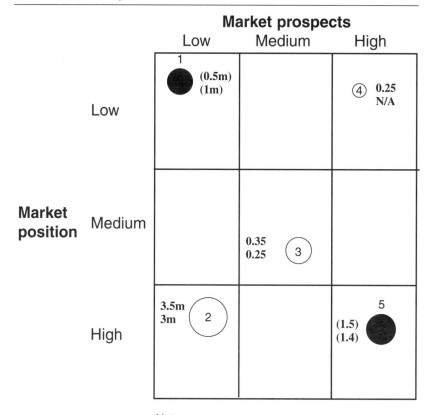

Figure 2.1 Example of portfolio chart

determinant of strategy, it is extremely useful as a way of getting an overview of a complex multi-business organisation. In Figure 2.1 we have used black circles for businesses losing cash in the last financial year and open circles for those gaining it. The figure for cash gain or loss is written against the symbol: the second figure shown is the average for the last three years.

Any information about known commitments for the future which will alter the pattern could also be signalled on the chart. An example might be a contract agreed for the building of a new factory in the following year, the capital costs of which have not yet hit the books.

Of course, it would be possible to do a simple listing of businesses detailing this information. The value of a portfolio chart is that it gives some indication of the quality dimension of each business, and although unspecific about future capital needs, it does distinguish those businesses likely to be heavy cash consumers from those that are not. The key point is that profits and cash generation are not always synchronised: a very profitable business in a high-growth situation may be going through a period where the annual cash used, for assets and working capital, may be greater than the cash generated.

Using an ROI Chart

A useful method for showing the economic structure of a business is the ROI chart, sometimes called a Du Pont chart after its leading initiator. The ROI chart, illustrated in Figure 2.2, combines the income statement and balance sheet, and gives a broad indication of the sources of profits and, ideally, the utilisation of financial resources.

The main difference between Figure 2.2 and the version which appears in many text books is that we suggest that *contribution to profits and central overheads* be used instead of profit, as in many organisations head office costs are allocated and apportioned to businesses on a somewhat arbitrary basis. This can make a business appear less profitable than is the actual case, but – worse than this – can make it appear that closure of the business is a sensible strategy: this is only true if the head office overheads also disappear. Frequently this does not happen, as they are not true direct costs, and this means that the same costs are now allocated or apportioned over a smaller base of businesses, which makes these businesses look less profitable. Using contribution instead of profit can therefore give a truer economic perception of the value of each business.

The ROI chart is an ideal tool for an organisation with five or six SBUs, or for an SBU with a similar number of sub-units. It becomes cumbersome with large, complex organisations, and may become difficult to read, although it may still be valuable at SBU level. Similarly, in small, single-business companies it may add nothing to what can be read off the final accounts. As with all ways

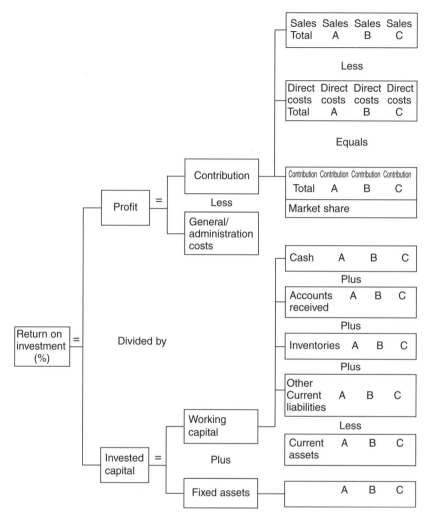

Figure 2.2 ROI chart to show economic structure of the business

of displaying information, the decision to use it should be based on the situation of the organisation.

A DEEPER UNDERSTANDING OF THE SOURCES OF PROFITS

At this stage of the appraisal we should have documented the overall position of the organisation, and know the cash generating or cash consuming propensity of each of the SBUs. We would also have first impressions of the level of profits, profitability and contribution of each SBU. Performance ratios will have been looked at against various internal and external comparators, so that we have an understanding of whether they are good or bad. We would also know our overall financial strength or weakness.

The next stage is to gain a deeper understanding of where the profits come from. This means getting to the level of products (or activities in the case of service businesses) and customers. And the first thing to do is to check out the way the organisation calculates the costs of products.

To managers used to taking the cost accountants' figures as accurate, this may seem like heresy. In reality it is not the accuracy of the calculations that should be questioned, but the validity of the assumptions that lie behind them. The following extract from Hussey (1999 pp. 43–6) explains the issue.

> In many cases the apportionment of costs between products is on some form of allocation basis. It is worthwhile studying the basis of apportionment and allocation since although suitable for many purposes it may be inadequate for this study. Many allocations assume that costs fall in a normal distribution; for example, that invoicing costs are a fixed percentage for all products. Inventories may be treated on the same basis. If costs are reallocated on the basis of actual transactions two things may become apparent:
>
> * a skewed distribution between products;
> * a skewed distribution between different customers.
>
> An example may make this clearer. A firm offering a lorry sales service is likely to express its sales/delivery costs as a percentage of the sales value, say 5%. The assumption is made that every £1 of sales bears the same percentage of cost: in other words that a normal distribution applies. In fact, everybody really knows that it costs less per unit to sell one customer 100 units than to sell 100 customers one unit each. In addition everybody knows that it takes more time and effort to reach a customer 10 miles away than one who is only one mile away. In other words costs do not fall in a normal distribution. Yet not all organisations arrange their cost data so that they can make any decisions on this basis.

One of the first people to argue for a different basis for costing was Drucker (1964), who suggested the transaction basis for cost allocation mentioned earlier. An example of this would be to allocate invoicing costs on the basis of the number of lines on the invoices when looking at products, and the number of invoices when assessing the costs of customers. This gives a

Table 2.1 Consultancy project costing sheet: two options

	1. Staff wholly in-house		2. Use in-house and part-time staffing	
Fees	17500		17500	
Expenses + 10%	1100		1100	
Total Revenue		18600		18600
Labour:				
10 days at £330	3330		10 days at £330 3330	
10 days at £250	2500			
Subtotal	5830		3330	
Overhead (115%)	6704		3830	
Total labour	12534		7160	
External consultant			4000	
(£400 per day)				
Reimbursables	1000		1000	
Subtotal costs	13534		12160	
Admin. burden (10%)	1353		1216	
Total costs		14887		13376
Profit		3713		5224
Profit (%)		19.96		28.08

much closer interpretation of the true costs than apportioning by value.

The transaction idea has been given a modern interpretation in the concept of activity-based costing (ABC). This tackles the indirect costs, by seeking to understand how they are generated (which enables them to be better controlled) and relating them to specific processes, activities or products.

> ABC assigns costs to products and/or customers upon the basis of the resources that they actually consume. Thus an ABC system identifies costs such as machine set-up, job scheduling, and materials handling. These costs are allocated according to the actual level of activities. All overhead costs are thus traced to individual products and/or customers, as the cost to serve all customers is far from equal. As a result, ABC forms an integral component in the strategic planning process and unlike conventional accountancy, provides a vehicle for assuming future costs rather than purely measuring past history. . . . ABC permits managers to identify actual cost drivers and address these, and so reduce fixed costs. (Channon, 1997, p. 5)

Any remaining overheads which cannot be allocated on ABC

principles should not be apportioned. Contribution to these over-heads and profits, rather than an arbitrary profit figure, should be used instead.

The nonsense that can result from apportionments is illustrated by an experience David Hussey had while undertaking a cor-porate appraisal with the UK company that made Ovaltine, among other things. On the UK market at that time there were two types of labelling, the large volume being in the label for the normal retail trade. The other, which was low volume, was for supply to hospitals. The only difference in the product was the colour of the label. Hospital Ovaltine was sold at a much lower price, and the only reason for the different pack was to prevent hospitals selling the product on to the retail trade, although why anyone should have thought that this would happen is a mystery. However, the accountants were well pleased with the hospital product, because the cost schedules showed that the factory cost was so much less than that of the retail variety, so despite the lower selling price, the gross margin was higher.

All anyone had to do to know that this was rubbish was to watch the product being made. As the only possible difference in costs was the paper label, the figures had to be wrong. But they were checked twice by the accountants, who confirmed their findings. Closer examination found that indirect factory costs had been allo-cated to all products on the basis of realisation, so the cheaper the price, the less it appeared to cost. What happened as a result of this was that the special label was dropped. As there were several pack sizes this also reduced the inventory of finished stock.

This was some time ago. Do any companies make similar errors today? Unfortunately, the answer is yes.

Another extract from Hussey (1999, pp. 46–7) shows one of the disturbing things found when he undertook an appraisal of a management consultancy on his appointment as its managing director.

> Table 2.1 provides another example of how a cost system which may be good for some purposes can give the wrong signals in others. The example comes from a management consulting firm: the figures are made up for the example but the method of calculation is real, as are the two overhead burden rates. This firm used an absorption costing system, where all overheads are charged to "products", in this case con-sulting assignments. The example is of the choice facing a project direc-tor who has gained an assignment to start immediately, but has the

choice of two ways of staffing it. One uses the project director and another employee: the other uses an equally competent external part timer, who is only paid for work performed. The accountant's schedule shows that more profit is earned if the outsider is used.

The main reason why it works out this way is that the 115% overhead is not added to the outsider. There is logic in this, as this burden is part-ly the cost of the consultants' downtime, and partly a share of space and secretarial costs: the outsider is only paid when employed by a client so no downtime is incurred, and works only on the assignment so uses (in theory) none of the space and support costs. So the accounting conven-tions tell you to use the staffing of case 2, to make more profit. But a moment's thought tells you that you earn less in this way than in option 1, because you have £4,000 additional expense going out of the busi-ness. You still have to pay the in house consultant who would not be used in example 2. So in the circumstances I have described it would be a silly choice.

This example shows the danger of using figures without thought. If the firm had conducted an analysis of its customers calculating the sales to and profit earned from each, and used these conventions, it might also mislead itself. For various reasons the client providing the highest accounting profit, might not be the most valuable client to the firm. Clients giving a lower profit might provide a greater contribution.

Although option 2 in Table 2.1 would not be in the economic interests of the firm, it is worth mentioning here – although HR issues are the subject of a later chapter – that the reward system drove project directors to make this choice. Total profit earned in the year on projects managed, as defined by the accountants, was one of the criteria by which performance was judged.

If an organisation already has an ABC system, this stage of the appraisal will be much easier to conduct. In the many which do not have such a system there will be much more work, which can bring a very different perception of the value to the business of products and individual customers, and may even change the perception of the profitability of the SBUs. In addition to the new strategic insight, which often challenges the existing perceptions held by managers, our experience has been that many immediate actions to improve results are identified and implemented.

Figure 2.3 gives an example of an analysis sheet, which can be adapted to specific situations, and expanded if necessary. We are not suggesting that all organisations have only seven products, nor do we imply that every minor product should be examined with the same intensity.

The analysis cannot be completed entirely from looking at the

Product		Sales			Profit contribution			Market		
Name	Life cycle	Value	Growth	% Sales	Value	% Sales	% Total	Share	Relative share	Growth
1										
2										
3										
4										
5										
6										
7										

Product		Financial assets		Factory		Human resources		Management	
Name	Life cycle	Fixed	Current	Capacity	%	% R&D	% Sales	%	Quality
1									
2									
3									
4									
5									
6									
7									

Figure 2.3 Related products to resource utilisation. (Source: D. E. Hussey, *Strategy and Planning: A Manager's Guide* Wiley, Chichester, 1999. © John Wiley & Sons, Limited. Reproduced with permission)

accounting information. In fact, only the columns looking at sales, profit contribution and financial assets could be filled in from what has been discussed so far. Later chapters will discuss issues related to the remaining columns. The point of the form is that it draws together a wide spectrum of information so that it can be looked at simultaneously.

The first two columns of each line are identical, and the repetition is to make it easier to read the form, as the width, which is restricted by the size of the book, and the need to avoid confusing readers with the abbreviations that would be used in practice mean that the rows have to be divided.

SPECIFIC AREAS OF RISK

The financial appraisal should also cover areas of real or potential risk. This is where certain events and trends in the external environment meet the internal elements of the organisation. The type of issue we have in mind here is the depth of exposure to exchange-rate fluctuations, or the assets and profits at risk through investments, major contracts or major customers in politically or economically unstable countries.

The aim here is to identify the big risks, and quantify them as far as is possible. It hardly needs saying that an organisation with half of its assets and earning power in a combination of Russia, Serbia, Indonesia, Sierra Leone and Zimbabwe would be facing more risk than a similar sized organisation whose efforts were concentrated on the EU, the USA and Japan.

THE FINANCE AND ACCOUNTING PROCESSES

So far we have looked mainly at the position of the organisation through its financial figures. However, in doing this we have also touched on matters which stand behind the figures, and which cause the organisation to interpret its results differently, or to behave in a particular way. Examples are the particular way in which the organisation judges itself (e.g. earnings per share, value-based strategy or some other approach), and its concept of cost accounting (e.g. absorption costing, ABC).

Competitive advantage can be gained or lost through the choices the organisation makes, so an important part of the financial appraisal is to identify these policies, concepts and conventions. It should not be assumed that the organisation's current choices are the best, and although all have advantages and disadvantages, in every unique situation some are better than others. The evaluation of whether what is done is the best choice has to take the context of the organisation into account.

One illustration of how the accounting system can become a weakness is indicated by research by Kaplan (1995). He found that many organisations have a "fundamental disconnect between the development and formulation of their strategy and the implementation of that strategy into useful action". Four major barriers to effective implementation were identified:

- Vision that could not be actioned, because it was not translated into operational terms.
- Strategy that is not linked to departmental and individual goals (incentives are tied to annual financial performance instead of to long-range strategy: only 21% of executive management and 6% of middle management have objectives that are tied to the strategy).
- Resource allocation is based on short-term budgets and not

the strategy (only just over a third of organisations have a direct link between the strategy and the budgeting process).
- Control is directed at short-term performance and rarely evaluates progress on long-term objectives.

Some of the aspects which might be considered are included in the checklist and questionnaire which appear in Appendix 2.2.

APPENDIX 2.1

METHODS FOR MEASURING FINANCIAL PERFORMANCE

Earnings per share (EPS) This is calculated by dividing the after-tax profits attributable to ordinary shareholders by the number of ordinary shares. The difference between the EPS at the start and end of a period shows the growth or decline. This method provides a measure of the value provided to shareholders, expressed in an easily understandable way that can be compared with other companies. However, EPS is based on accounting conventions, which can vary between organisations, and does not take account of the market value of shares.

Margin on sales Net profit divided by sales, expressed as a percentage.

Market value (of a quoted company) The generally accepted definition is the current stock market price per share times the number of issued ordinary shares.

Price/earnings (P/E) ratio Market price per ordinary share is divided by the earnings per share, to give a ratio which takes account of share prices. However, it has the deficiencies of the EPS method, plus the fact that the method of calculation in the financial press uses the last reported EPS, and it is making a big assumption that this figure is a constant until the next company report.

Return on investment (ROI) There are several different ROI methods, but they are all based on calculating profit as a percentage of capital. It is the definitions of these which vary with the purpose. The ROI can be calculated both pre- and post-tax:

traditionally British companies have preferred the former, and US companies take the latter as the norm. Two of the most used ROI measures are given here, but there are others.

Return on assets (ROA)   Net profit as a percentage of total assets. It measures the profitability in relation to the assets, without being concerned with how those assets are financed. For this reason it is useful for comparing the performance of units within the organisation, when these units have no responsibility for how the finances are organised.

Return on owners' equity (ROE)   Measures the return gained on the shareholders' equity in the firm. It is a performance measure which is of interest to senior management and shareholders, although it does not measure the full extent of shareholder value.

SHAREHOLDER VALUE METHODS

There are a number of methods which examine strategies for their value to shareholders. They all start from the economic premise that cash flow is what is important, at the level of the whole organisation and of each of its business units, thus avoiding many of the traps. They use discounted cash flow (dcf) methods to evaluate the future cash flows of the strategic options, which is similar to how dcf has been used, for around 40 years, for the assessment of capital investment projects. This approach therefore takes account of the time value of money, and also insists that all strategies are designed to earn more than the organisation's cost of capital.

Cost of capital   The weighted average cost of capital is the most commonly used method. This takes the cost of debt, preference shares and equity, weighted by the proportions in which they occur in the capital structure of the organisation. Debt and preference shares can be costed relatively easily. Equity is somewhat harder, as it represents the opportunity cost to shareholders, or what could be gained by investing in other organisations with similar risks. It can be argued that for equity there are three components to consider: the interest rate that could be gained from a risk-free investment, compensation for the expected rate of inflation, and a risk premium which is related to the additional risks of this investment.

Valuation methods   (Sources are given at the end of each description.)

Equity-spread approach   The equity-spread approach to valuation focuses on the difference between the return on shareholders' equity (the change in share price, plus dividends, divided by the initial share price) and the cost of equity (the shareholders' expectation for return, based on the element of risk). If the equity spread is positive, then shareholder value has been created; if negative, then it has been destroyed.

Share price theory assumes that the share price is influenced by a company's expected equity spread as well as its growth prospects. Managers will do best, then, to focus investment for growth in positive equity spread businesses. The technique's value is limited because it is based on accounting value, with likely distortions. It also ignores some very important sources of value, such as deferred taxes and terminal value at the end of the planning period, and is also very sensitive to financial leverage. (Handler, 1991)

Market value multiples   This approach seeks to find a business unit equivalent of the market/book multiple. This approach lends itself to simulating both the beginning and ending market values of a business unit on the basis of the book value of its assets

To establish the multiple it is necessary to determine what are the measurable indicators or drivers of the market value. These variables (combinations of returns, growth, R&D expenditure, etc.) are given weighted values, with the help of specially developed models and databases to help predict share price based on book value.

The key advantage of this approach is that its accuracy can easily be tested with historical data. A test of a sample of 600 US firms found that value-creation estimates based on multiples of either assets or sales corresponded more closely to actual shareholder value creation than the accounting measures of ROI and EPS (Reimann, 1988). One of the disadvantages of the method is that book values (the base to which the multiple is applied to predict the "value") can be affected by many accounting factors which could distort the picture, so it does not necessarily prove a reliable base. (Handler, 1991)

Economic value added approach The economic value added approach is the product of the equity spread (the difference between return on equity and the cost of capital) and the total capital employed in the business. The objective is to increase the economic earnings derived from the existing or projected capital bases. (Unfortunately, if the equity spread is negative, then the approach is "economic value lost').

This approach is frequently used at the portfolio planning stage; and some companies only use it for making strategic decisions at the group level. (Handler, 1991)

Positive-value and negative-value business unit approaches These approaches are simply the opposite sides of the same coin. Like the economic value added approach, they are used to make portfolio decisions about business units, and in making acquisition and divestment decisions – adding to or growing those businesses for which economic returns exceed the cost of capital (positive net present values). Businesses with negative economic values will be restructured or eliminated, with capital diverted to positive-value business units.

The Q-ratio approach The Q-ratio approach also focuses on economic value. Developed in the 1960s by James Tobin, the Nobel Prize winning economist, the approach calculates the relationship of the market value of a company's assets to the cost of replacing those assets in current money. This Q-ratio is, thus, an M/B multiple with the book value of assets in the denominator adjusted for the effects of inflation. The rationale is that investors adjust their expected returns for anticipated inflation when analysing alternative investments. Therefore, the true or "real" value of a business should also reflect this inflation factor. (Reimann, 1987)

SOME LIQUIDITY RATIOS

Current ratio (expressed as a ratio) Current assets divided by current liabilities.

Debt/equity ratio (expressed as a percentage) Total liabilities divided by shareholders' equity.

Debts/capitalisation (expressed as a percentage) Non-current liabilities divided by (non-current liabilities plus shareholders' equity).

APPENDIX 2.2

CHECK LIST AND QUESTIONNAIRE

The aim of this appendix is to aid the application of the approaches discussed in this chapter. It is divided into two parts. The first is a reminder of the work that should be done on the numbers themselves. The second asks questions about the finance and accounting processes and policies, with suggestions for scoring the answers based on good practice observed in a variety of organisations. These questions are not meant to be answered by guesses. Adjust the checklist and questionnaire to fit your business, but do not reject anything without very careful thought.

PART 1: CHECKLIST

Prepare an analysis sheet recording the following minimum information. Do not let this prevent you from calculating additional ratios if you think these might be helpful

1. Key figures for each year for at least the last three, and preferably five years, at both corporate level and for each SBU or major subsidiary in the group
Sales
Operating profit
Cash loss or gain
Profit before interest and tax
Net profit after interest and tax

2. Indices for each of the above (year 1 = 100)
Index series are suggested because they make it easy to compare performance across business units, and to examine growth/decline patterns.

3. Performance ratios at corporate level, by year: make appropriate internal and external comparisons
Year-end market value
High and low values during each year
Earnings per share
P/E ratio
Return on assets

Return on equity
Cost of capital

4. Performance ratios at business unit level, by year: make internal and external comparisons
Return on assets
Gross margin
Cash lost/gained

5. Sources of profit (possibly by business unit)
Products: list in descending order of profit contribution, showing revenue, profit contribution, and for each the percentage of the total. If cumulative percentage columns are added, it is possible to read off the position in approximate deciles.
Customers: similar Pareto analysis by customers. For most organisations it would be impracticable to list all customers.
(See also Figure 2.3 for another useful analysis.)

6. Financial resources/flexibility
List the conclusions from this section of the analysis.

7. Specific areas of risk
List and quantify the revenue and profits exposed to risks of political instability and abnormal fluctuations in exchange rates.

8. Conclusions
List the conclusions that can be drawn from the analysis.

PART 2: QUESTIONNAIRE

Possible answers, from "no competitive advantage for the firm" (1) to "excellent or significant competitive advantage for the firm" (4), are given below each question. They are examples derived from various firms. Use them as an aid in assessing the questions.

1. What performance concept is the driving force for strategic decisions?

In light of your assessment, how do you evaluate its competitive impact on the organisation?

No competitive   Significant competitive
advantage   advantage

1   2   3   4

Examples:
1. We use a number of measures, but none has any particular strategic impact.
2. We use ROI measures, because if we get these right we will satisfy shareholders.
3. Our measures try to take account of shareholder value (e.g. EPS, P/E ratios).
4. We use value-based methods.

2. To what extent is management in agreement about the firm's critical success factors?

In light of your assessment, how do you evaluate its competitive impact on the organisation?

No competitive   Significant competitive
advantage   advantage

1   2   3   4

Examples:
1. We make no such analyses; the bookkeeping takes care of itself.
2. As long as profits are satisfactory, we have no use for discussing our strong and weak sides. If profits fall, we try to lower production costs.
3. At least once a year, we critique the value of assorted products, both their expense and marketability. This gives a pretty good indication of the firm's strong and weak points.
4. We closely examine where our strengths lie (what we are good at), and where we are least strong. In light of market challenges and our strategy, we seek to develop our strong points even more, and we improve the weak, thus furthering development.

3. How systematically does the firm work with long-range financial and strategic plans?

In light of your assessment, how do you evaluate its competitive impact on the organisation?

No competitive advantage		Significant competitive advantage	
1	2	3	4

Examples:
1. The firm has no long-range planning effort in place.
2. In connection with large loan applications and other essential dispositions, the firm's management tries to forecast business for the following year.
3. The firm's management has definite goals for the firm's production, its sales, and earnings for the next 3 to 5 years.
4. The firm's management and employees jointly have defined our desired market position 3 to 5 years hence, and on this basis have definite plans for various products, market developments and investments. Derived from this are definite yearly surplus and financial goals.

4. What form of short-term financial planning does the firm use?

In light of your assessment, how do you evaluate its competitive impact on the organisation?

No competitive advantage		Significant competitive advantage	
1	2	3	4

Examples:
1. We have no proper financial planning, not even for the short-term.
2. On the basis of the yearly balance sheet and income statement, we try to estimate the necessary business for next year if earning goals hold. At the same time, we estimate whether or not the firm has adequate resources to achieve these goals.
3. The firm's management prepares a pro forma balance sheet, income statement, capital budgets, and liquidity forecasts, partly from information in the previous year's accounts, and partly from an evaluation of the future market and competitive situation.
4. Based on market developments and our strategic plan, we set goals for the coming year in quarterly plans. This is the basis for periodic budgets for operation, assets, investments and liquidity.

5. To what extent are the detailed actions needed to attain our longer range strategies included in the budgetary process, and the way management performance is assessed?

In light of your assessment, how do you evaluate its competitive impact on the organisation?

No competitive advantage		Significant competitive advantage	
1	2	3	4

Examples:
1. We assume that managers have done this, and expect them to meet the budget
2. We tell managers to do this, but in any conflict situation the current year's planned profit is what has to be met.
3. The strategic actions are seen as important, and managers have to explain any deviations, but the planned profit is very important.
4. The control system forces managers to take a strategic view, and managers are held accountable for taking the actions and achieving budget. Performance assessment covers both aspects.

6. How well is the firm's accounting system designed with respect to giving management information, e.g. for cost estimates and budgets?

In light of your assessment, how do you evaluate its competitive impact on the organisation?

No competitive advantage		Significant competitive advantage	
1	2	3	4

Examples:
1. The accounting system accomplishes the minimum required in terms of providing management information.
2. The accounting system does not give management any current information, but the yearly statements are analysed, and this analysis forms the basis for future dispositions.
3. Monthly statements are prepared and it is possible to go back in the records and get information about individual product groups and markets.

4. The accounting is primarily built on the basis of budgets, thus allowing budget control.

7. How systematically do you perform budget control?

In light of your assessment, how do you evaluate its competitive impact on the organisation?

No competitive   Significant competitive
advantage   advantage
1   2   3   4

Examples:
1. There are no budgets and no budget control.
2. The budget is compared with the annual report.
3. Quarterly or monthly budgets and accounts are compared, and the variance calculated. We also do yearly estimates.
4. The budget and accounts are run together and, deviations from the budget are discussed by management and relevant employees.

8. Is the firm's cost analysis method valid and reliable?

In light of your assessment, how do you evaluate its competitive impact on the organisation?

No competitive   Significant competitive
advantage   advantage
1   2   3   4

Examples:
1. We neither estimate nor perform post hoc cost analyses.
2. We estimate approximate costs based on last year's accounting information.
3. We estimate standard costs, but do not use ABC.
4. We estimate standard costs, revise for variance in volume, and use ABC methods.

REFERENCES

Channon, D. F. 1997. Activity based costing, in Channon, D. F. (ed.) *Blackwell Encyclopedic Dictionary of Strategic Management*, Oxford, Blackwell.
Drucker, P. F. 1964. *Managing for Results*, London, Heinemann.

Handler, S. 1991. *Value-Based Strategic Management: A Survey of UK Companies*, London, Harbridge Consulting Group.

Hussey, D. 1998. *Strategic Management: from Theory to Implementation*, 4th edn, Oxford, Butterworth-Heinemann.

Hussey, D. 1999. *Strategy and Planning*, 5th edition, Chichester, Wiley.

Kaplan, R. 1995. *Building a Management System to Implement Your Strategy: Strategic Management Survey*, London, Renaissance Solutions.

Reimann, B. C. 1987. *Managing for the Shareholders: An Overview of Value-based Strategic Management,* Oxford, Blackwell/The Planning Forum.

Reimann, B. C. 1988. Decision support software for value-based planning, *Planning Review*, March/April.

3

The Marketing Audit

INTRODUCTION

Managers may have a number of reasons for undertaking a marketing audit. Among them might be:

1. The introduction of a new product.
2. As part of a profit enhancement exercise.
3. Assessing whether the firm has:
   - the right pricing policy,
   - the bundle of goods and services appropriate for the market,
   - an appropriate channel strategy.
4. As part of a regularly scheduled marketing planning process.

The marketing audit is a comprehensive and structured examination of the firm's market and the forces impacting the market, the firm's activities and performance, as well as the processes by which marketing decisions are being made. The outcome of a marketing audit should highlight the opportunities and challenges for the firm's marketing and suggest recommendations for improvement, and a plan for achieving superior performance.

It is necessary to follow a structured approach when assessing the company's market performance. This helps the marketing audit team work through a comprehensive and systematic diagnosis.

The audit will generally start with a meeting of the marketing audit team and key officers of the firm, in order to establish the

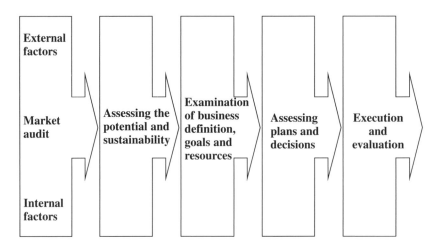

Figure 3.1   The marketing audit process

initial reason the for audit and the objectives to be answered by the marketing audit. Limitations in terms of depth, coverage, reporting format (written reports consume many resources; effective presentations few) and time period to be covered should also be agreed up-front. Such a meeting should be followed by a detailed plan, under considerations of timeliness and costs.

INTRODUCING THE MARKETING AUDIT PROCESS MODEL

We believe the marketing audit process should follow a five-stage process, as outlined in Figure 3.1. Each phase consists of a number of elements that must be investigated in detail.

The first step, the marketing audit, can generally be divided into two parts: external and internal analysis. These two parts cover six key areas of analysis:

1. *Customers.* This part of the investigation must cover an analysis of the current, past and future customers, their needs and preferences, segment differences, demands of different segments, buying patterns, development in application of core and augmented products, and similar issues.

2. *Competitors.* Who are the major competitors, current and future? What are their strategies and objectives, competencies and capabilities, market share, profitability, and technology base?

3. *Channels.* How are products and services brought to market? What are the channels? What is their share, concentration, ownership, profitability, efficiency, ability to satisfy current and future customer needs, trade practices, and similar issues?

4. *Context.* This element covers the macro-economic, demographic, political, ecological, public and regulatory conditions under which the market is operating. For firms operating internationally, this element must be reviewed with care, as it can be particularly tricky for the marketing activities of the firm.

5. *Company's competencies.* The firm's own strengths and weaknesses must also be considered as part of the marketing audit. Not only must the competencies be evaluated, but also their relevance in terms of generating competitive advantage. The firm's organisation, structure, marketing information, reporting, planning and control systems are also important.

6. *Costs and profitability.* What are the profitabilities of the firm's different market segments, products, territories and channels? (See the remarks on product costing and profitability in Chapter 2.) What is the cost structure and how does it compare to competitors?

The first four elements are part of the external analysis and the last two part of the internal analysis. Conveniently, all six elements start with the letter "C", and marketers often refer to the list as "the 6 Cs of marketing". The marketing audit results provide the input for assessing the potential and sustainability, which is our next step.

ASSESSING THE POTENTIAL AND SUSTAINABILITY

Based on the 6 Cs analysis of the marketing audit, the task is now to establish the basis for future demand and competition. The key questions to answer from the previous analysis are (Figure 3.2):

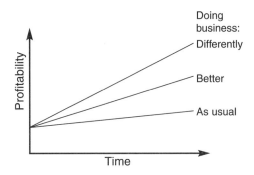

Figure 3.2   Assessing the future performance gap

1. What will be the forecast for our products and services if we
    continue to conduct business as usual?
2. What happens to the future demand if we improve what we
    are currently doing?
3. What would happen if we started to do business in a very
    different way?

As part of this analysis, we must also examine the sustainability of
performance. To what extent is the current level of performance
dependent on unique technology, cost structure, trade relationships, or customer "lock-in"? The fundamental issue to be
addressed is the *attractiveness* of the market and the segments
being served. By attractiveness, we are considering the fundamental growth and profitability. If the answer is positive, the following question is, of course, what forces might threaten the
attractiveness. If a negative response is concluded from the
analysis, we must ask what can be done to make the market
attractive.

EXAMINATION OF BUSINESS DEFINITION, GOALS AND RESOURCES

The previous analysis provides the basis for examining the fundamental business definition and the stated goals, and assessing
the resources made available. Here a number of questions may
challenge the current definition of the customers, the market

coverage, the technology base, the aspiration level and the means to reaching the goals. Typically, the auditing team will ask questions, such as, "How do we define our business?", "What do we want to make our business?", "How do we want to conduct our business?" etc. This discussion will naturally be linked to a fundamental discussion on the objectives which the key decision makers believe will be necessary to achieve at the behest of the company's shareholders. However, the discussion must also include other important constituents, such as employees, customers, partners in the distribution channel, local, national and international governments, suppliers and other "stakeholders'.

Box 3.1

A recent study at a large, international producer of industrial refrigeration revealed that its current definition of products and market scope would yield insufficient growth over the next 10 years. This led the management team to examine a redefinition of the business to more aggressively include an expanded service business that moved the firm outside the fundamental refrigeration business.

The establishment of specific goals will naturally flow from an examination of the relevant sets of objectives. The goals can be quantitative as well as qualitative. In recent years, more firms are starting to consider a broader set of financial as well as non-financial measures. Even with the financial goal set, we are starting to see firms use a more sophisticated set of measures, which are then linked to the remuneration packages of management. For the marketing management team, this means that merely achieving sales targets will likely be inadequate. Achievements of market share, channel penetration, shelf position, brand recognition, customer loyalty indices, sales force effectiveness, advertising effectiveness, repeat purchase benchmarks and similar factors may also be part of the goal set.

The evaluation of the firm's goal set, and particularly of their prospects for achievement and their future relevance, will necessitate a discussion of the current resource allocation, as well as the likely resource availability. This will, in turn, create a new discussion on the future goals to be achieved.

ASSESSING THE MARKETING PLAN AND KEY MARKETING DECISIONS

The discussion of goals and resource utilisation is essentially a prelude to an assessment of the current marketing plan's effectiveness and efficiency. This phase will also include an examination of the firm's segmentation approach and the choice of the target customers. The marketing audit provides an overview of customer developments, but an analysis of the chosen segment and developments for this group of customers will also be necessary, for several reasons:

1. The firm's marketing activity may have altered customer expectations, and new initiatives will now be appropriate.
2. Competitors' actions may have changed the dynamics within and between segments.
3. Customer preferences may have developed due to outside trends.

New technological and channel developments may also be part of the forces that have challenged the assumptions that were the basis for the firm's current marketing plan. In light of the market developments of the preceding period and the prospects for the future assessed in the marketing audit, it behoves the audit team to analyse the specific aspects of the company's "marketing mix". The marketing mix is a term used by marketing professionals to describe the critical marketing decisions which in concert are the manifestation of the firm's marketing strategy. The marketing mix is generally thought to consist of five critical decisions, all of which flow from the marketing audit:

1. *Positioning decision.* This decision relates to the distinctive perception desired of the firm's bundle of goods and services, in the minds of customers in the chosen market segment. For example, Volvo's positioning, in the minds of its chosen customer group, is that of a safe family vehicle.
2. *Product/service decision set* The decision concerns the bundle of product features and augmented service offerings that the firm has chosen to be part of its commercial endeavour. The decision include both the depth and range of the product/service portfolio and must include not only an

evaluation of volume, profitability and development, but also an assessment of the fits with customer needs and expectations for the chosen segment.

3. *Pricing decision set.* This decision set focuses on the firm's pricing strategy, but must also include assessment of volume discounts, year-end bonuses, trade support, non-financial incentives, return policy, financing offerings, back-purchase etc., which may all influence the customers' cost experience.

4. *Promotion decision set.* This decision deeply concerns the firm's efforts to communicate its value proposition to its targeted customer group, including public relations efforts, general awareness creating activities (such as television promotions and print media activities) and interest enhancement efforts (such as trade shows, dispensing of sales force campaigns and in-store campaigns).

5. *Place/distribution decision set.* The decisions concerning the management of the firm's channel strategy must also be examined. The impact of the Internet has made these decisions more difficult today, and in previous years. Rooted in the customers preferences of where and how they choose to buy the firm's offering, the channel strategy must manage the potential conflicts among the various avenues to the end customer.

These five critical sets of marketing decisions, often referred to as the 5 Ps of marketing, must be viewed in totality, and thus examined for their internal consistency. The segment choice and the totality of marketing decisions in unison form the marketing strategy of the firm.

The marketing audit team must also consider the robustness of the current plan, its internal consistency, and its analytical and creative composition. The group may examine whether alternative strategies are available to the organisation, and the reasons for selecting one as opposed to others. Contingency plans are an inherent part of the general plan, and should also be evaluated.

EVALUATION OF EXECUTION

The final phase of the marketing audit process is the examination of the firm's execution of the marketing plan. The basis for this phase rests in the key marketing decisions that are the core of the marketing plan. The execution is grounded in the specific pro- grammes and projects of the critical marketing decision frame. The auditing team must consider the consistency and relevance of the programmes and projects, and how each initiative links the de- cisions to the goal achievement. The associated budgets for each programme and project should also be evaluated against the actu- al resources expended, and the goal achievements associated with each programme or budget. Finally, the delegation of responsibil- ity for each programme or project, the timeliness, and the desired impact will also be part of the marketing auditing team's scrutiny.

IMPACTING THE MARKETING MANAGEMENT PROCESS

The marketing audit is not merely intended to examine the achievement of current marketing results and suggest changes in the decisions which may have led to the marketing results. The marketing auditing process should also lead to an evaluation of the firm's marketing management, the processes used to generate market intelligence, and the processes for analysing and dissemi- nating the results to the relevant decision makers within and outside of the marketing function. Recent research suggests that these processes are vital to spur market orientations in firms, resulting in higher business performance, greater customer satisfaction and more satisfied employees, but also examine the degree to which the market intelligence and analyses are used in responsive decision making (Jenster and Jaworski, 2000).

As suggested by Figure 3.3, this research suggests that three key drivers are vital to achieve market orientation. The first driver is a set of senior management factors. These factors are mainly about the senior executives' concern and involvement in ensuring that market intelligence is undertaken in a timely fashion, that the analytical work has a sufficient level of rigour, and that key de- cisions are being supported by facts and analyses and not merely anecdotal evidence. In the words of one executive, "If the top doesn't ask the question, nobody will provide the answer". The auditing team must address the issue of senior executives' drive for market orientation, and suggest any desired corrective action.

The second critical set of factors relates to the inter-functional

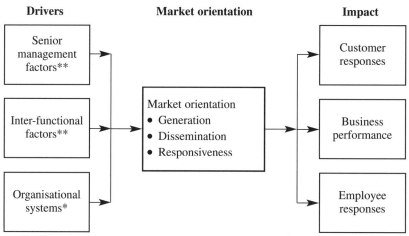

| Drivers | Market orientation | Impact |

Senior management factors**

Inter-functional factors**

Organisational systems*

Market orientation
• Generation
• Dissemination
• Responsiveness

Customer responses

Business performance

Employee responses

* Significance at 90% confidence interval.
** Significance at 95% confidence interval.

Figure 3.3 Recent research of 198 international industrial firms suggests different relationships. (Source: P. V. Jenster and B. Jaworski, Driving forces in market orientation: a study of international industrial organisations, *Journal of Strategic Change*, **9**(6), 357–62, 2000. © John Wiley & Sons, Limited. Reproduced with permission)

dynamics of the firm. To what extent do serious functional barriers prevent information from flowing between departments? Do different professional groups have the social and linguistic ability to cross functional demarcation lines?

The third driver of market orientation consists of various organisational and systems factors which may impact the market orientation. The firm's organisational structure, the budgeting and planning process, the reward and remuneration systems, and the IT system may all impact the degree of market orientation of the firm.

The marketing audit should also address these fundamental drivers of market orientation as part of the review process.

This chapter has covered the marketing audit process, and has discussed the critical areas of analysis to be performed during the various phases of the process. The extensiveness of the marketing audit is a function of the specific needs of the firm and the purpose decided on prior to the start of the process. The process can be performed by an internal team. However, following good auditing practices developed in accounting, it is very useful for one or more outsiders to participate or to monitor the efforts.

APPENDIX 3.1

MARKETING AUDIT QUESTIONNAIRE

Analysing a company is a challenge even for the most skilled managers and consultants. Where should we start? What are the key issues to focus on and the most important areas to investigate? The following questions have been used over the years to uncover important areas where firms either excel or fall short in comparison with their competitors. Obviously, these questions should not be generalised to every firm or business unit. However, although these questions focus on issues related to traditional, small- to medium-sized manufacturing organisations, they are relevant to service and high tech firms.

The following process should be followed as you or your representatives apply these questions to the firm.

1. Read all of the questions to get an idea of the area covered by the checklist.
2. Think of the critical success factors as they apply to the strategy you have or think is necessary to follow in the industry. (See Chapter 9 for more information on critical success factors.)
3. Read the individual questions and think about the situation in your own firm. Does this situation provide you with a competitive advantage or disadvantage? Use the sample answers or responses as an indicator and not a key in the evaluation of your own firm. Note down comments and issues as you go along.
4. Finally, evaluate the firm's situation in the entire area covered by the checklist. This can be done by evaluating the importance of the individual questions for your firm. The result should be a realistic evaluation, not just an average of checks in from the various scales. Where does the firm stand and what are the areas which need more attention?

Note that the examples following each question are sample responses that have been found in various organisations and may not necessarily apply to your firm. They contain examples of situations that are important for some firms, and are only expressions of the thoughts behind the questions.

Good luck.

PRODUCTS AND SERVICES

Possible answers, from "no competitive advantage for the firm" (1) to "excellent or significant competitive advantage for the firm" (4), are given below each question. They are examples derived from various firms. Use them as an aid in assessing the questions.

1. Are the firm's products or services commodity items or unique in character?

In light of your assessment, how do you evaluate its competitive impact on the organisation?

No competitive advantage		Significant competitive advantage	
1	2	3	4

Examples:
1. Commodity items.
2. Commodity market items, although with a few improvements.
3. Products not a result of our own development, but we have added improvements, making them some of the best in the market.
4. Highly differentiated, internally developed and produced to the specific needs of a targeted segment of customers.

2. Can the firm's products or services be copied, or are they protected, e.g. by patents, special technology or because imitation requires special development work?

In light of your assessment, how do you evaluate its competitive impact on the organisation?

No competitive advantage		Significant competitive advantage	
1	2	3	4

Examples:
1. Every firm in the field can make a substitute.
2. Technical knowledge is required to make the products.
3. Main products are protected by exclusive licences.
4. Special development work together with unique processes and know-how are required to make the product.

3. Do price and quality fit the expectations of the customers the firm has chosen to serve (please provide evidence from customer surveys)?

In light of your assessment, how do you evaluate its competitive impact on the organisation?

No competitive   Significant competitive
advantage   advantage

1   2   3   4

Examples:
1. We concentrate on moving the product at the current price and quality level. We don't know very much about the customers and their price and quality requirements.
2. Quality is somewhat worse (or much higher) than the customers apparently want.
3. There is good agreement, but we haven't decided whether we should work with an exclusive market with high quality or with a broader market and lower quality and price.
4. The firm has positioned itself at the best price to quality level for our customers, who recognise our higher price and our superior quality.

4. Is the market for current products or services expected to grow or shrink?

In light of your assessment, how do you evaluate its competitive impact on the organisation?

No competitive   Significant competitive
advantage   advantage

1   2   3   4

Examples:
1. Sales of most products are falling. Products may soon be outdated.
2. Sales are seriously threatened by new technology or materials, but are still holding steady.
3. Sales are steady and we plan to further develop our product portfolio to our market share.
4. Revenues are increasing from carefully managed market share expansion.

5. How profitable are the individual products or services?

In light of your assessment, how do you evaluate its competitive impact on the organisation?

No competitive advantage		Significant competitive advantage	
1	2	3	4

Examples:
1. We don't know the profitability of individual products, only that overall profits are unsatisfactory.
2. Overall profits aren't good enough, but we know which products aren't profitable and are working to change them.
3. Profitability is systematically investigated, and we are well on the way to solving problems with unprofitable products.
4. Our product portfolio is constantly monitored and the ones that are less profitable are constantly subject to cancellation, redesign or repositioning.

6. When your firm develops new products, what is the impetus for improvements or innovations?

In light of your assessment, how do you evaluate its competitive impact on the organisation?

No competitive advantage		Significant competitive advantage	
1	2	3	4

Examples:
1. New products are introduced when customers demand them.
2. New products are introduced when another firm comes up with an idea we can use.
3. New products come from our in-house technical development.
4. We internally design and produce our products. New products are developed regularly in accordance with our planning.

7. How does the range of products/services produced affect your firm's overall performance?

In light of your assessment, how do you evaluate its competitive impact on the organisation?

No competitive   Significant competitive
advantage   advantage

1   2   3   4

Examples:
1. The number of products is large, giving constant production and delivery problems. We can neither improve nor develop.
2. We are trying to limit products, but have large commitments to deliver old models: 20% of our line accounts for 80% of revenues.
3. We keep track of revenues for individual product groups. Almost all groups do a reasonable business.
4. Sales of individual products are closely followed, and elimination is prepared for when sales fall.

8. Does the firm have a problem with returned goods/rework compare to other firms in the field?

In light of your assessment, how do you evaluate its competitive impact on the organisation?

No competitive   Significant competitive
advantage   advantage

1   2   3   4

Examples:
1. Yes, we have a much higher return rate than competitors.
2. There are many complaints. We take a lot of returned goods.
3. There are some returns attributable to transit damage.
4. We almost never have returns or complaints.

COMPETITION

Possible answers, from "no competitive advantage for the firm" (1) to "excellent or significant competitive advantage for the firm" (4), are given below each question. They are examples derived from various firms. Use them as an aid in assessing the questions.

1. How does the firm's market share compare to that of the competition?

In light of your assessment, how do you evaluate its competitive impact on the organisation?

No competitive
advantage

Significant competitive
advantage

1   2   3   4

Examples:
1. We haven't calculated our market share or undertaken corresponding analysis.
2. Even though sales are rising, our market share is declining, when we compare our sales with industry sales according to public information.
3. Our market share is very stable.
4. Market share is growing at the level we have set in our long-range plans.

2. How well does the firm's management know the critical success factors affecting the firm's position in the market?

In light of your assessment, how do you evaluate its competitive impact on the organisation?

No competitive
advantage

Significant competitive
advantage

1   2   3   4

Examples:
1. We have succeeded so far in selling everything we make, so we haven't examined these conditions.
2. Other than price as a key customer consideration, we are not aware of any other factors affecting market share
3. We think there is a connection between price and quality and our position in the market, so we attempt to match price with quality level.
4. Through a number of analyses of the effect of price changes, quality changes, customer service, changes in advertising etc., we have found these factors to be important.

3. How much of a leadership role does the firm take with regard to new products, new design, new packaging etc.?

In light of your assessment, how do you evaluate its competitive impact on the organisation?

No competitive   Significant competitive
advantage   advantage

1   2   3   4

Examples:
1. We are usually the last company to introduce changes, as we feel that as long as the product can be sold as it is, there is no reason for change.
2. If the ideas of others are successful, we will try to follow as well as we can.
3. We try to find the leading firms and follow them as closely as possible.
4. We spend a fair amount on market and product analysis and always try to be ahead of the competition.

4. How sensitive is the firm to price competition?

In light of your assessment, how do you evaluate its competitive impact on the organisation?

No competitive   Significant competitive
advantage   advantage

1   2   3   4

Examples:
1. It has already been necessary to lower the price to stay in the market, but we can't take another reduction.
2. If the price is further reduced, we will have to cut into our reserves.
3. We don't want to move from our current prices. Instead we can improve quality quickly or, if necessary, shift to other products.
4. We are sensitive to the customers' demands for better pricing and are able to lower prices appropriately with improved efficiencies without cutting into margins.

5. How is the firm able to meet quality competition?

In light of your assessment, how do you evaluate its competitive impact on the organisation?

No competitive advantage

Significant competitive advantage

1   2   3   4

Examples:
1. We have constant difficulties with design and production quality.
2. We can usually convince customers that we are at least "as good" as competitors' products.
3. Improvements in quality can be implemented very quickly, since plans are complete and method changes are always prepared.
4. We have always led the field in quality and are constantly trying to maintain that position by product analysis and development.

6. To what degree are pricing, credit policy, and discounts determined by competition?

In light of your assessment, how do you evaluate its competitive impact on the organisation?

No competitive advantage

Significant competitive advantage

1   2   3   4

Examples:
1. Our prices are determined by what others are charging.
2. On the whole, we have to align our prices with those of others in the field, but in our service-oriented field, customer goodwill is more important than prices offered by other firms, in maintaining sales.
3. We have meaningful freedom in setting prices, because we have built relationships with many of our customers and because some of our products are so special that comparison with other firms is impossible.
4. Our products must be seen as unique. We constantly develop products, and prices are more determined by what the market can bear than by what competitors are doing.

7. To what degree does the firm use opportunities for co-operation with the competition?

In light of your assessment, how do you evaluate its competitive impact on the organisation?

No competitive advantage		Significant competitive advantage	
1	2	3	4

Examples:
1. We haven't attempted any cooperation.
2. A few attempts at cooperation have failed, but we continue discussions.
3. Cooperation most often takes a multilateral form. Forces are in place leading toward more structured cooperation.
4. Cooperation in production and sales are relatively well established.

8. How well does the firm know the future plans of its most important competitors?

In light of your assessment, how do you evaluate its competitive impact on the organisation?

No competitive advantage		Significant competitive advantage	
1	2	3	4

Examples:
1. Absolutely no knowledge.
2. We have a bit of knowledge acquired more or less randomly.
3. We constantly try to judge the external (e.g. price and advertising) and internal (e.g. purchasing and hiring) actions of our competitors.
4. We maintain systematic current knowledge of developments in the field, and we have good knowledge of competitors' development and plans for the future.

CUSTOMERS

Possible answers, from "no competitive advantage for the firm" (1) to "excellent or significant competitive advantage for the firm" (4), are given below each question. They are examples derived from various firms. Use them as an aid in assessing the questions.

1. How stable is the firm's customer base?

In light of your assessment, how do you evaluate its competitive impact on the organisation?

No competitive advantage | Significant competitive advantage

1   2   3   4

Examples:
1. We have never really given it much thought.
2. Although we have tried, it seems that we only have a limited number of steady customers.
3. We have a number of steady customers who return again and again.
4. Our customer base is well understood, very stable and is continually growing.

2. How dependent is the firm on a single or a few major customers?

In light of your assessment, how do you evaluate its competitive impact on the organisation?

No competitive advantage | Significant competitive advantage

1   2   3   4

Examples:
1. We only sell to a couple of major customers as second or third level supplier.
2. We have to reduce production if we lose one of our major customers.
3. About 20% of our customers buy 80% of our products.
4. We would definitely notice the loss of a couple of our major customers, but it is not likely and the firm's existence would not be in danger.

3. How good is the contact with important customers in the market?

In light of your assessment, how do you evaluate its competitive impact on the organisation?

No competitive   Significant competitive
advantage   advantage

1   2   3   4

Examples:
1. We haven't developed any contacts.
2. We only have contact with our own customers, and they aren't the largest in the market.
3. We have developed contact with the customers whom we feel are the most important.
4. We have systematically developed in depth contacts with the major customers in the market from a predetermined marketing plan.

4. How is the liquidity of your customers?

In light of your assessment, how do you evaluate its competitive impact on the organisation?

No competitive   Significant competitive
advantage   advantage

1   2   3   4

Examples:
1. Apparently, not too good because the loss on debts is rising steadily.
2. We don't know too much about it, but we have extended credits and the cash discount rates aren't working.
3. Apart from a few losses, we have no problems and customers keep their obligations to us.
4. We always perform credit checks on new customers and sort out the risks. Old customers are investigated as soon as they don't make timely payments.

5. How complete is the management's knowledge of the profit from each customer group?

In light of your assessment, how do you evaluate its competitive impact on the organisation?

No competitive   Significant competitive
advantage   advantage

1   2   3   4

Examples:
1. It is the bottom line which counts and we don't divide profits for each customer group.
2. We have difficulty pinpointing cost of sales to each group, and their subsequent contribution margin.
3. We have a good sense of the customers who don't show much profit, but haven't really investigated it.
4. We know the profit margin for each of the major customer groups.

6. To what extent is the firm's customer base a reflection of systematic understanding of needs and planning?

In light of your assessment, how do you evaluate its competitive impact on the organisation?

No competitive   Significant competitive
advantage   advantage

1   2   3   4

Examples:
1. We haven't had much influence on who became our customers.
2. We haven't used formal marketing planning efforts as the customers have come to us.
3. Our effort has been "semi-formal" in that we have focused on certain customers, yet we have never said no to a customer if we are able to satisfy an order to his wishes.
4. Our market and production planning as well as product development must be seen as a whole, and the present customer base reflects a conscious effort of integration.

7. Is the firm able to deliver during seasonal changes in demand?

In light of your assessment, how do you evaluate its competitive impact on the organisation?

No competitive advantage		Significant competitive advantage	
1	2	3	4

Examples:
1. We aren't able to meet demand during our peak seasons and lose many orders and customers.
2. Delivery time varies with the season, and demand in excess of the normal season gives us delivery problems.
3. Our delivery time is usually less than the competition, and even in periods of fluctuation, we are able to deliver quickly.
4. Seasonal fluctuations are incorporated into our planning so that customers can get prompt delivery.

MARKET PLANNING

Possible answers, from "no competitive advantage for the firm" (1) to "excellent or significant competitive advantage for the firm" (4), are given below each queston. They are examples derived from various firms. Use them as an aid in assessing the questions.

1. To what extent does the firm engage in systematic market analysis and planning?

In light of your assessment, how do you evaluate its competitive impact on the organisation?

No competitive advantage		Significant competitive advantage	
1	2	3	4

Examples:
1. We don't use any formal market plan but serve customers as we receive orders.
2. We haven't used formal market planning to identify customers, but we advertise in various places to develop the necessary contact.

3. Senior management considers developments in the marketplace in the yearly budgeting process.
4. Through regular market research, we have gained much knowledge about our customers and strengths in our production. This knowledge is used to develop the short-term and long-term market plan.

2. How is market information collected?

In light of your assessment, how do you evaluate its competitive impact on the organisation?

No competitive advantage

Significant competitive advantage

1	2	3	4

Examples:
1. We haven't collected much information.
2. We have developed sales statistics as our source of our market information.
3. We use sales statistics and customer files as the basis for information gathering. This information is gathered sporadically.
4. We use our own sales statistics, as well as industry and public statistics. The customer files are always kept and we collect information on market conditions. We use professional analysts on a regular basis.

3. Who in the firm is directly involved in market planning?

In light of your assessment, how do you evaluate its competitive impact on the organisation?

No competitive advantage

Significant competitive advantage

1	2	3	4

Examples:
1. We don't do any formal market planning.
2. Top management only.
3. Top management and selected members of the sales department.

4. Since market plans are the basis for other functions in the firm we include members from all these functions and departments.

4. What elements determine the size of your marketing budget?

In light of your assessment, how do you evaluate its competitive impact on the organisation?

No competitive   Significant competitive
advantage   advantage

1   2   3   4

Examples:
1. We don't have a separate budget for marketing efforts.
2. When production costs are covered and depreciation is determined, we decide how much marketing we can afford.
3. For old products we decide a fixed percentage for marketing. For new products, we have a separate budget.
4. The budget is determined by relative profit margins of products, position in the product life cycle, competitive activity and market potential for each product.

5. How are the firm's distribution channels chosen?

In light of your assessment, how do you evaluate its competitive impact on the organisation?

No competitive   Significant competitive
advantage   advantage

1   2   3   4

Examples:
1. Distribution of the old products hasn't changed, and new products follow the old channels.
2. We try to follow our competition.
3. Top management's personal connections often determine our distribution. For new products, market analyses determine the appropriate distribution channel.
4. Our distribution system is evaluated on a regular basis, and if certain points are seen as ineffective, we proceed to make appropriate changes.

6. To what extent has the firm developed policies and guidelines for the prices and sales practice?

In light of your assessment, how do you evaluate its competitive impact on the organisation?

No competitive   Significant competitive
advantage   advantage

1   2   3   4

Examples:
1. We don't have any guidelines.
2. Only top management is involved in sales, so we don't need any policies.
3. Our sales price is determined by a set of rules regarding calling frequency, account priorities, entertainment expenses etc.
4. The policies and guidelines follow the market plan and the sales team is briefed regularly on these procedures.

REFERENCE

Jenster P. V. and Jaworksi, B. 2000. Driving forces in market orientation: a study of industrial firms, *Strategic Change*, **9**(6), 357–62.

FURTHER READING

Hollensen, S. 1998. *Global Marketing – A Market Responsive Approach*, Hemel Hempstead, Prentice Hall.
Jenster, P. and Carlos J. 1994. *Internationalizing the Medium-size Firm*, Copenhagen, Handelshøjskolens Forlag.

4

Appraising Production

Production, as used here, is the process of making the product or service. For some organisations it may mean manufacturing, which is perhaps the first image that comes to mind when we read the word. For a supermarket it is the retail outlets and the warehouses that support them. In a management consultancy, it is the service that is actually provided for the customer. In civil engineering contracting it is the building of roads, bridges and other structures.

So whether the organisation makes products or provides services, there is a process of production, which requires analysis during the corporate appraisal. Not all organisations may think of their activities in quite this way, as the critical factors vary immensely between different types of industry, and different sizes of organisation within each industry.

Success for a hairdresser depends more on the skills of the person providing the service than on the limited equipment used in the process. This makes a dramatic contrast to a Ford or a Nissan, which takes a global view of its production, with factories in various locations, all coordinated as part of a global sourcing programme. The enormous variety of companies and industries makes it difficult to give guidance that can be applied universally. The approach taken here is to make manufacturing the prime example, but then show some of the variations that would be applicable to different types of service business. From this we hope that the reader will be able to derive a satisfactory investigation of his or her own business.

CRITICAL FACTORS IN PRODUCTION

A recommended first step is to define the critical factors, which are derived from the critical success factors for the business as a whole. These are the things which production has to get right, if the organisation is to satisfy its customers, develop its competitive position and achieve its overall goals. The critical factors provide one standard against which actual performance can be compared, and are a useful starting point.

Although there may be some factors that are common to many businesses, there will be others that are more specific to the particular business. For example:

- *A manufacturer of lifts.* Two critical factors are *on-time delivery* and *quality performance*. The factory has to be in a position to ship all the required sub-units of a contract to the field installation unit at the date specified in the contract. The sub-units might include several lift cars, doors, architraves, controllers and motors. If the factory is late in delivering even one sub-unit, it may delay the completion of the whole building. The same effect can be caused if one of the sub-units does not meet the quality standards and has to be replaced. Besides losing the goodwill of the contractor, architect and building owner, delay means additional costs in the field, and exposure to penalties.
- *A contract packer of own-label detergents.* Own-label manufacturers provide a substitute for branded products. Their customers include the major supermarket chains, whose brands appear on the products. Critical factors for this business include *flexible production*, so that requirements for new products can be met speedily, *manufacture to a tight production cost* and the *ability to meet the volume requirements* of customers.
- *A management training organisation.* Two critical factors for an organisation providing in-company training courses, in addition to the expected capabilities in training skills and subject knowledge, are about keeping customers. A feature of this type of consultancy is a relationship with the client, which can last for many years. So the first production criterion is to be able *to meet each client's needs for the number of times a course is to be run,* and the time and place where it is to be run. This does not mean that there will be no flexibility at all over dates,

but if the client's needs cannot be met there is a high chance that another consultancy will be brought in instead. It is better to decide not to bid to a new client than to decline to teach some of the programmes an existing client requires. A second criterion is *continuity of professional staff.* This does not mean that no changes can be made over time, but changes that are over-frequent, or the withdrawal of the professionals who have built the relationship, can cause dissatisfaction.

In a well-run organisation many critical factors will have been included in the formation of the management information system. However, they may not all be easily capable of conversion into routine summary information. For example, the contract packer needs a careful approach to continuous production planning to ensure that customer volume needs can be met, and bare performance statistics will not replace this.

When the appraisal is part of a due diligence study, the buyer has to be careful not to fall into the trap of assuming that what is critical in his or her business is all that matters for success with the acquisition. This can be a particular danger when the business being acquired has similarities with, but is not the same as, the business of the buyer. It is not just that the wrong criteria can be used for assessing production performance, but any wrong assumption may lead to poor post-merger integration actions, and ultimately disappointment with the acquisition.

If there is any doubt about the critical production factors, you may gain inspiration from Figure 4.1. This shows what Johansson et al (1993) call the new metrics for establishing customer value. If you know which of these are critical for your organisation's strategy, you should be well on the road to determining what the critical requirements from production really are.

GETTING THE FACTS

There are two different areas to audit: the basic facts, which include the operating results, and the production strategy. Although logically the facts are the outcome of the strategy, they also indicate its effectiveness, so looking at these first makes the task of appraising the strategy somewhat easier.

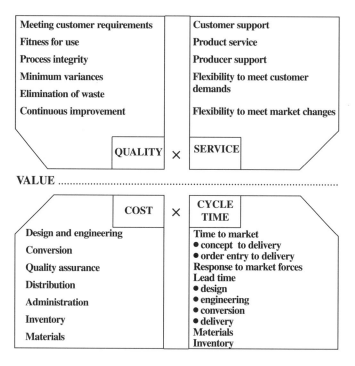

Figure 4.1 Customer value criteria. H. J. Johansson, P. McHugh, A. J. Pendlebury and W. A. Wheeler, *Business Process Reengineering*, Wiley, Chichester, 1993, p. 4. (Source: © John Wiley & Sons, Limited. Reproduced with permission)

What Is the Capacity of the Present Production Unit(s)?

This is a relevant question for both service and manufacturing units. It is not always an easy question to answer, particularly in a manufacturing plant where the same machinery can produce different products, some of which may take longer than others. There are often trade-offs; for example, the plant can produce either 100 units of product A or 200 units of product B. There are other qualifying statements to be made, such as the number of shifts worked, or maximum production with and without overtime working. In a manufacturing environment, there is a finite capacity, even if it is difficult to quantify.

In service operations capacity is also fixed at any one time. An airline has a finite number of seats available on each flight. This can be reconfigured, within limits, to allow for more or less space per passenger according to class of travel, but – like manufacturing – at any one time there is a finite capacity.

The same sort of situation applies whether the organisation is a retailer, a professional undertaking such as a firm of solicitors or general practitioners, a hotel, or a central heating service engineer. However, there may be a difference between theoretical capacity, and practical capacity. For example, the theoretical capacity of a consulting firm might be taken as the number of working days in a year, multiplied by the number of consultants in the firm. However, in practical terms it is not possible for every consultant to work on client assignments for 100% of the working days in any lengthy period. To do so assumes that no person has any gaps between assignments and that no clients ever change dates of appointments, and it allows no time for gaining new work, administrative tasks or personal development. So the practical capacity is somewhat lower than the theoretical.

Capacity can be expressed in physical terms, in money (e.g. factory cost, revenue earned or gross margin). And, of course, any organisation may have more than one unit of production making more than one product or service. Only in the simplest of organisations would we want to look only at a total figure, something which becomes even more important when we seek answers to the next question.

What Was the Capacity Utilisation?

Capacity utilisation is obviously important, and, like capacity, there may be several ways of looking at it. For example, an organisation with several plants making the same product may have had a reasonable average capacity utilisation, but there may be a different interpretation if the analysis shows that for individual plants utilisation varies between 20% and 100%. And the interpretation could be different if the market is expanding than if it is contracting.

Then there is seasonal variation in utilisation in some industries, and it is possible for production to run below capacity for half the year, yet not be able to meet demand in the other half: a typical problem in, for example, the holiday hotel industry. And just to

complicate things further there may also be a seasonal variation in
capacity, because of the impact of holidays.

What Are the Implications for Increasing or Reducing Capacity?

The capacity utilisation figures should be supported by an understanding of what is required to increase capacity (or reduce it, if
this is more relevant to the situation). The relevant issues to consider are the minimum size of increments in capacity, costs (capital and revenue) and the time needed to bring more capacity on
stream. To these we should add opportunities for outsourcing, and
actions such as extra shifts. There is a vast difference in time, costs
and minimum increment from, for example, extending capacity in
an oil refinery, compared to a professional services firm. An airline may be able to charter extra planes quickly, depending on the
state of the charter market and its landing rights, but a compar-
able option may not be available to a hotel whose attraction is its
building and location.

What about Productivity?

Everyone would agree that the recent trends in productivity, and
the indications for the future are important. What is more difficult
is how to measure it. If asked, most of us would probably say that
it is our output in relation to the inputs we have to provide to
attain it. A survey (PA/CBI, 1988, p. 8), gave examples of some of
the measurements found in practice:

- Output value/labour cost
- Output volume/material cost
- Plant availability
- Total cost/unit of output

Total factor productivity (TFP) was suggested by Hayes, Wheelwright and Clark (1988, pp. 378–89), as a means of measuring the
overall performance of a factory, department or other productive
unit. Although they were writing about manufacturing, the

method can be used in service businesses. The final analysis is expressed in terms of money, at the values of the base period taken for the study, in an attempt to remove inflation.

The formula is expressed by Hayes, Wheelwright and Clark as:

$$TPF_A = \frac{\text{Output of product A}}{\text{Sum of the total resource inputs}}$$

They suggest that output be the number of units valued in real terms at either manufacturing cost or sales price. The four inputs are materials, energy, labour and capital. The first three are first expressed in physical units, and valued (with adjustment for inflation. Capital, under their definition, is net book value of machinery (their preference, although gross book value could be used). It is valued by first adjusting the value for inflation, and then calculating the annual cost of this capital by multiplying the capital value by the firm's cost of capital (inflation adjusted). The reason for this is that it approximates the period costs of the machinery.

Ratios of output/input can be calculated for each of the four factors, and for the total, and the base period can be compared with subsequent periods, and the improvement or deterioration expressed in percentage terms.

Although productivity calculations are at their most complex in a manufacturing organisation, or in a service industry with an industrial type of environment, they are equally important for most other service businesses. However, more imagination may be needed to determine ratios that make sense in situations where output cannot be converted to money. For example, we would not argue that a teacher is now three times more productive because someone has increased class sizes from 25 to 75 pupils: it ignores the results which cannot be measured in money, and are related to personal development of the pupils within the limits of their individual capabilities and potential.

DELIVERY PERFORMANCE

This was mentioned in an earlier section, and may not be critical for every business. Where it is important, performance data should be included in the appraisal.

THE PRODUCTION STRATEGY

There are numerous options within a production strategy, whether for a manufacturing or a service organisation. Understanding the path that is being followed, and considering whether it is the most appropriate way of doing things, is a valuable part of any appraisal. There may be strengths in the way things are done, but there may also be weaknesses. There has been a tendency in Western business to assume that "either manufacturing was totally compliant to the requirements of marketing or finance, or that its contribution to new thinking would be relatively limited" (Pendlebury, 1990, p. 101). Although Pendlebury's comments refer particularly to manufacturing, they are relevant to many service businesses as well.

Our approach is to discuss a few concepts which seem to us to be particularly important, and to follow this with a broader checklist which suggests rating what is done using a scale of the competitive advantage gained.

World Class Production

World class performance should not be restricted to production. Knowing whether you are world class or not is just a comparison, but a decision to become world class is strategic. Knowing where you are requires comparisons, not necessarily against competitors, as other organisations with similar processes may be more effective in those processes than competitors. Moving on from merely comparing ratios to attempting to understand how the results are achieved, and bringing the lessons back to the organisation, is called benchmarking. Benchmarking is not necessarily a signal that the organisation is striving to become world class, as it can be used to seek improvement without any long-term aim. A determination to be world class implies a longer term strategic commitment.

Hayes, Wheelwright and Clark (1988) define world class manufacture as "Basically this means being better than almost every company in your industry in at least one important aspect of manufacture." (p. 21). This definition need not be restricted to manufacture.

A four-stage journey to being world class was postulated by Hayes, Wheelwright and Clark:

- *Stage 1* they term "internally neutral". The task is seen as just to "make the stuff", or provide the service without surprises. The organisation at this stage is likely to set its standards on the basis on its own past performance. It may be seeking to improve its performance, but without reference to anything outside the organisation's own interpretation of what should be achieved.
- *Stage 2* is "externally neutral". The reference is taken with regard to competitors and the industry, and the task is seen as to meet the standards of main competitors, following industry practice, and using the same materials and suppliers of plant as the industry. Many organisations at stage 2 restrict their comparisons with competitors to those manufacturing within the country.
- *Stage 3* is "internally supportive". It is no longer seen as appropriate just to copy competitors, and the organisation moves beyond this, with its actions being related to the specific strategies of the whole organisation.
- S*tage 4*, "externally supportive", is when the whole organisation seeks not merely to be better than competitors, but to be the best in the world in every important thing that it does. The comparison is no longer just with the industry, but with any organisation from any industry that is best at any of the relevant processes. However, being the best means much more than copying. It requires continuous, creative attention to every aspect of the organisation.

Global or Local Production

Global thinking is well established in many organisations, but this does not always mean that production has kept up with the changing requirements. We can imagine a continuum which has purely local operations at one end and full global integration at the other. Two points could be marked on this continuum: the most appropriate position for the organisation, and where it actually is. Ideally, the two points would be identical, but in practice this is not always so.

The factors which lead to the appropriate position on the continuum begin with the requirements of customers, and are followed by the nature of the technology. Production has to meet the needs of the customers, yet itself is subject to a number of factors which affect its optimum organisation.

Factors which are purely related to production include:

- *Scale efficiencies.* High efficiencies of scale bring an economic incentive for a few large centres of production. Very low efficiencies of scale remove this incentive.
- *Procurement economies of scale.* Where these are low, the incentive for concentration is low. The converse applies when they are high.
- *Experience curve.* The experience curve means that production costs in a plant fall as cumulative production volume rises. Where the curve is steep, such as in the manufacture of many electronic products, there is another incentive to concentrate in a few factories.
- *Nature of raw materials.* Where the raw materials are perishable, as in the quick freezing of vegetables or the production of wine, the economic incentive is likely to be the sources of raw materials, rather than seeking the benefits of global production.
- *Transport costs.* High transport costs in relation to the value of the product are likely to pull the decision towards local plants. Where costs are low, there is less disincentive for fewer plants operating on a global basis.

The factors listed above are more likely to be relevant for manufacturing, where industry after industry has moved further towards the global end of the continuum (for example, motor cars and consumer electronics). This is because customer requirements can be met from this type of industry regardless of the location of production.

Globalisation takes a different form with many service organisations, where production itself has to be local because of customer needs. What often happens here is that although the service has to be provided locally, the customer organisation may be global and requires the same service across the world in all its locations. This brings a need for coordination of multi-local operations, with common standards of service, and the ability to meet the client's global needs. Many firms in many industries increasingly operate in this way: examples can be found among accountants, advertising agencies, hotels, car hire and business travel agents, as well as numerous other industries.

In manufacturing, the incentive to move towards the global end of the continuum is driven by customer requirements, technology and manufacturing advantages. In service industries the driver comes mainly from the customer or, less frequently, the technology (for example telecommunications).

The Focused Factory

The idea of focus in manufacturing is not new, and the quotation used here comes from Skinner (1978), from concepts developed as long ago as the 1960s. Our reason for including the concept, is that it is still being "discovered" by various organisations. Skinner (p. 70) argued:

> A factory that focuses on a narrow product area for a particular market will outperform the conventional plant, which attempts a broader mission. Because the equipment, supporting systems, and procedures can concentrate on a limited task for one set of customers, its costs and especially its overheads are likely to be lower than those of the conventional plant. But more important, such a plant can become a competitive weapon because the entire operation is focused to accomplish the particular manufacturing task demanded by the company's overall ʿ strategy and marketing objective.

Focus avoids at least three manufacturing problems:

1. Equipment is obtained which is optimally suited to what it has to produce. Where there is no focus, equipment bought for a different manufacturing task may be used, and although the product can be made on it, it is not necessarily the most effective method of production.
2. People who are trained to be excellent at a particular thing may be expected to change their standards when making the next product. Defence and aeronautical parts may have to be made to extremely high tolerances and with zero defects. The machinery may well be capable of making products which require less stringent standards. To produce them to the higher standard means that the cost of production is higher than it

need be, but to keep telling the workforce to change the standards they apply depending on the type of contract causes confusion and leads to failures in both product areas.

3. The main line of importance may have to be interrupted because of a need to make other products. This causes more downtime and set-up costs, as well as disruption. A common example is the production of spares on the main line used to produce the original equipment, particularly as the spares may be for products that are no longer made. A result is failure to meet the manufacturing objectives of either, and there is often a conflict over which to produce. The issue is not what can be produced on any given line, but what should be produced.

Skinner recognised that it was not always possible on volume grounds to have completely separate plants for every different product line, and suggested that when this was the situation the concept should be extended to establishing "plants within the plant". In other words, parts of the factory would be dedicated to specific products, and operated as if they were completely separate plants. The "plant within a plant" concept may make sense for smaller organisations, but the expansion of global operations means that more organisations have the volumes needed to set up focused plants. An example is Ford, which is transferring car assembly from a factory in the UK to Cologne in Germany, but is making the UK plant a centre of world excellence for the production of engines.

The concept of focus is not restricted to manufacturing. It may also be appropriate for industrial-type service businesses, and for other service activities like transport and warehousing. There may be marketing reasons why other types of service business focus production. But the concept has its widest application in manufacturing, and if your organisation takes pride in the fact that it can meet any challenge in any of its plants, this is probably a weakness and not a strength.

Outsourcing

Organisations have always bought in some products and services which they could have made themselves, usually because it is cheaper to do this, or it avoids a capital investment. Additional reasons for outsourcing have developed over the past 10 to 20 years, related to the total quality management (TQM) concept of cooperative relationships with suppliers, which treats suppliers as if they were more strategic partners than adversaries.

Although it is convenient to consider outsourcing in Chapter 4, on the appraisal of production, it is a corporate-wide concept which is by no means restricted to production. Services that have been outsourced in many organisations have included internal audit, security and the routine parts of information technology, as well as many aspects of production.

The main reasons for considering outsourcing, and why the current situation should be assessed as part of the appraisal, are:

- *Flexibility.* The problem of managing peaks and troughs is reduced as far as the organisation is concerned, because its own employees are fewer in number. The problem of managing the fluctuations is shifted to a specialist supplier.
- *Reduction of risk.* This may be related to flexibility, but may also be a reduction in exposure. A highly integrated operation means that a number of corporate eggs are in one basket. If some of these can be removed, and the risks passed to someone else, the organisation may be in a healthier position.
- *Cost.* An external organisation which is focused on a particular product or service can often deliver cost reductions because of the economies of scale it can achieve.
- *Inventory reduction.* In some situations outsourcing can lead to a reduction in the inventory of raw materials and work in process, particularly if just-in-time methods are used.
- *Focus.* The removal of important, but peripheral, areas of activity means that the organisation can focus on the things that are important, and which it can really do well.
- *Quality.* Specialised suppliers should be able to provide products and services to a high quality standard.

There are pitfalls to avoid. Things which are core to the organisation's future success should be protected, and should not be outsourced. This includes core knowledge. The last thing that is wanted is to set up a new competitor.

The appraisal of outsourcing should look at the current state of affairs, the opportunities for further outsourcing, and areas currently outsourced which are core and which should be brought back into the organisation.

APPENDIX 4.1

PRODUCTION CHECKLIST AND EVALUATION

The purpose of this set of questions is to aid you in evaluating the organisation's production strategy, policies and methods.

Possible answers, from "no competitive advantage for the firm" (1) to "excellent or significant competitive advantage for the firm" (4), are given below each question. They are examples derived from various firms. Use them as an aid in assessing the questions.

PRODUCTION STRATEGY

1. At which stage is your organisation on the journey to world class performance?

In light of your assessment, how do you evaluate its competitive impact on the organisation?

No competitive   Significant competitive
advantage   advantage

1   2   3   4

Examples:
1. Stage 1. We seek improvements from inside the organisation without any knowledge of what the industry is
   achieving.
2. Stage 2. Our aim is to meet the standards of the industry. We
   ensure that we are always as effective as competitors in
   every area where it matters.
3. Stage 3. We monitor the industry, but use our own creative
   approaches to achieve a superior performance. We want to
   be better than competitors, not just copy them.
4. Stage 4. Our whole company is striving to be the best in the
   world. We seek out the best performers from any industry
   and establish why they are in the forefront. In addition, we
   continually drive to improve performance in all areas, applying new methods and through our own creative thinking.

2. Is your organisation operating in the appropriate position on the continuum from local to global production?

In light of your assessment, how do you evaluate its competitive impact on the organisation?

No competitive advantage		Significant competitive advantage	
1	2	3	4

Examples:
1. We operate in our own traditional way and have given no thought to the global implications.
2. We are aware that there are global implications, but have done little to ensure that our production matches the need.
3. We are doing most of the right things to meet the challenge of global requirements of our business.
4. We are confident that we have a near perfect match between the way our production is organised and where it should be to enable us to produce effectively and meet the needs of customers.

3. Does your organisation follow the concept of the focused factory?

In light of your assessment, how do you evaluate its competitive impact on the organisation?

No competitive advantage		Significant competitive advantage	
1	2	3	4

Examples:
1. Our plants are charged with the task of making any product that they are capable of producing.
2. We are considering ways of achieving more focus in our plants.
3. We have achieved a reasonable degree of focus, but still have a few things to sort out.
4. Each plant is focused on a limited set of manufacturing objectives (or we have established the "plant within a plant" concept).

EQUIPMENT AND PRODUCTION TECHNIQUES

1. To what extent does your firm's production facility or facilities match current and future needs?

In light of your assessment, how do you evaluate its competitive impact on the organisation?

No competitive   Significant competitive
advantage   advantage

1   2   3   4

Examples:
1. The facilities are not well suited for production. The location of machines is inadequate and storeroom and transport conditions are inefficient.
2. The facilities accommodate current production needs adequately, but there is no room for future expansion if it is needed.
3. The firm's facilities are large enough for our current needs, and there is some possibility for expansion.
4. Our production facilities were designed to accommodate current levels of demand and also to grow according to market anticipations and strategic manufacturing plans.

2. How well is machinery able to meet desired production output?

In light of your assessment, how do you evaluate its competitive impact on the organisation?

No competitive   Significant competitive
advantage   advantage

1   2   3   4

Examples:
1. Machines are occasionally too complex for easy maintenance and breakdowns stop us from meeting production goals.
2. Machines are good in and of themselves, but they are outdated and often hinder our ability to meet delivery requirements.
3. Machinery is well suited for present production as well as for forecasted needs for the near future.

4. Machines are suited to production under consideration for expected development. We frequently estimate the profitability of renovation or purchase of new equipment.

3. To what extent is production space utilised effectively?

In light of your assessment, how do you evaluate its competitive impact on the organisation?

No competitive advantage		Significant competitive advantage	
1	2	3	4

Examples:
1. No analysis has been done to determine space use in relation to production needs.
2. In some places we lack capacity, and in others machines stand idle. We are working with the question of adaptation.
3. We have dealt with the question, and although we still don't utilise all of the machine space well, our capacity problems are limited.
4. Production space is used to maximise each machine's capacity usage according to our overall plan to achieve most effective and efficient production processes. Periodic capacity utilisation and workflow studies are undertaken, resulting in rearrangement of machinery or machine replacements.

4. How do the present production techniques compare to other alternatives?

In light of your assessment, how do you evaluate its competitive impact on the organisation?

No competitive advantage		Significant competitive advantage	
1	2	3	4

Examples:
1. The production method is archaic and more labour intensive than that of our competitors.

2. We try to renovate our machines and follow developments of new approaches as best we can, but there is no systematic consideration of new production methods.
3. We follow technical development closely, but in some areas production is not great enough to warrant investing in the newest technique.
4 We follow new manufacturing developments very closely, working systematically with the latest methods and using the best techniques. At the moment we have enough demand to afford investing in new production technology and machinery to keep our lead over the competition.

5. Who handles maintenance?

In light of your assessment, how do you evaluate its competitive impact on the organisation?

No competitive   Significant competitive
advantage   advantage

1   2   3   4

Examples:
1. Maintenance is done whenever the quality of production declines or when break-downs stop production.
2. The foreman is responsible for maintenance, and he/she calls a repair person when necessary.
3. Machines, motors, etc., are maintained according to a regular schedule. Major repairs and maintenance are performed on an on-going basis, following a time-table or during an annual factory "shut-down".
2. Each machine operator is responsible for regular maintenance and repairs in accordance with his/her quality control process. Only with large repairs do we need a repair person. Routine maintenance and repairs are done at the end of each production shift.

6. How do you utilise the prospective possibilities for "sourcing" of components and product modules outside the firm (buy versus make)?

In light of your assessment, how do you evaluate its competitive impact on the organisation?

No competitive
advantage

Significant competitive
advantage

1   2   3   4

Examples:
1. We haven't tried.
2. We don't take this into much consideration, but in some areas we have bought from without because it was profitable.
3. We frequently prepare estimates and catch up with sales, so we survey the advantages of outside buying.
4. The question of whether to buy from the outside or manufacture in-house enters into consideration of investing and production preparation. Our own production concentrates on those areas where we are best.

7. Is the firm's production equipment ahead or behind in comparison with other firms in your industry and with the available technical possibilities?

In light of your assessment, how do you evaluate its competitive impact on the organisation?

No competitive
advantage

Significant competitive
advantage

1   2   3   4

Examples:
1. We find it difficult to keep up with the latest production techniques used by other firms.
2. Production apparatus standards are maintained, but there is little real improvement. In certain areas others think that we could invest more wisely and expediently.
3. The firm has not been able to follow in all fields but, with specialising, we have limited ourselves to fewer areas in which we have considerable advantage in relation to others.
4. We have been in a position to closely follow technical development and are supposedly among the best equipped in our area of speciality.

PRODUCTION AND QUALITY CONTROL

1. What basis do you use for production planning?

In light of your assessment, how do you evaluate its competitive impact on the organisation?

No competitive   Significant competitive
advantage   advantage

1   2   3   4

Examples:
1. We do not estimate or register time utilisation.
2. We prepare estimates and compare with earlier similar jobs.
3. Time and material use is calculated in detail on the basis of data from earlier similar work.
4. We systematically register time spent on all operations as well as material use, waste etc.

2. To what degree is the production scheduled efficiently?

In light of your assessment, how do you evaluate its competitive impact on the organisation?

No competitive   Significant competitive
advantage   advantage

1   2   3   4

Examples:
1. We don't have a production schedule; we build to order, thus in peak season we're swamped and in low times we have lay-offs.
2. We use "standard time" and estimated changes, trying to estimate the time of delivery, but due to miscalculations, we are often wrong in our lead-time estimates and end up being late.
3. We use a planning system and sectional planning for "bottleneck" machines.
4. We undertake long- and short-term planning that on an ongoing basis corrects for changes based on the contacts between purchase, production and sales. We are currently considering moving some of our production to a just-in-time system.

3. Do rush orders cause problems?

In light of your assessment, how do you evaluate its competitive impact on the organisation?

No competitive   Significant competitive
advantage   advantage

1   2   3   4

Examples:
  1. Our sales force calls each order "rush" even if it's not, just to be sure we get it out on time, as we normally miss shipping promises. This causes us to miss even more schedules.
  2. Our frequent rush orders are essentially the cause of our poor delivery record.
  3. A production plan is set for a specific period, i.e. we take rush orders first when they can fit in the plan without breaking the flow of operations. We do try to accommodate our premier customers.
  4. Rush orders are not a problem. Planning is so good that they are handled by customer service and become part of the plan for the following period.

4. To what degree are production schedules monitored and controlled?

In light of your assessment, how do you evaluate its competitive impact on the organisation?

No competitive   Significant competitive
advantage   advantage

1   2   3   4

Examples:
  1. There is no systematic monitoring of a work schedule.
  2. The foreman receives all the orders and makes a casual assessment of the best way to accommodate the production schedule and delivery time.
  3. We systematically register and log production time. The schedule variance does not fluctuate much from week to week.
  4. The production schedule is constantly monitored and updated.

5. Is material work flow satisfactory?

In light of your assessment, how do you evaluate its competitive impact on the organisation?

No competitive   Significant competitive
advantage   advantage

1   2   3   4

Examples:
1. There is no plan for material supply. Each operator must procure materials from various places in the warehouse.
2. Material supply is somewhat orderly. Materials are found at designated places. The operator can get assistance with the logistics.
3. Supply works fairly well. The principal materials are supplied by inventory on schedule, and the remaining by requisition.
4. The delivery of materials enters into planning, so that materials and tools are found at the workstations when they are needed.

6. How well do materials flow throughout the manufacturing area?

In light of your assessment, how do you evaluate its competitive impact on the organisation?

No competitive   Significant competitive
advantage   advantage

1   2   3   4

Examples:
1. There is always a large accumulation of work at various work areas: too much work in progress.
2. There is often a long waiting time between operations and stockpiling at individual machinery.
3. Material flows through the factory very smoothly. There is seldom accumulation and transport aisles are normally free.
4. Machinery layout, production technologies and personnel are constantly examined to make improvements needed to speed-up turn-around time for production.

7. Is the plant organised and tidy?

In light of your assessment, how do you evaluate its competitive impact on the organisation?

No competitive   Significant competitive
advantage   advantage

1   2   3   4

Examples:
1. There is no satisfactory order with regard to the placement of materials and tools.
2. There are specific places for materials and tools, but workers are not held to account for orderliness.
3. Satisfactory order and tidiness. Tools are always in their specified places.
4. The plant is very orderly and tidy given that each work group is responsible for and rated for how well they keep things in order.

8. Is there any organised form of quality control?

In light of your assessment, how do you evaluate its competitive impact on the organisation?

No competitive   Significant competitive
advantage   advantage

1   2   3   4

Examples:
1. None in-house. We respond to the complaints on product quality as they arise.
2. There is end-of-the line quality control before shipping, but no set standards for this control.
3. There is control of some essential phases of production and systematic end-control of products according to specific instruction.
4. Quality control is done by each machine operator or work area team according to written instructions concerning quality and testing. Complaints are systematically examined and improvements made to solve problems.

9. What is the basis of production with respect to drawings, standards, tolerances, preparations, instructions etc.?

In light of your assessment, how do you evaluate its competitive impact on the organisation?

No competitive
advantage

Significant competitive
advantage

1   2   3   4

Examples:
1. We are poorly organised and do not have procedures in place. Tolerances vary a great deal and a uniform product is never certain. We cannot supply spare or replacement parts without adjustment.
2. We use drawings and models, but dimensions and adjustments are left to the individual operator's experience.
3. Each product is well documented with exact production standards, tolerances, drawings etc.
4. The basis of production is completely developed with respect to production type, so there is no question with respect to quality.

10. Are measurement and quality control techniques satisfactory?

In light of your assessment, how do you evaluate its competitive impact on the organisation?

No competitive
advantage

Significant competitive
advantage

1   2   3   4

Examples:
1. No specific quality measurement or control techniques are used; this depends on the individual inspector's experience and judgement.
2. Only calibrated and specified measuring tools are used, although there are product aspects that cannot yet be tested.
3. The firm specifies all measuring tools, including systematic control and maintenance. The same holds for measuring techniques.
4. Measuring techniques and equipment are completely developed. We carefully consider which measuring equipment is advantageous for the individual operations. We are moving towards a zero-defect approach to our processes.

PURCHASING AND INVENTORY MANAGEMENT

1. On what basis do you evaluate your firm's vendors?

In light of your assessment, how do you evaluate its competitive impact on the organisation?

No competitive advantage		Significant competitive advantage	
1	2	3	4

Examples:
1. We haven't evaluated vendors recently; we continue to use those we have historically used in the past.
2. We evaluate vendors by their prices and buy from whomever is cheapest at the moment.
3. When we consider quotations from vendors, we compare interested vendors with respect to prices and discounts and get an understanding of the range of quality available on the market.
4. We make a complete evaluation of vendors with respect to price, discount, quality and delivery time. For all goods for which quality and delivery time are determined significant, we try to build a permanent vendor relationship.

2. Does the supply of materials to the firm work satisfactorily?

In light of your assessment, how do you evaluate its competitive impact on the organisation?

No competitive advantage		Significant competitive advantage	
1	2	3	4

Examples:
1. Material supply is one of our biggest problems. Apparently our vendors never learned to keep delivery terms.
2. Material delivery isn't bad in terms of timeliness. However, often the goods/parts delivered are below our expected quality levels.
3. In places where we know problems might arise, we make advance orders from production and purchasing plans. Material supply works perfectly, except that we store an unbalanced quantity of raw materials.

4. Our vendors deliver parts and materials to us on a just-in-time delivery schedule, minimising our raw material inventories.

3. Do you perform systematic receiving control with regard to quality and quantity of purchases?

In light of your assessment, how do you evaluate its competitive impact on the organisation?

No competitive   Significant competitive
advantage   advantage

1   2   3   4

Examples:
1. It is random who receives purchased goods. There is no special control other than to verify the invoice.
2. When receiving goods, we get the invoice and control the quantity.
3. Receiving is part of our system; quantity is always controlled and, when necessary, quality.
4. We have strict policies for receiving goods in which we have specified quality testing of specific types of purchases.

4. How are materials and production tools purchased?

In light of your assessment, how do you evaluate its competitive impact on the organisation?

No competitive   Significant competitive
advantage   advantage

1   2   3   4

Examples:
1. One of the foremen does the purchasing.
2. We handle all of the large purchases; each function or division is responsible for buying its own tools and small items.
3. All purchasing is done through the purchasing function.
4. The purchasing function manages the relationship with vendors and internal buyers.

5. How does inventory control work?

In light of your assessment, how do you evaluate its competitive impact on the organisation?

No competitive advantage		Significant competitive advantage	
1	2	3	4

Examples:
1. Periodic inventory is taken manually, and actual quantities rarely match with recorded quantities.
2. We maintain the stock list for large raw materials, which is compared and manually adjusted by shipping and receiving. With tools and other goods there are no control.
3. There is a single foreman responsible for this; what is delivered to stock is registered. We occasionally take test samples in agreement between actual and registered stock and make necessary corrections.
4. Inventory levels for raw materials, parts and in-process work, and tools are maintained by computer; withdrawals and incoming goods are keyed in by code, so that our production planning system is integrated with the inventory system.

6. How do you evaluate purchasing and stock order sizes?

In light of your assessment, how do you evaluate its competitive impact on the organisation?

No competitive advantage		Significant competitive advantage	
1	2	3	4

Examples:
1. We try to obtain a certain quantity discount and buy the amount necessary to receive the discount.
2. We have a manual system for minimum order levels, and order according to the reordering charts for each product group.
3. We try to keep inventory low through our computer system, and try to attain advantages in discounts and delivery time.
4. The production plan forms the basis of the purchasing plan. We compare discounts we can obtain with stock shipment costs, and, for the most important goods, calculate quantity and delivery time together with stock size.

REFERENCES

Hayes, R. H., Wheelwright, S. C. and Clark, K. B. 1988. *Dynamic Manufacturing: Creating the Learning Organisation*, New York, Free Press.

Johansson, H. J., McHugh, P., Pendlebury, A. J. and Wheeler, W. A. 1993. *Business Process Reengineering*, Chichester, Wiley.

PA/CBI 1988. *UK Productivity: Closing the Gap?,* London, PA Consulting Group/Confederation of British Industries.

Pendlebury, A. J. 1990. Manufacturing strategy for competitive advantage, in Hussey, D. E. (ed). *International Review of Strategic Management*, vol. 1, Chichester, Wiley.

Skinner, W. 1978. *Manufacturing in the Corporate Strategy*, New York, Wiley.

5

Auditing Technology and Innovation

We have included technology and innovation in the same chapter because they are often, but not always, related. However, we should make it clear that this chapter does not cover information systems/technology, which, because it is a requirement of almost every organisation, has a chapter to itself. Not all industries will have technology high on the priority list, and certainly not all will be innovators in the development or application of technology. But when technology is important, it can be a critical factor.

Those organisations in high-tech industries depend for their survival on the application of complex technologies. But they are not the only industries where technology is important, as products with lower levels of technology may use up-to-the-minute technologies in the production processes. For all these industries, future success may depend on the strategies developed for technology, and the way technology is integrated into the total corporate strategy.

Of course, an organisation can employ a mix of technologies, and still not be particularly innovative, just as it is possible for innovation to occur in organisations or functions which have little connection with a particular technology. All organisations should be concerned about innovation: many should be concerned about technology.

Despite their many differences, it is easy to see that corporate success will be affected by the choices organisations make about the technologies that lie behind their products and processes, and their capability to innovate. Both are important, and both are often neglected areas of the corporate appraisal. From first-hand experience in both areas, we believe that the technology aspect is neglected in many organisations which should give it more attention because it is difficult and moves into realms of uncertainty. Innovation is often excluded because of a common misconception that it is the same as creativity. As we will see, creativity is a key component in an organisation's capability to innovate, but it is by no means the whole story.

TECHNOLOGIES

Let us begin with a dictionary definition:

> *Technology*: "the practice of any or all of the applied sciences that have practical value and/or industrial use: technical methods in a particular field of industry or art." (*Chambers Twentieth Century Dictionary*)

Although our focus is on the internal aspects of the appraisal, technology – like marketing – is a topic where we have also to look outside the organisation in order to be able to interpret what we have found. An example of this comes from our collective experience, a consulting assignment at corporate level with a merchant banking organisation which had a number of subsidiaries in various industries. One of these subsidiaries was a photographic processor, which at that time provided central processing services to many of the high-street shops. This subsidiary was seen as very effective in its technology, and indeed it had to be in order to keep its contracts with the big high-street names. At that time there was a commercial vulnerability, in that there was a high dependence on a few key customers, who had the resources to set up their own central processing laboratories. There was also a concern over the potential impact of the emerging digital technologies (at that time it was video). All this was enough for the decisions that were made at the centre about whether it was time to sell what was currently a profitable business.

However, there was another threat which emerged later: the change in processing technology which has enabled fast in-store development of films and the production of photographs. We do not know whether the management of what had been the subsidiary saw this change in good time, but it is easy to imagine the uselessness of assessing the current technological competencies as strengths without taking into consideration the impact of the emerging changes in technology.

In broad terms, what is needed is a way of auditing the technology situation and then identifying the strategic implications of what has been uncovered. The principle is similar to the approaches taken in various other facets of the corporate appraisal. The difference lies in the peculiar complexities of defining technologies in useful ways, in classifying them and in constructing useful quantitative information which is not always readily accessible.

What Is the Technology Audit?

A number of authors have written about the technology audit. We have found the books and articles mentioned here of particular value. Because the approaches are all somewhat different, there is something of value that can be found in all of them.

Henry (1990) suggested a four-step approach to looking at technology:

1. Technology audit
2. Strategic implications of the technology portfolio
3. Technology implementation plan
4. Technology monitoring programme.

Parts of this approach go beyond the scope of this book. Our concentration is on the first two steps, although we find it easier to think about them together. However, for those who have a need to make the technology audit a continuous part of the management process, the rest of his framework is of interest.

Henry (1990) argues that technology is a value-adding activity: an asset which enables organisations to leverage resources to meet the needs of the market. He looks at the chain which stretches from the factors of production (labour, materials/natural resources, and capital) to the final consumer. The steps in this chain move from material acquisition through all the activities of productions, distribution and marketing. At various points there are nodes, where technology is used to connect various business links to improve efficiency or give a particular advantage.

> A technology-asset audit focuses on determining the real or perceived value that any technology node, or its individual technology links, has in the business benefit–cost chain – from raw material acquisition, to the supply of the produce or service, to the customer. (Henry, 1990, p. 139)

Henry suggests that comparisons should be made against the competitors, and offers a checklist of questions that should be considered:

> What are the basic technology assumptions in the company's current business strategy?
> What are the basic technology assumptions in competitors' strategies?
> Is the customer's perception of the technological qualities of the company's products important?
> What value, if any, do the customers place on the technological qualities of the competitors' products?
> Is corporate R&D contributing to improvements in the company's current technology position, or are improvements starting to take longer and cost more?
> Are competing technologies becoming costs-effective? Are competitors making gains ahead of the company?
> How does the company manage information related to these questions? (Henry, 1990, p. 140)

Lindsay (1994, p. 2) provides a statement of the objectives of a technological audit which is helpful here.

- To identify and evaluate the organisation's technological resources and capabilities
- To assess and evaluate the market significance or potential of the organisation's strategies
- To assess the organisation's competitive position in its technologies
- To understand and identify how the organisation can develop and exploit its technologies in order to build and maintain sustainable competitive advantage.

Ford (1988) offers a framework and a number of questions which need answering. We have followed some of his thinking in our own advice on the technology audit. He too makes the point that the audit should become a continuous management process.

Content of the Audit

1. Product or Production?

The key technologies may be used in the production methods the organisation uses, or they may be the products it offers, or a mix of both. A critical success factor may therefore be the way technology is applied to make the product to higher quality standards and at lower costs.

An example is the modern steelworks, where complex technology is used to produce what is a lower technology product. In another organisation the basis of success may lie in the ability to offer something unique in the product itself. An organisation concerned with the application of engineering principles to new applications, up to and including the installation of the proven prototype, may produce a new application of technologies, such as a new method of tethering North Sea oil platforms. It is the application of the product, rather than the production processes by which the prototype is made, which gives the strategic advantage.

The processor used in PCs offers an important technology to those who buy it, and at the same time can only be made using key technologies. In such organisations, the strategic advantage may be gained through both the production and the product, and the organisation may have patents for both.

When we begin to audit the technologies in an organisation, a first step is to separate our findings under these two headings.

2. Further Classification

Ford (1988) suggests looking at technology under three headings: the technologies which are *distinctive* to the organisation, those which are *basic* (without these the organisation could not enter its markets), and those which are *external* to the organisation. The distinctive technologies are the ones which are the foundation of the organisation's success and which give it distinct competitor advantage. Basic technologies are important, but the organisation is a user rather than a developer. External technologies are bought in, for example as sub-components, and are not the area where the organisation gains distinctive advantage.

Personal computers offer an example. It is possible to find small organisations which will assemble a computer for you. Every component is external bought-in technology. The main basic technology is the ability to mix and match the various components and assemble a finished product which matches the customer's requirements, and works. There is no distinctive technology in either the production or the product itself. At the other extreme there are the large organisations like Compaq, IBM, Dell and Gateway. These, too, rely on many external sources of technology. In addition they have certain distinctive technologies which are important to their success. These may lie in the area of production, design or in some of the elements that make up their computers. Although they all have access to the same component suppliers, and the same basic technologies, the distinctive technologies are among the tangible factors which enable them to differentiate their products.

If these three headings were applied to the two main groupings of production and product, the result would be a strategic understanding of what each technology means to the organisation. But this begs another question. How do we identify technologies?

3. Identifying the Key Technologies

One of the practical problems is to desegregate generalised descriptions of technologies into more precise elements which have meaning in the organisation. This can be very difficult for a non-technical person even to attempt, so one of the first requirements is that the team undertaking the audit should include members who have knowledge of the technologies.

Nakamura (2000) illustrated one approach, using similar but slightly different groupings to those suggested in the previous section. It takes the form of the technology tree shown in Figure 5.1. The roots are the basic technologies which provide the firm with a foundation for technological development. The trunk represents the core technologies which are growing out of these roots. The branches are the derivative technologies growing from the core. Leaves and fruits are the products which have sprung from each derivative technology. His description envisages the fusion of branches, to develop more applications.

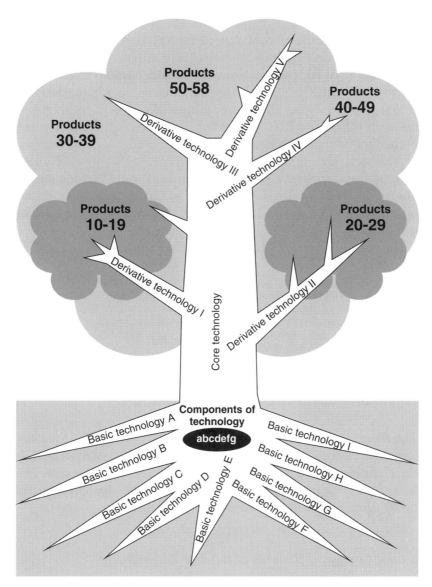

Figure 5.1 Technology tree of KGS Group – its breakdown and proliferation. (Source: G.-I. Nakamura, *Niche-Focused Strategic Management in Search of the "Only One Firm": Challenges for the KGS (Group) towards the 21st Century*, H & I. Tokyo, 2000. Reproduced by permission of H & I Inc.)

The figure comes from Nakamura's consulting assignment with a particular Japanese company, and the published version does not give away critical confidential information. Some organisations have several technology trees, from different strategic business units (SBUs), and one role of the audit should examine the degree to which the trees themselves intertwine. Our experience is that it can be very difficult to obtain synergy in technologies between different SBUs, even when there are certain similarities in the technologies applied.

Although the numbers on Nakamura's tree are somewhat sketchy, it is possible to see how the concept could provide a technology analysis of products, which would enable quantitative information to be derived showing the significance of the various technologies through their impact on sales and contribution.

Hussey (1998, p. 407) describes another approach:

> [Figure 5.2] illustrates a way of trying to define and examine technologies across an organisation. This particular example is derived from an assignment of mine in an unusual organisation which was a cross between consulting engineering and process engineering, although neither term is an accurate description of the activity. In essence the business was concerned with the application of engineering principles to new applications, up to and including the installation of the proven prototype. The technical strands of a business such as this are of great importance in defining future strategy. To preserve confidentiality I have extended it to a completely different industry.

The figure relates the technologies to the products and their different markets, and it is possible to calculate the significance of the technologies by inserting the numbers for sales and contribution. Not too much should be made of the specifics of the illustration, as it is only to show the principle.

4. The Costs and Benefits of the Key Technologies

This point links to the second section of this chapter, which deals with innovation. Failure in capitalising one's own technologies can be because innovations are killed by the internal inertia, and the good ideas never reach fruition. On the other hand, success may occur because there is something about the way the organisation is run that enables sound ideas to be properly tested and evaluated,

Markets	Products	Fats and oils	Surfactants	Emulsifiers	Skin chemistry	Flavouring
Consumer	Laundry soap	*	*			
	Soap flakes	*	*	*		
	Toilet soap	*	*		*	
	Cleaners		*	*		
	Fabric softener		*	*		
	Shampoo		*		*	
	Toothpaste		*	*		*
	Mouth wash		*			*
	Deodorant				*	
	Skin care				*	
Hotel	Toilet soap	*	*		*	
	Shampoo		*		*	
Laundry	Detergent		*	*		
	Fabric softener		*			
Industrial	Detergents	*	*	*		
	Cleaners		*	*		
	Toilet soap	*	*		*	

Figure 5.2 Technology appraisal: generalised example

and ensures that the winners are backed. 3M is the world's prime example of an organisation that is able to benefit from its distinctive technologies, and develop new areas of distinction.

However, failure may also occur because of problems with R&D. If new products or processes with commercial value are not developed in good time, or are not effective when put into use, the problem may lie with the objectives given to R&D, the resources allocated to it, the calibre of the researchers or the way the function is managed.

In the audit we need to try to look at past patterns of costs and benefits, to collect quantitative data to support the analysis. For example:

- Number of patents registered (but remember that patents are a means, not an end in themselves)
- Annual contribution from new products
- Annual contribution from process improvements

- Annual income from licence agreements granted
- Annual costs.

Past and current performance is helpful in highlighting strategic issues, but should be expanded by notes which relate the results to the current strategy that is being followed.

Does the company fully exploit its technologies? This question may be more important for a multi-SBU organisation, where there is potential synergy to be obtained between the technologies of various business units, but somehow this is not obtained. Sometimes the reason for this lies in the difficulty of defining technologies in precise enough terms, so that the possible areas of congruence are not perceived. Sometimes the problem is organisational, in that no one has time to coordinate technology with other businesses, and there is no one with overall responsibility for doing this. There may be "not invented here" attitudes, or a belief that "this SBU spent the resources to develop its present position, so why should it hand the results to someone else?". The audit should first establish whether there are unexploited opportunities, and then explore why they are not exploited.

There is a related issue. Can we release value on some of the patents and know-how which we possess? This may be through sale or licence, or it could be through joint ventures with other organisations, or setting up a business to use some of the technology. Examples of the latter are the Danish brewery which has a subsidiary offering an independent consultancy service to the industry, and the airport operator which acts as a consultant in airport design and operation.

5. The Life Cycle Position of the Key Technologies

This is a requirement which is rarely capable of a precise answer, but it is still an important issue to consider. The approach suggested under heading 1 above and Figure 5.2 would give a view of the current importance of each technology to the organisation, although it needs to be qualified by information about any changes that are expected in the near future. For those technologies which are seen as key, it should be possible to assess where the technology life cycle is, if only on one of four points: emerging, growing, maturing or declining. (Note: Lindsay (1994, p. 19) uses the headings emergent, viable, high growth, mature and declining.)

The results of this assessment feed back into the assessment of the organisation's R&D activity, discussed under heading 4, above. Although precision in this analysis is difficult to attain, it is not hard to see how the audit might bring to top management attention various situations which should be dealt with.

Between us, we can think of a number of examples from client organisations where there was an apparent lack of awareness that a shift in technology was taking place. For instance:

- A company that made bottle washing equipment, and had failed to consider that the growth of the non-returnable plastic bottle would change their market for their product. In fact it was worse than this because the son of a director had been foisted on them. Management resented and disliked him, and so chose to disregard a study that he had made of the likely effect of the then new bottle.
- The manager of a manufacturer of machines for printing tin plate for cans made on a three-stage process, who was in denial that the then recently introduced two-stage aluminium can, which printed the can as it was drawn, would have any impact on his market.

6. Emergent Technologies Not Yet Used by the Organisation which May Be Important

It is self-evident that this is an important question for many businesses, but it is not always one that can be answered easily. There is a relationship with the previous point, in that one reason for a change in the life cycle position of a technology could be because of new technologies. Indeed, both the examples were of organisations that had either not seen, or would not see, how a new technology was affecting the life cycle of their product. The aim is to see the situation before it becomes critical.

However, the ability of an organisation to do this depends on information, so the audit should consider the management process. How do we keep informed about emerging technologies, changes in current technology, likely developments for the future, and the position on the technology life cycle? Relying on people to dredge up an assessment for the annual planning cycle is a recipe for missing much of what matters. So the intelligence needs to monitor patents, other competitor activity, changing customer needs and new research trends. This requires technically qualified people, leavened by others with knowledge of markets and products. The questions that need answering are what sources of information are used, how regularly the intelligence is reviewed, who does it, and what happens to the results.

7. Which Are the Phases of a Development Project where Top Management Spends Most of its Time?

This point was inspired by Gluck and Foster (1975). It requires looking at the phases of development (study, design, development, production, marketing and post-marketing). Top management can exercise most influence on the final outcome if it is involved most heavily in the first two phases and the early stages of the third. In many companies this is the opposite of what happens and most top management effort is put into the final three phases. However, by this time, the major technological strategic decisions have been taken, usually by someone quite low in the organisation. It reminds us a little of a presentation once given by a mid-level person from a city's town planning department. He declared that he alone determined the whole town planning strategy. Yes, there were elected councillors, he had several managers above him, and they thought they were making the decisions. But he set all the assumptions on which the strategy was based, and no one had ever questioned them. These assumptions determined the strategies that could be followed, and eliminated many others. In technology it cannot make sense for the paths that the company will follow to be determined by people who have no responsibility for the overall vision and strategies of the firm.

8. Understand the Gap between the Technological Knowledge of the Company and that of its Key Customers

Ford (1988) argues that initially a firm which develops a new technology will posses a much greater level of knowledge about that technology than the customer, and because of this may be able to charge a premium price because it sets the standards. As customers gain in experience, and begin to add developments of their own, the gap narrows and the customer begins to find other sources. The margin therefore tends to drop. Following this argument, it is useful to obtain a view of where the organisation is in relation to its customers. However, there is a counter consideration, which is that if the gap is too wide, customers may be reluctant to buy the product, because of uncertainty over the benefits of the technology.

It is difficult to see how this information can be more than an estimate of the gap, and the trend it is following, so it has the dangers inherent in all such assessments, that wishful thinking can affect the result.

The dangers of thinking of the world as you would like it to be, rather than as it is, are illustrated by this example from the chemical process contracting industry. The particular organisation had high standing in the industry, and following a change of policy by one of its important customers was bidding to be the preferred supplier in its particular field. It had worked with the customer as a leading supplier for many years, and there had been some cross-licensing of technologies. They were convinced they would win. You can imagine the blow when they lost out to another supplier. The reason for their failure was nothing to do with their performance. It was simply that the customer did not want a closer relationship with an organisation that believed that in all areas it had greater technical knowledge that its client. Possibly in these particular areas it had once been ahead of the client, but those days had passed, although the organisation had not noticed.

Even Low-Technology Businesses Can Feel the Effects of Changes in Technology

It may be tempting to think that an audit of technology is only a matter for the high-technology companies, and can be ignored by all others. This is true only for as long as the technology stays static. A few examples worth mentioning of where new technologies have taken over a market, and frequently led to the collapse of some or all of the traditional players, are typewriters, which have been to a great degree replaced by computers, electro-mechanical telephone exchanges, which are now an obsolete technology, and home cine cameras and projectors, which have almost completely given way to video.

At the low-technology end, plastic windows frames and doors have replaced wood to a large extent, and with plastic cladding on exposed wood on buildings have reduced the volume of business available for professional house decorators. The task of painting the outside of a house may not on the surface appear to be affected by leaps of technology, but the available market has certainly changed.

One purpose of the technology appraisal is to help the organisation "leverage the company's technology assets to meet tomorrow's business objectives as defined by the current strategic plan" (Henry, 1990, p. 140). However, we believe that the need is more complex than this, in that the results of the audit should be used to help identify where new strategic decisions need to be taken. Current strategy may be a useful basis of comparison, but the analysis should also highlight areas where current strategy may appear to be inappropriate.

The purpose of the appraisal is to assist in the development of sound strategic decisions. At one level this means the strategic decisions appertaining to technology, in order to make a success of the corporate strategy – a reactive role. At another, it is the way technology will influence the overall corporate strategies – an active role. While the purpose of the appraisal is not to make strategic decisions, it will have little value if it does not give a clear indication of where there are issues that should be considered.

Matrix Techniques

Various matrix techniques have been proposed to enable organisations to look at the technology implications of the portfolio in ways that gives different perspectives to the types of analysis we have looked at so far.

Neubauer (1990, p. 80), suggests a technology grid, which is illustrated in Figure 5.3. This has *technology position* on one axis, moving from weak to strong. The other axis shows *technology*

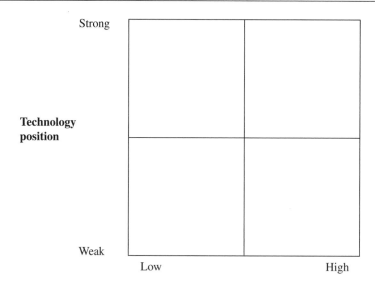

Figure 5.3 Technology grid

relevance ranging from low for old technologies of little value to high for new technologies where many applications are possible. The factors suggested for each axis are:

Technology position	*Relevance*
Patents	Breadth of application
Licences	Speed of acceptance
Development lead times	Developmental potential
Personnel	Application in other industries
R&D budgets	Environmental acceptability

Each SBU is plotted on this matrix. In our opinion, although the SBU may be appropriate in some situations, there are others when positioning in this way is to combine chalk and cheese. In these cases it may be desirable first to plot the main product groupings of the SBU, and then to combine these into larger "bundles" which share common characteristics. Otis Elevators could be seen as an SBU of its parent United Technologies, in that all of its products have a strong potential relationship with each other. It is possible for a large building contract to require lifts, escalators and moving walkways (think of an airport). However, the technologies of electric lifts, hydraulic lifts, escalators and moving walkways are not the same, and combining them on the Neubauer matrix could conceal valuable information.

The suggestion is that the final matrix would be used to check that current investment in technology matches the need, and that priorities are shifted; for example, to reduce investment in low-relevance technologies, and increase it in businesses where the company needs to catch up or maintain leadership.

Rowe, Mason and Dickel (1994, pp. 116–21), suggest a slightly different matrix. This positions the portfolio according to technical position and technology importance. It may be that for one axis both authorities have the same thing in mind, and that we should not read too much into the different meanings of relevance and importance. There are differences in the position index, where Rowe, Mason and Dickel use a concept of high = leader and low = follower. They offer a different perception in the labels attached to each of the four boxes:

- High importance/high position: a *technological leadership* position, which has to be pursued aggressively if it is to be maintained.
- Low importance/high position is labelled *over-engineering*. Businesses in this category may well be spending more than is appropriate, and should consider reducing the level of technological commitment.
- High importance/low position: *catch up or get out*. The argument is that this is not sustainable in the long term, and that either resources have to be committed to moving technology into the high position box, or the activity should cease.
- Low importance/low position: *technology adopter*. Businesses in this box beg questions about how the technology should be supported. The initial implication is that it should be acquired from external sources, and that major internal resources should not be spent on this area.

The questions raised from these and similar matrix analyses are indicative. The purpose of the corporate appraisal is to provide one of the foundations for strategic thinking. Although we are not treading much farther along the path of actually forming technology strategy, we will conclude this section with a few more ideas.

Ford (1988) suggests three different types of technology strategy. First there is a technology acquisition strategy. He adds the caution that there is a need to examine the position on the life cycle of the technologies or sub-technologies acquired.

There also needs to be a strategy for exploiting technology. This goes deeper than the issue of the strategic business portfolio, and includes an aggressive approach to finding other ways of gaining benefit, such as licensing others to use the technology.

Finally Ford suggests that there is a need for a strategy to manage technology, which implies making decisions on all the issues identified in the audit process.

INNOVATION

(Note: parts of this section have been modified from Hussey, 1997.)

Innovation may well have been covered in part by any organisation that has appraised its technology, but even in these organisations there may be innovations that are not related to technology, which may require objective scrutiny. All organisations rely on innovation to a greater or lesser extent to ensure that they renew themselves. The two aspects to audit are whether the organisation is innovating as successfully as it should, and, if the answer to this is negative, whether the management processes in the organisation are appropriate for the task.

Creativity

It is reasonable to suggest that creativity is a prerequisite for innovation, but it is not reasonable to assume that all an organisation needs to do to improve the quality and quantity of innovations is to harness creativity. Somehow the two are often confused. This is a point which we will come back to, as it lies at the heart of any attempt to audit an organisation's ability to innovate.

In normal usage, there are many meanings to the word creativity, and it is easy to slip into the trap of thinking only of the creative genius of a Leonardo da Vinci, or an Einstein, forgetting that quality of imaginative thought which is possessed to a greater or lesser extent by all human beings.

Jones (1972, p. 7) suggests: "Creativity is a combination of flexibility, originality and sensitivity to ideas which enable the thinker to break away from the usual sequence of thought into different and productive sequences, the result of which gives satisfaction to himself and possibly to others".

Creativity needs to be taken in context. Almost all of us have a creative spark within us, but the context in which this bursts into flame is not always that of the organisation. The cleaner may appear to be a stolid, plodding, work-horse in the office, but at home may produce delicate embroidery or tend a beautiful garden. What is happening is a harnessing of creative ability to a degree of technical mastery. These manifestations of creativity may have no value in the organisational context, but in any case would be unlikely to flower in a situation where work is routine and without stimulation, there are few problems to overcome, and expectations of the contribution of the worker are very low: which is precisely how we perceive and manage many office cleaners.

Of course the degree of creative ability varies from person to person, and the highly creative individual may be in the minority. Although those endowed with a high level of creativity may produce more and better ideas and concepts, it is also possible to harness the latent creativity of the less well endowed. This is one of the benefits that may spring from a well-run total quality management (TQM) concept. Although few of the many innovations that may result are likely to be of major strategic value, the cumulative impact of many small innovations can be significant. Maslow (1943) argues that the fullest (and healthiest) contribution to creativeness may be expected from people who have reached the self-actualisation stage: that is, their physiological, safety, love and esteem needs are already met. Perhaps we might simplify this by arguing that empowered people who operate in an organisational climate which encourages creativity are most likely to be able to produce creative solutions for the benefit of the organisation.

The need for an organisational climate which fosters creativity is important, and there are differences between the creative organisation and others which are more stolid in their acceptance and application of the new. One of the reasons behind the need for a sympathetic climate is that the creative process is not completely logical. Although parts of the process can be directed so that the mind is focused on a specific problem area, the solution cannot be guaranteed. Indeed, it is uncertain whether an idea of any value will emerge at all. Motivation and the encouragement of creativity are important elements in the process, and will not occur in a hostile environmental climate.

An innovation might be described as a creative idea that has been made to work. Webster, (1990, p. 209) says:

> Simply put, *innovation* is a better thing to do, or a better way to do it, that increases an organisation's ability to achieve its goals. This does not mean change for change's sake. To qualify as an innovation, a change must be visible to others and must offer a lasting impact. Innovation can occur, and should be encouraged, at all levels within a company, from top level executives to lower level managers and individual contributors. An innovation can be as basic as a procedural change in a distribution system or as complex as entry into a whole new market.

So an innovation may be a product, a process, a method or a system, but is more than an idea. It has to be converted from the idea to action.

Some years ago Drucker (1964, pp. 216–20) commented on the fact that creativity was not the bottleneck: "There are more ideas in any organisation, including business, than can possibly be put to use. What is lacking as a rule is the willingness to look beyond products to ideas. Products and processes are only the vehicle through which an idea becomes effective". Although this management classic might be considered old in terms of the speed at which management thinking has developed, his statement is remarkably similar to the conclusions from her research which led Webster (1990) to her definition. It was not lack of ideas that was the problem, but the ability to convert them into innovations.

The entrepreneurial process means that an idea has to pass rigorous tests. Drucker emphasised that it has to have operational and economic validity, and must meet a further test of personal commitment:

> The idea itself might aim at social reform, but unless a business can be built on it, it is not a valid entrepreneurial idea. The test of the idea is not the votes it gets or the acclaim of the philosophers. It is economic performance and economic results. Even if the rationale of the business is social reform rather than business success, the touchstone must be ability to perform and survive as a business.

The strategic importance of innovation is emphasised by Drucker, who sees ideas as part of the process of making the future: "tomorrow always arrives", and those companies which fail to innovate will suddenly find that they have lost their way. This is a rephrasing of the words of the sixteenth-century philosopher Sir Francis Bacon: "He that will not apply new remedies must expect new evils: for time is the greatest innovator".

How Effective is the Organisation at Innovating?

This is the first question that the appraisal should attempt to answer. It is not always easy to quantify the answer. Although it may be relatively simple to look at the number of new products launched in a period, and the sales and contribution gained from each, this begs the question of whether they were copycat products or something which had genuine originality. This means that each new product should be looked at objectively, to see whether it counts as an innovation.

But as we saw from the Webster definition, innovations can also take place in systems, processes and the machinery used to make products, and not all will be as visible in the accounts as a new product. To help us interpret information on successful innovation, we also need to know about the attempted innovations that fell by the wayside. And to have real meaning we should look at the phase where they fell, and also look at the patterns of success or failure of the new products. The phases of an innovation might be considered under the headings of:

- inspiration (having the idea),
- initiation (getting the idea accepted),
- implementation (putting the idea into practice),
- inspection (checking that it has produced the expected results).

Since, in most organisations, the available information will not give insight into every phase, the only solution might be some sort of survey, either through getting selected managers to complete a formal questionnaire, or by arranging meetings with groups of managers and other key people to complete the analysis as they see it.

Pinpoint precision is not needed. In the end we need to have a view of whether the organisation is innovative enough for the conditions in which it operates, and the success rate of new innovations.

Does the Way the Organisation Operates Encourage or Inhibit Innovation?

In order to be able to examine the processes of innovation in an organisation, we have to think about what the processes are. The outline here is based on research undertaken and concepts developed by management consultants Harbridge House, modified by our own experience. (For those who want to be closer to the original, Owen (1990, p. 296) describes the Harbridge House approach.)

There are three elements to consider.

1. The Individual, Alone or in Small Groups

This is where the inspiration starts, and the main requirements are creativity, any appropriate technical competencies and various individual characteristics (such as a willingness to challenge the status quo).

2. The Interface of those Promoting the New Idea with the Influencers and Decision Makers in the Organisation

The components of this activity cover the initiation, implementation and inspection phases. The activity here is a form of change leadership, complicated by the fact that few of the people who have to go along with the change report to the initiator, and many may be senior to him or her. The initial letters of the words chosen to describe the steps in the change leadership process spell EASIER.

- *Envisioning*. This is the process of developing a coherent view of the nature and importance of the innovation. The vision may cover such things as size, what the innovation will do for the organisation, its future scope, and how it fits the overall corporate vision.

It is the person who is responsible for moving the idea to an innovation who should define this vision, and the greater the potential opposition to the idea within the organisation, the greater is the need to give attention to this part of the process.

The leader who cannot articulate the vision in a way that has meaning to others will find it harder to ensure that everyone pulls in the same direction. It is particularly important when the driver of the innovation is not at the top levels of the organisation, because it will be necessary to carry more senior managers along. 3M, which has an enviable reputation for innovation, is reported to have a system in which the originator of every potential major innovation has to have a Board-level sponsor. Getting over even this first hurdle is difficult unless there is clarity of vision.

• *Activating.* Envisioning is a difficult process, because the border line between empty platitudes and meaningful descriptions is very narrow. Activating is even harder. It is the task of ensuring that others in the organisation understand, support and eventually share the vision. The vision cannot be understood unless it is communicated, and it cannot be communicated unless it is defined in a coherent way. Initially the task is to develop a shared vision among the key players in the task of implementation, but in many organisations there are benefits in reaching deep into the organisation.

A widespread commitment to the vision makes it easier to see the relevance of the innovation, and underlines the importance of coordinated efforts.

The well-known story of Post-it Notes at 3M shows that the approach to getting commitment to the vision of the prospects for the product can itself be creative. The glue on these pieces of paper, which many of us now find indispensable, was reputed to be a failed research product, but someone saw the potential for a permanent, but removable, marker for documents. The recognition of the possibility is accredited to an employee who wanted something to mark the places in his hymn book when he sang in the church choir, and from that those involved formed a vision of a wider potential. To gain commitment to the product, against initial opposition, they made up a stock of the little pads, and issued them to various managers in the company. Once everyone was hooked, they discontinued this special supply, and said that the product would not be available unless it was launched. By this time everyone in the company was convinced that the product was essential, and would succeed

- *Supporting.* Good leadership is not just about giving orders and instructions. It is much more about inspiring people to achieve more than they otherwise might have believed possible, and providing the necessary moral and practical support to enable this to happen. The envisioning and activating steps in implementation are about sharing and sustaining inspiration. The supporting step is about helping others to play a key part in the implementation process.

  To achieve this the leader has to have a strong empathy with the people he or she is trying to inspire, and the imagination to see things from their point of view. There needs to be an understanding of both their present capabilities and their potential. While giving support to help a subordinate reach a tough new goal, the leader has to be able to recognise the problems the person faces, without ever implying that there is the slightest doubt that the person will succeed.

  Supporting needs a base of respect, trust and integrity, and fails when these essentials are lacking.

- *Installing.* This is the process of developing detailed plans to enable the innovation to be implemented and controlled.

  The nature and shape of those plans will vary with the complexity of the innovations, and their nature. In only rare circumstances will it be a task that should be totally undertaken by the leader of the innovation project, and in most cases the process would benefit from the involvement of the key people who are expected to carry out the actions that will implement the innovation.

  The instruments that may be used will also vary, depending not only on the complexity of the strategies, but also on the time scale for implementation, but the basic reasons are constant. They are to:

  - ensure that all the consequences of implementing the innovation are understood, in so far as they can be foreseen.

This includes the impact on the organisational variables discussed earlier.

- identify all the actions that have to be taken to bring about the change. This usually requires much more attention to detail than would be appropriate for any formal strategic plan or boardroom presentation.
- allocate responsibility for the various actions that have to be taken.
- establish the priorities of the various actions, in particular those that will hold up the whole process if not done to time.
- provide the budgets needed to ensure implementation of the plans.
- set up the teams and structures needed to implement.
- allocate the right human resources to the tasks (if necessary recruiting additional people or using consultants).
- determine any policies that are needed to make the implementation process work.

There is nothing unique or special about any of these individual requirements, nor the instruments such as plans, budgets, critical path analysis, Gantt charts and other tools which have to be developed to ensure that nothing is overlooked, and that everything is coordinated. These are all the regular instruments of management.

In most organisations this stage will require a hard-nosed view of the economic prospects for the innovation. 3M, which does more than most companies to stimulate the creative process, even to the extent of expecting that everyone will "bootleg" a significant amount of time to the development of new ideas, has the final check where the Board considers the business plan for all significant new activities, and nothing sloppy is likely to pass this scrutiny

- *Ensuring.* Plans, structures for implementation and policies may be formulated, and on paper the organisation may have covered everything. But this is not enough, and consideration must be given to the monitoring and controlling processes that will ensure that:

    - all actions are taken on time, unless there is a conscious, justifiable decision to change the actions.

- where actions are changed, there is both good reason for the change, and re-planning for the new circumstances.
- the results of actions are as expected, and if not corrective action is taken.
- plans are still appropriate if the situation has changed.

All organisations have monitoring and controlling processes, but those that currently exist may be inadequate to monitor the new strategies. One of the actions in the implementing phase might therefore have been to establish supplementary controls so that timely information is made available on a regular basis.

Monitoring and control processes also provide a reason for the various players in the implementation game to meet, thus providing another way of reinforcing the commitment to the vision.

- *Recognising.* This means giving recognition to those involved in the process. Recognition may be positive or negative, and should be used to reinforce the change, and to ensure that obstacles to progress are removed.

Although recognition may include financial reward, this may be the smallest part of what is needed. Public recognition (among peers and senior managers) of the part played by a particular manager may show that what has been done is appreciated. That small word "thanks" may have great motivational value when expressed sincerely by a leader who is respected by the person.

3. The Organisational Context

Every organisation establishes a context within which everything has to work. This context may encourage innovation, be neutral or actively prevent it. The three elements to consider are the organisational culture, the structure, and the strategic direction.

The best way to appraise the innovation process and the organisational context is to track through how a few recent innovations, or attempted innovations, have been managed. What you find can then be compared with the approach recommended here, and any significant areas of concern noted.

REFERENCES

Drucker, P. F., 1964, *Managing for Results*, London, Heinemann (page references are to the 1967 edition, Pan, London).

Ford, D. 1988. Develop your technology strategy, *Long Range Planning*, **21**(5), October.

Gluck, F. W. and Foster, R. N. 1975. Managing technological change: a box of cigars for Brad, *Harvard Business Review*, September/October.

Henry, J. P. 1990. Making the technology–strategy connection, in Hussey, D. (ed.) *International Review of Strategic Management*, vol. 1, Chichester, Wiley.

Hussey, D. 1997. Creativity, innovation and strategy, in Hussey, D. (ed.) *The Innovation Challenge*, Wiley, Chichester.

Hussey, D. 1998. *Strategic Management: From Theory to Implementation*, 4th edn, Oxford, Butterworth-Heinemann.

Jones, T. P. 1972, *Creative Learning in Perspective*, London, University of London Press.

Lindsay, J. 1994. The technology management audit: a company self assessment, in Buckner, K. (ed). *The Portfolio of Business and Management Audits*, Uster, Strategic Direction Publishers.

Maslow, A. H. 1943, A theory of human motivation, *Psychological Review*, **50**, 370–96 (reproduced in abridged form in Vroom, V. H. and Deci, E. L., *Management and Motivation*, Harmondsworth, Penguin, 1970).

Nakamura, G.-I. 2000. *Niche-Focused Strategic Management in Search of the "Only One Firm": Challenges for the KGS (Group) Towards the 21st Century*, Tokyo, H&I (this book was published in Japanese and English as part of the 45th anniversary of KGS Group. It is not available from book shops).

Neubauer, F.-F. 1990. *Portfolio Management*, Deventer, Kluwer.

Owen, P. 1990. Fostering innovation in organisations, in Lom, C. (ed.) *1990 Technology Strategy Resource Book*, Zurich, Strategic Direction Publishers.

Rowe, A. J., Mason, R. O. and Dickel, K. E. 1994. *Strategic Management: A Methodological Approach*, 4th edn, Reading, MA, Addison-Wesley (summarised in Channon, D. (ed.) *Blackwell Encyclopedic Dictionary of Strategic Management*, Oxford, Blackwell).

Webster, B. 1990. Innovation: we know we need it, but do we know how to do it?, In Hussey, D. and Lowe, P. (eds) *Key Issues in Management Training*, London, Kogan Page.

6

HRM, Management Effectiveness, Culture and Structure

Although the four areas of this chapter are by no means the same thing, they are related, and human resource management (HRM) appears first because, to a degree, it touches on all of them. In all four areas there is a case for comparing some of the performance measures against external criteria, but it is even more important to evaluate the policies and actions against the vision, values and strategies that the organisation is pursuing. It is this strategic comparison which is often overlooked.

Figure 6.1 provides a partial explanation of why we believe this to be so important. Models like this have been around for some time, the most famous being the McKinsey 7S model, but we believe the originator of this type of thinking was Leavitt (1964). He argued that structure, task, people and technology were closely related, and that actions taken on one of these had an impact on the others. The main difference in our model is that *technology* has been subsumed into the broader term *strategy*, and *culture* and a number of different aspects of *systems* have been added.

The argument summarised through this figure is that the intended strategy should drive the other organisational variables. If there is a mismatch, the other variables may instead supplant the strategy. In other words, what happens will not be what was intended to happen. Obviously there are degrees to which a mismatch can be tolerated, but everything that works against the

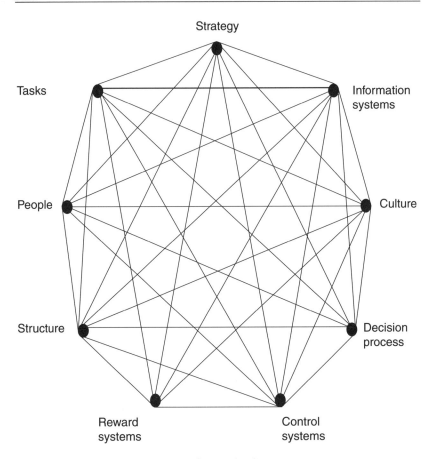

Figure 6.1   An integrated view of organisation

strategy makes implementation more difficult, and increases the possibility of a total failure of the strategy.

If the corporate appraisal is made before a new strategy has been decided, the comparison can only be made against the current strategy, and it would be desirable to re-examine the conclusions in the light of any major changes that might afterwards be decided. However, much of the work will have been done, and it should be possible to make the reassessment with a minimum of delay.

The methods described here should bring strengths and weaknesses to the surface. In many organisations the problems lie concealed in the background where they cannot be recognised and solved. If you have any doubts about the validity of these comments, turn back to page 39 in Chapter 2, and read the management consulting example in the light of Figure 6.1. It is easy to see how the combination of the information coming from accounts and the reward system was driving behaviour in the opposite direction to the strategy. The research in Kaplan (1995), also quoted in Chapter 2 (page 43) demonstrates that a mismatch of processes and the strategy is by no means an isolated event. It happens in well-run organisations.

HUMAN RESOURCE MANAGEMENT

Looking at the Numbers

We begin, as we did with finance, by establishing the factual base. Although not all HR strengths and weaknesses can be read from looking at figures, many can. For example, recruitment and labour turnover figures can reveal whether the organisation has difficulty attracting and retaining particular types of employee, and high absenteeism figures may point to various other problems.

The following description of the minimum information that should be collected is adapted from Hussey (1996).

Most organisations know how many people they employ, but even that is sometimes an easier question to ask than to answer, because of definition problems and timing issues. But there are legal requirements which demand that these figures are available for at least some points in the year. For a detailed understanding of the organisation we need to have much more statistical data than just total numbers. In fact the use of totals without an underlying depth of knowledge can mislead. A simple example is that a bald employment total gives us no idea of how many people we might expect to have to recruit next year, just to maintain the same size. And the real-life situation is much more complex than this.

In all cases the statistics are more helpful if they are in a time series, so that a run of several years can be compared and, where there are seasonal factors, relevant lesser periods, such as by month or by quarter, can also be examined. The following subsections outline some of the statistics which should be collected as a first stage of the HR appraisal.

Detailed Analysis of Actual Employment Numbers

Employment numbers should be broken down by business area, country, location within the country and department. The reason for this group of headings is obvious. If you do not know how the employees are dispersed by location and organisational unit, it is not possible to assess the impact of some of the changes in activity which are intended to take place. Similarly, the fact that there is a full complement of highly skilled people in the US operation does not solve a shortage in a third-world country.

There are other headings that should be investigated to give more insight into what the numbers really mean. For example, it is important to get an understanding of certain types of employee in the overall totals. Traditionally many organisations have kept statistics on the basis of direct and indirect employees, hourly paid and salaried, productive and non-productive. In the USA there is also normally a breakdown of exempt and non-exempt, which is a legal requirement related to terms and conditions of service. These breakdowns take us a little further forward, although most emerged more from an accounting need for cost information, than for HR actions. The separation of *direct* from *indirect* workers is less meaningful than perhaps it once was, because of the replacement of numbers of direct production employees by automation, which requires the support of more indirect experts.

The next level of resolution is concerned with seniority and skills. The first point can be more easily covered if the organisation has a grading system, because there is at least some chance that every employee has been put into a grade. This gives us some good information to build on. However, information on level in the organisation does not tell us what people do, and it is not really meaningful to combine sales managers, when sales managers are easy to recruit or promote from within, with scientists on the same grade, when there are few others in the organisation with the same disciplines and there is a world shortage. In this situation, we could double the number of sales managers without a problem, but this may not be true of the scientists. So we need to have access to some statistics which describe jobs in a broad but meaningful way that is suitable for aggregation. It is possible to go further, to try to break down employees by skills and competencies. Such databases can be very useful but are also extremely difficult to establish and keep up to date, and unless there is such a database already it may be impracticable for a larger organisation to make this analysis. It is also harder to keep the information in the same way as the other statistics, as each employee may fall under several headings in the analysis. A simple example is that when I used to analyse the saleable skills of employees of a consultancy which I managed, I always had more skills than people. When we added language fluency the list extended again. This was a useful and simple exercise in a consultancy employing 20 full-time staff and about 10 part-time associates, where all the people knew each other, but would be very complex and more difficult to apply to a very large business.

The final levels of resolution are gender and ethnic minorities. The main purpose is to ensure that the organisation's anti-discrimination policies are operating in a satisfactory way, although the statistics are not the whole answer to this question. However, they will give a preliminary indication of whether the organisation operates a "glass ceiling" with few women or people from ethnic groups able to move beyond a certain level. Such statistics have to be read with care, as the fact that a plant in Bradford has more employees from minority ethnic groups than another in Horsham, West Sussex, may be more to do with the make-up of the population in the area than any policies applied by the organisation.

Age and Length of Service

Other statistics are needed to give more insight into potential human resource issues and problems. A starting point is an analysis of age of employees by grade and by length of service. Table 6.1. has been compiled to indicate the type of problem that can be revealed by age analysis. It is deliberately kept simple, and assumes that the organisation has three grades of manager plus a managing director. Grade 3 is the most senior grade, and these are the executive directors. If we relied only on the bottom line of totals by grade, we would see that there is an issue, in that the proportion of women moves from just over a third in the lowest grade to nil in the highest, but it would not give any insight into where to look next, nor would it have given any indication of the other problems that can be seen from the age analysis. What the detail shows is that the organisation seems to have done something about achieving a measure of parity in the entry-level grades, but there it ends. It also suggests that unless particular attention is given to this issue, it will be many years before there is a more appropriate proportion in the next grades. A companion length-of-service analysis would bring more insight. If, for example, it showed that in grade 1 75% of the 36–40-year-old males had at least ten years' experience, but that 50% of women had less than five years, it would indicate that either the organisation has greater difficulty in retaining women, or that when vacancies have arisen it has taken deliberate efforts to have a fairer recruitment or promotion policy. In grade 2, we would make different deductions if the length-of-service analysis showed that most of these managers had spent their whole careers with the organisation, than if there were a healthy mix of service periods, which showed that not all promotion was from within.

The main strategic problems revealed from Table 6.1 are around management succession, impending changes at the top, and the potential career management issues for those in grades 1 and 2. Length-of-service statistics would give further understanding.

Apart from the insight such analyses give to the organisation, they provide a basis for calculating retirements, and may indicate weaknesses in succession planning.

Table 6.1   Example of age analysis

Age	Grade 1			Grade 2			Grade 3		
	M	**F**	**Total**	**M**	**F**	**Total**	**M**	**F**	**Total**
61–65	2		2	1		1	4		4
56–60	3		3	2		2	5		5
51–55				18	1	19			
46–50	12		12	12	2	14			
41–45	38	8	46	11	2	13			
36–40	49	40	89	15	5	20			
31–35	7	3	10						
26–30	21	25	46						
21–25									
Total	132	76	208	59	10	69	9		9

Labour Turnover Analysis

There are two elements to labour turnover statistics: how many people leave and why they leave. Statistics should be capable of being presented under all of the headings discussed so far, so that it is possible to compare areas of the organisation, grades and age/length of service. For forecasting and for policy purposes it is important to know the broad reason for leaving, such as death, retirement, health, redundancy, other organisational initiative and resignation. Although not representing termination from the organisation, it is useful to be able to add those who have left a grade or area on promotion (or for other reason) elsewhere in the organisation, an analysis which might have more complexity in a multinational that moved people into different businesses and countries.

The cause of the turnover is very important. Projecting historical ratios of all turnover is not safe when there is an abnormality in the situation. The retirement pattern of the past few years may not continue, for example, because the organisation has had a policy of early retirement and there are now few people left who are over 50 years of age: there may have been major redundancies in each of the past three years, but the organisation is now slimmed down, and these abnormal events are not expected to recur.

What is revealed about resignations at different levels or areas of the organisation can be important for the understanding of the situation. It may also indicate a need for further investigation, such as surveys to find out why people resigned.

Turnover by grade and age can be particularly revealing, in that an apparently healthy rate for the whole can conceal major problems in certain areas. An overall rate of 10% might hide the fact that in some areas it exceeded 100%. While turnover rates should be expected to vary across the organisation there are limits to what should be seen as healthy.

Overtime

This has been a long-standing way of giving some flexibility of resources to the organisation. and boosting the income of employees. Typically, figures will only be available for overtime for which the organisation pays and therefore excludes most management and much clerical and secretarial time. Extra time, willingly given, to deal with a particular problem or project may be a sign of a motivated organisation. A situation where people stay at their desks, regardless of whether there is work to do, so that they are seen to be there long after closing time, is a sign of low morale and an unhappy, distrustful atmosphere.

Lost Time Analysis

Time may be lost for unavoidable reasons. However, sometimes it can be as a result of either low morale, or the working situation itself. It is important to know the patterns of time lost in different areas of the organisation, and whether these can be changed. Because there may be large differences by location, grade and type of job, it is not appropriate to assume that overall ratios can be applied universally. Categories under which information might be analysed include days lost because of:

- Industrial disputes
- Accidents
- Occupational illness
- Other illness
- Time off in lieu of overtime (where the organisation has such a policy)
- Other approved reasons (e.g. unpaid leave, education)
- Absenteeism.

Holidays have not been included in this list because they are an entitlement.

Non-employees

Most organisations have people working on site who are not employees, but for whom some services have to be provided. They may be temporary staff, who are the employees of an agency, contract staff, some of whom may be self-employed, but where the organisation has responsibilities to collect tax and national insurance, and contracted-out services, such as security, internal auditing and IT operations. It would be wrong to ignore these categories of people, and I would suggest that the minimum information needed is the total hours they provide, and the maximum and minimum numbers of people each month.

Remuneration Levels

What is needed here is not great schedules or what the organisation pays its employees in cash and benefits, but a summary analysis which explores the variation between practice in the organisation and the industry. For certain level of people, such as senior managers, and skills which span many industries, a broader basis of comparison may be needed. The figures cannot be interpreted in isolation from the profit situation. For example, an organisation which pays the highest rate in the industry for its factory workers and has the lowest profitability of the industry may have a serious weakness: however, if its profitability were to be higher than any other firm in the industry a high wage policy might be a strength.

The External Environment as it Affects HRM

Although generally in this book we have not tried to cover the appraisal of the external environment in all its aspects, in the HR area it is not always possible to interpret the internal statistics without some consideration of what is happening externally. For example, an inability to recruit sufficient numbers of people with certain specific skills could be because:

- the organisation offers remuneration packages which are below the average; or
- the organisation has a poor reputation as an employer; or
- there is a national shortage of people coming out of the universities with the appropriate qualifications.

One of these causes is totally internal, another may be a mix of internal and external factors, and the third is related to wider environmental issues. For this reason we suggest that Figure 6.2 be used as a checklist for considering the environment. Of course it should be amended to fit the particular situation, and you will need more space than we have provided to record the answers.

HRM, Vision and Strategy

Earlier in this chapter we stressed the need to compare current HR policies and practices with the requirements of the vision of the organisation and the strategies it was following. In this section we suggest a number of tools which will assist this process, and later we will suggest the steps needed to look in depth at one area of HRM, management training. With modifications, this way of thinking can be extended to other HRM activities, and we believe that the detail we provide on management training will point the way.

A Diagnostic Questionnaire

The first tool is a diagnostic questionnaire which can be used at corporate or business unit level. It examines the overall philosophy of HRM in the organisation, and can give a good indication of the degree to which HRM is a good strategic partner to the other management functions. Although this could be completed by one person, more might be gained by having several managers in the organisation fill it in from their own perspectives. Some thought should be given to each of the questions: if no one in the organisation can see their relevance, you can assume that HRM does not act strategically, and is not allowed to do so anyway.

More can be gained from the questionnaire than the crude scores suggest. An interpretation sheet, which analyses the answers in more detail, appears at the end of this chapter. It is separated from the questionnaire to ensure that it does not influence initial thinking about the questions themselves.

Change Type	Examples	HR Implications	Importance Rating
Demographic	Population structure		
	Migration patterns		
	Population size		
	Diversity of population		
	Labour availability		
Economic	Growth/decline		
	Inflation		
	Unemployment levels		
	Wage/salary levels		
	Taxation		
	Black economy?		
	Exchange rates		
Legal	Employment law		
	EC employment law		
	Health and safety		
	Specific industry regulations		
	Information disclosure		
	Equal opportunity laws		
	Case law (e.g. stress)		
Technological	Information technology		
	Manufacture process		
	Manufacture methods		
	Product life cycle		
	Cycle time		
Infrastructure	Education: schools		
	Education: higher		
	Education: post-experience		
Ecology	Pressure groups		
	Smoking attitudes		
Social	Ethical issues		
	Work attitudes		
	Cultural differences		
	Educational values		
Political	Government changes		
	Industry-specific concerns		

Figure 6.2 Environmental issue and HR activities.
(Source: D. Hussey, *Business Driven Human Resource Management*, Wiley, Chichester, 1996. © John Wiley & Sons, Limited. Reproduced with permission)

Questionnaire: How business-driven is your HRM activity?

	A	B	C	D
1. Is HRM consulted while strategies are being considered?	Never	Rarely	Often	Usually
2. Does this advice have any impact on the decisions?	Never	Rarely	Often	Usually
3. Is the HR role proactive?	Never	Rarely	Often	Usually
4. Will risks be taken to give unpopular advice?	Never	Rarely	Often	Usually
5. How many specific examples can be given where HRM has contributed to the strategic success of the business in:*				
5.1. Overall HR	None	1 or 2	3 to 5	Over 5
5.2. Remuneration	None	1 or 2	3 to 5	Over 5
5.3. Recruitment	None	1 or 2	3 to 5	Over 5
5.4. Management development	None	1 or 2	3 to 5	Over 5
5.5. Training	None	1 or 2	3 to 5	Over 5
5.6. Succession	None	1 or 2	3 to 5	Over 5
5.7. Others	None	1 or 2	3 to 5	Over 5
6. Is there a clear strategy and policy for each HR area?	No	Some	Most	Yes
7. Does this derive specifically from business strategies etc.?	No	Loosely	Partly	Totally
8. When were all HR policies and strategies last reviewed?	Don't know	Years ago	Last year	This year
9. Are such reviews made regularly?	No	Infrequently	Periodically	Yes
10. Does top management play a part in such reviews?	No	Not much	Informally	Formally
11. Is line management involved in such reviews?	No	Not much	Informally	Formally
12. Have performance criteria been set for HR?	No	A few	Most areas	All areas
13. Are the criteria derived from the business needs?	No	A few	Mainly	Totally
14. Do you know the costs of activities in HRM?	No	A few	Some	All
15. Do you measure HR time spent on key projects?	No	Roughly	In part	Fully
16. Are HR actions such as training evaluated?	Never	Rarely	Sometimes	Often
17. How are priorities decided when setting the HR budget?	None	Whim	Gut feel	Corp need
18. Are HR actions in different parts of the organisation coordinated to give priority to business needs?	No	Rarely	Sometimes	Always
19. What sort of image does your organisation have as an employer?	Don't know	Poor	Good	The best
20. How do the HR performance measures compare with:				
Competitors?	Don't know	Badly	Same	Better
World class organisations?	Don't know	Badly	Same	Better
21. Do line managers think HRM is a good strategic partner?	No	Sometimes	Mainly	Yes

* Scores for these sub-questions should be averaged

SCORING RULES
Score A = 0, B = 1, C = 2, D = 3
Maximum score 21 × 3 = 63
Minimum score 0

Score

Contribution of HRM to the Business Needs

Figure 6.3 offers one way of beginning to get into the detail, and if required can be used in a working session with managers to crystallise their perceptions. The headings to the rows can be adapted to include other areas of HRM activity. The space under each row heading is intended for the specific detail of what is being considered, as the headings are too broad to be useful. For example, the reward system might be considered under headings like top management, first-line managers, sales and shop floor. Management training might also be considered by level. What is actually listed should be related to the needs of the organisation, and it is unlikely to be the same for every organisation.

Once the areas to be explored have been identified, the next question to ask is whether what is being done helps or hinders the organisation's strategy. A rating scale is suggested. Identifying an issue in general terms is not always helpful, so the next question invites specific attention to what could be improved. The final column identifies obstacles. For example, it might be that a new agreement would have to be negotiated with a trade union, or solving a problem faced in department A would cause a problem for department B.

The summary, which is what Figure 6.3 represents, should not lead anyone into the trap of a simplistic form-filling approach. Those using this tool must have knowledge of the HR activity being considered and of the strategy it is being examined against. Clearly if there is no knowledge of either, this particular approach will not be useful.

Using the Integrated Organisational Model

The model presented in Figure 6.1 is more than a concept, and can be actively used in a detailed analysis of the components of HRM. Figure 6.4 uses this model to explore what new needs are called for as a result of a new strategic initiative. With adaptation it could be used to review an existing strategy. It is not just the strategies that might change, so the recommendation is that the analysis covers vision, values and objectives as well. We define these as follows:

- *Vision* is top management's expression of what the organisation is striving to become, and incorporates what in earlier

HR activity	Rating					What could be improved?	What obstacles to be removed?
	Hinders		Neutral		Helps		
	1	2	3	4	5		
Reward system							
Managers							
Sales							
Shop floor							
Culture							
Internal							
Intercultural							
Internal communication							
Briefing groups							
Company newspaper							
Email							
Recruitment							
Managers							
Clerical							
Technicians							
Industrial relations							
Company policy							
Works councils							
Performance management							
Top management							
Managers							
Clerical							
Technicians							
Management training							
Senior							
Middle							
Junior							

Figure 6.3   Contribution of HR activity to the business needs. (Source: modified from a figure in D. Hussey, *Business Driven Human Resource Management*, Wiley, Chichester, 1996. © John Wiley & Sons, Limited. Reproduced with permission)

literature used to be called mission statements. A vision is semi-permanent. It is likely to outlast any strategic plan that may be prepared, but will not last forever.

- *Values* are the moral and ethical principles which guide the organisation in its decisions and actions.
- *Objectives* relate specifically to the key targets for each of the next few years, set in the context of the vision, and which are markers that help indicate progress towards the vision.
- *Strategies* are the means by which an organisation moves to attain its long-term aims

Relating HRM to the Business

Figure 6.5 illustrates another approach, which will be discussed further in the detailed examination of management training which follows. It requires that the organisation has some clarity in its strategic thinking: if no one can define the elements of the strategy, it will not be possible to look at how it might impact each of the areas of HRM.

The intention of the approach is that the key elements of the strategies, values, visions and objectives would be written out in the left-hand column. Strategies appear first, not because of the logic of how they were formulated, but because they should be more concrete than values in HR terms, and values in turn are likely to be more concrete than vision. There may indeed be little to write at all under objectives, since all the actions may already have been identified at an earlier stage.

The HR area headings are indicative, and should be changed and expanded to fit the particular business. The figure does not attempt to list them all. The space under these headings is intended for the specific issues to be recorded. We would not attempt the impossible, to literally write in every detail in a minute space, and instead would prepare a separate schedule of each of the HR activity areas. The summary chart would use symbols to show the state of the issues found in the supporting analysis: none, minor or serious.

In broad terms we know that every one of the activity areas is likely to be relevant to every strategy, but what we are looking for is three specific things:

Use a separate questionnaire for each strategy or element of vision etc. Combine them afterwards to see if any of the strategies require HRM to pull in different directions at the same time.

1. Describe the strategy, element of vision, value etc.

   . . . .

2. Is this an incremental or fundamental change?

   . . . .

3. How does the strategy, vision or value affect the organisation (using the headings from Figure 6.1)? What HRM needs are revealed?

Aspect of organisation	What is the issue?	What is the HRM impact?
Strategy		
Tasks		
People		
Structure		
Reward systems		
Control systems		
Decision processes		
Culture		
Information systems		

4. What obvious issues can be identified from this stage of the analysis?

   . . . .

Figure 6.4 Applying the integrated organisation concept

Vision etc.	HR areas impacted					
	Management Develop	Succession planning	Recruitment	Reward	Work force planning	Other (specify)
Strategies						
Values						
Vision elements						
Objectives						

Figure 6.5 Relating HRM activities to the business

- A mismatch of the current HR policy with a particular strategy etc., on the lines of the integrated organisation discussion given earlier.
- An aspect of a current strategy etc. which should lead to specific HRM actions, but has not done so.
- The implications of new strategies, and the impact these might have on the existing situation.

Going Deeper into HRM: An Audit of Management Development

A really serious appraisal should go somewhat deeper into each HRM activity area. The sort of analysis described above should provide considerable insight, but there will also be many activities within HRM which should be probed in depth. The ideal would be to undertake a complete audit of each activity area, but if this is not practicable we recommend a selective audit of those areas which are like icebergs, and have much more of the detail hidden than is visible. And like icebergs they have the power to do damage to an organisation.

Management development is only one of many activity areas which could have been chosen to illustrate a detailed methodology for an audit. We selected it because it is an area which could contribute more to strategic success than is the practice in many organisations. It is also an area where organisations spend considerable sums of money without knowing whether they are receiving any benefit. Because there may be thousands of different initiatives ongoing, many of which may have become institutionalised over the years, it is usually an area which will repay study.

The framework and questionnaires used here can be modified easily to fit other activity areas (see Hussey, 1996), and indeed may need to be modified for any particular organisation. The bias here is towards management training.

An Overall Framework

Figure 6.6 provides an overall framework which describes the logic of the steps outlined here. Although only the top four elements of the model are about the audit itself, in the interest of completeness we touch briefly on the remaining parts of the model. Our bias is to drive the audit by the needs of the organisation. This does not mean that we will ignore the needs of individuals, but we will look at them in a particular perspective.

Step 1 What the Organisation Needs

The questionnaires discussed earlier are appropriate here, and should have yielded information which is directly relevant to this HR activity area. When considering the needs of the organisation which may be met through management development, it is worth remembering that management training, for example, can be used to help people understand and become committed to a significant

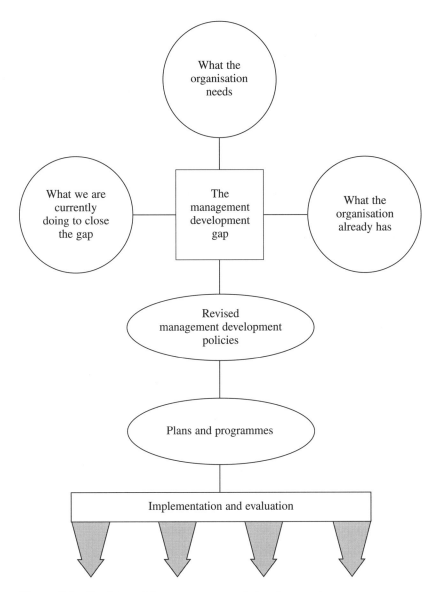

Figure 6.6 Business-driven management development.
(Source: D. Hussey, *Business Driven Human Resource Management*,
Wiley, Chichester, 1996. © John Wiley & Sons, Limited. Reproduced with
permission)

change, as well as providing skills and competencies that are important if people are to be able to play a full part in making the change a success.

Matrix approaches can be helpful in analysing the implications for management development of particular aspects of vision, values and strategy. An example of one matrix (in simplified form) is given for illustration in Figure 6.7, and this is followed by a blank form for completion. The example assumes that the organisation

STRATEGY	CORPORATE NEED	PRIORITIES BY LEVEL OF MANAGEMENT		
		1	2	3
EXPAND IN EUROPE				
	NEW NEEDS			
	Specific country knowledge		A	B
	Intercultural differences	A	A	A
	World class manufacturing	C	B	A
	Market planning	A	A	B
	EXPANDED NEEDS			
	Project planning		C	A
	Transformational leadership	A	A	C
DELAYERING				
	NEW NEEDS			
	Empowerment	A	A	A
	Career management		A	
	Outsourcing skills	A	A	B
	Internal corporate communication	A	B	
	Change management	A	A	A
	EXPANDED NEEDS			
	Performance management	A	A	A
	Situational leadership		C	B
	Interpersonal communication	A	A	A
STRATEGIC ALLIANCES				
	NEW NEEDS			
	Financial assessment	A	A	C
	Managing alliances	A	A	B
	Understanding culture	A	A	A
	EXPANDED NEEDS			
	Evaluating operational performance	A	A	C
	Visionary leadership	A	A	C

Figure 6.7   Getting to grips with organisational needs

has three new strategic actions: a major expansion into Europe, delayering the organisation and the building of strategic alliances.

Real-life situations are more complex and subtle than this, and more than one matrix may have to be developed. The principle remains valid. Be ready to develop a more detailed analysis showing the number of people who require the skills listed. Also

Vision etc.	Resulting organisational need	Priorities by management level		
		Level 1	Level 2	Level 3
Strategies				
Values				
Vision elements				
Objectives				

Figure 6.8 Use this to begin to identify the implications for management development. Questionnaire: How business driven is your HRM activity?

consider whether a management training or other development initiative might deliver added value to the organisation as a tool to help implement the strategies. For example, if new strategic alliances are forged, would a joint workshop of managers from both parties help both sides to understand cultural differences, and as important, to begin to develop a working relationship?

In a real situation we should expand the analysis to include vision, values, strategies and objectives. This is what Figure 6.8 and its supporting questions attempt to cover.

1. Use the concepts of the blank Figure 6.8 to begin your analysis.
2. What are the implications of your findings?
3. For each of the organisational needs identified, list the skills and knowledge that are required at each level of management using the form below. Use the following letters to indicate whether these are new to the organisation (N), already existing but in need of enhancement (E), or already existing but needing to be maintained (M). Modify and extend the form for your own situation and the levels of management in your organisation. You may need to break skills etc. into competencies.

Outline form (Abbreviated)

1.1. Organisational need..
     List skills/knowledge by level

Level 1	Level 2	Level 3

1.2. Organisational need..
     List skills/knowledge by level

Level 1	Level 2	Level 3

Notes:_____

_____

Step 2: What the organisation already has

In this context we mean the skills, knowledge and competencies that are already possessed. It is possible, for example, that all the requirements identified are already possessed, in which case the organisational need is to maintain those skills, and equip people for promotion. For corporate appraisal purposes it would be a great strength, albeit a somewhat unlikely one, if all the requirements were in place. There could also be a major weakness revealed if the organisation were setting off on complex strategic paths without having people with the right skills in the right numbers.

During this step we have to uncover what skills exist, and what training needs have been identified. Initially this means reviewing the sources of information available inside the organisation, although it may indicate a need to undertake special studies, and to change the regular methods the organisation uses.

Task 1: determine which of the following methods your organisation uses:

- Annual appraisal of subordinate by his or her boss
- Special training needs assessment surveys
- Assessment centres
- 360° annual appraisal systems
- 360° feedback systems for collecting training needs information.
- Other (specify).

These sources will indicate identified training needs which may or may not match with the strategic requirements identified. They will also identify a number of requirements for the future development of people, and what we might term "maintenance requirements", needs which may not appear to be strategic, but which are important to enable the organisation to continue to operate effectively.

Task 2: list the training needs identified, by level of management. Classify these into those which:

- meet the identified organisational needs (S)

- meet longer term needs such as developing people for promotion (L)
- meet the personal objectives of managers, but are peripheral for the organisation (P)
- have no obvious value (O).

Training or development need...
List needs by level and type

Level 1	Level 2	Level 3

Task 3: assess the implications of the analysis so far.

Task 4: what can be concluded about any organisational needs which have not been identified in the assessment? Is this because they were not considered in the evaluations, or is the organisation already proficient in all these areas.? Or do we not know? We need to reach a decision. It may be necessary to undertake an additional survey to establish the facts.

Task 5: Assess the implications from the analysis of what the organisation has, and identify actions that should be considered.

Step 3: What Are we Currently Doing to Close the Gap?

Actions already being undertaken may include training and development programmes, coaching and the recruitment of people with additional skills. Before we can begin to assess the gap between what we have and what we need, we need to audit the actions already under way. The concentration in this checklist is on training and education, but in real situations the other initiatives should also be considered. Typically, an organisation has many programmes and initiatives in place, aimed at various levels of management. The questions below concentrate on the training and education aspects of development, but the concept should be extended to other management development actions.

Task 1: analyse the present, past and planned future annual expenditure on management training and education. The following format provides a guide.

In theory this should be an easy analysis to make. However, we know from our own experience, and from various published surveys, that not all organisations could easily turn up these figures from the management accounts, and if your organisation is one of these you will have identified a serious weakness.

Part of the reason why some organisations do not appear to have a full understanding of their total expenditure on management training is the multiplicity of ways in which costs are incurred for each initiative. Some costs are incurred by head office, and may or may not be charged out to profit and cost centres in various ways. Others are incurred directly by the cost and profit centres. Some are mixed: for example, the costs of the programme itself may be funded centrally, but the travel and accommodation costs may be paid by the participants and repaid by the unit where they work on an expense claim. Ignorance of the full picture often means that poor economic decisions are made.

Very few organisations outside the civil service and professional services firms like management consultants have any idea of the cost of those who attend programmes, and even fewer attempt to consider the opportunity cost.

Task 2: audit the overall training programme. An examination of the total spend should yield useful information, but there is much more that we need to know. Expenditure and effectiveness are very different things, and what we have to begin to establish is:

• What did we get for our money?
• Did the aims of the initiatives match the strategic needs of the organisation? (Did we spend money on the right things?)

Suggested format for establishing management training expenditure

EXPENDITURE IN £000	Year				
By type of expense	Last – 1	Last	Current	Next	Next + 1
Direct Costs					
Development costs*					
Teaching costs					
Meeting room hire					
Travel and hotel: course leader/tutors					
Travel: participants					
Food and lodging: participants					
Participants' time					
Other direct					
Total direct					
Total indirect					
Total full costs					
Opportunity costs of delegate attendance					

* i.e. development of new initiatives, training materials etc.

- Did the right target population attend the programmes?
- What were the real benefits achieved from each initiative? (Were the benefits what we expected?)

To answer these questions requires a detailed operational analysis, as well as an examination of information from the management accounts. A number of organisations would have difficulty answering these questions without a number of special exercises, which is surprising considering that large organisations may spend many millions of euros on management training and development.

Typical findings in practice are that with some work the costs of the various initiatives can be calculated. However, although the aims of some programmes match the corporate need, many do not. Often the programme is set up in relation to the needs of specific people, but it is others who attend the programmes, so the real need is not met. And in most organisations the only assessment made is the completion of happy sheets, at the end of each programme, which measure neither learning nor changes in behaviour

The analysis suggested overleaf is not meant to imply that all organisations run only two programmes, and in real situations the number of columns should be extended and additional pages should be used. Some of the questions posed in the example are to establish the basic facts: others are detailed probes into every aspect of the programmes the organisation is running.

It would be appropriate to include initiatives planned but not yet run, although in these cases some of the questions would remain unanswered.

Not every point that needs investigation is included in the above example, and there are a few more that require attention.

- In support of the analysis so far we need to establish the topics in each initiative and the time given to each. This is because otherwise we may not be able to match programmes to the strategic needs which we have identified. It is also possible for a topic to be covered, but not with the depth that is really required.

- What are the present policies for training? This question should be divided into general policy, provision of training and assessment of benefits.

- Who decides what new training initiatives are needed? It may be that the decisions are being taken at the wrong levels, and that because of this training is not reaching its target population.

- How does the organisation ensure that the right people receive training? It may be that a measure of compulsion is needed.

Example of an analysis sheet for training initiatives

Item	Prog............................	Prog............................
Objectives		
How were the objectives determined?		
Vision, strategy, value or objective supported		
What other corporate needs were met?		
Any other rationale for the initiative?		
What are the measurable targets for the initiative?		
Target population		
Number in target		
How target population identified		
How are people selected to attend		
Number of participants who have attended: Year.... Year.... Year....		
% attendees from target population: total to date		
When did the initiative start?		
How is it resourced?		
Number of events held Year.... Year.... Year....		
Costs per event: Year.... Year.... Year....		
Average event ratings		
How are the benefits measured?		
Does the initiative meet all the objectives?		

- What is the policy for who pays for training (corporate, divisional, business unit, individual etc.).
- How is performance of the training unit measured? (If the only measure is the average number of training days per person provided you will know you have another weakness).
- How are the benefits of initiatives determined?
- What is the policy on personal development (e.g. professional examinations, sponsored degree courses etc.)?

Step 4: Assess the Management Training Gap

It is now time to interpret the gap from the analysis undertaken so far.

1. What organisational needs are not being met?

   Needs   *What should be done?*

2. Which needs are only being partially met

   Needs   *What should be done?*

3. Which initiatives fully meet organisational needs?

   Initiatives   *What should be done?*

4. Which initiatives partly meet organisational needs?

   Initiatives   *What should be done?*

5. Which initiatives do not appear to meet any needs?

   Initiatives   *What should be done?*

6. Which policy areas require review?

7. What solutions other than training may be used to fill the gap?

The Remaining Steps

Figure 6.6 includes three further steps which might loosely be called implementation. They cover the actions which are likely to result from the appraisal. The first of these steps is called revised management development policies. The appraisal could, of course, demonstrate that all the current policies are appropriate, but frequently changes will be indicated. For example, there might be a need for a different policy towards development which can be directly related to corporate needs, than towards development which meets only the personal aspirations of employees. Such policy changes might cover the nature of the development which will be offered, the proportion of the budget which will be spent on each, and changes in how people are selected to receive the development.

After the policy changes, the next logical move would be the detailed actions to support the policies. In the training example we have been using, this might mean dropping some of the training programmes offered, changing the content of others, adding new programmes, altering the target participation and changing the frequency of events. It might involve replacing some training events with a different method of management development.

The final stage of the model is to implement these plans, and to monitor the results.

The detail of these last three steps is outside the scope of this book. More information can be found in Hussey (1996), which also has chapters applying a similar model to other areas of HR activity.

Conclusions to the HRM Appraisal

We hope that the brief coverage of the HRM appraisal has shown that not only is there a lot to do, but that the conclusions reached can have a far-reaching impact on the future of the organisation. This is particularly so if the organisation has not previously taken a strategic approach to HRM. It is not just strengths and weaknesses which will be revealed, but areas where costs can be saved, money spent more effectively, and more accountability placed on HRM.

Our remarks should not be read as applying just to the HR department. In many organisations some HRM activity is delegated to operating management and to line managers. The principles described here are relevant, no matter where in the organisation HR is managed, or how that responsibility is divided.

MANAGEMENT EFFECTIVENESS

The effectiveness (or lack of it) of the management resource is one of the most important strengths or weaknesses of any organisation, but is probably one of the most difficult things to assess. Most modern companies have performance management systems, which will provide very useful data, but not always what is required.

One reason for this is that performance is generally assessed in relation to the current job, whereas the corporate appraisal should be looking forward in the light of the new challenges the organisation may be expected to face. A second reason is that, generally, one could expect that problems of effectiveness identified by line managers will have mostly been dealt with in the normal course of events. Following the logic of this, some might argue that there is nothing to appraise, because the performance management system will have ensured that all problems are solved. So by definition, no organisations have weaknesses in management, only strengths! And if you believe that, you will believe anything.

We have covered part of the problem through some of the suggestions made for auditing HR against the vision and strategies of the organisation, but here our emphasis was on the skills, knowledge and competencies needed. The underlying attitude was that anything missing could be solved by recruitment, development or outsourcing. We were not particularly discussing how effective the key managers were, only whether they had the capabilities needed. Effectiveness is about how those capabilities are applied.

The driving force of any organisation is provided by the top management teams at the centre, and in each of the major business areas, and it is these people whose effectiveness to take the organisation forward is our main concentration. This is what makes it difficult, as these are the same people who might already have decided that the major corporate strengths are the competence of the chief executive and the top team.

One method that might be used might be for the chief executive to look at every member of this top team, against the needs of the organisation as he or she expects them to emerge, and from this assessment we might come to a fair understanding of the strengths and weaknesses of this team. However, the validity of this exercise would depend on the competence and objectivity of the chief executive. If he or she is not up to the mark, we are unlikely to find out much by this method.

A variation on this approach might be for the appraisal to be undertaken by a task force of non-executive directors. Provided they really understand the business and the directions it is moving in, this could be the best approach to use. Certainly it is practical, and can be done quickly.

A more accurate method might be to run assessment centres for all the top team. The disadvantages are that this would be costly and time consuming in any organisation of size.

Culture

Culture is intangible. We know it is there, and we know that it affects how a company performs. We know that cultural differences between two companies which come together in a merger or strategic alliance can be a cause of failure. In a way, it is a little like temperature: we can tell whether it is hot or cold, but can only find a precise way of defining these terms when we have an instrument that will measure temperature with some precision. Until we have this, how we judge the temperature is affected by personal differences in whether we feel hot or cold, whether we are mobile or static, and our state of health. In addition, there is no precision in our feelings about what the temperature really is.

It is possible to make a judgement about culture, to know that the way people behave as a general rule in the organisation is helpful or a hindrance to the strategies the organisation is trying to follow. Observation will tell us in broad terms whether the culture is bureaucratic or entrepreneurial, or if people normally take decisions or avoid accepting responsibility. However, it is usually difficult to determine what needs to be done as a result of such judgements, they may not reveal important differences between the various business units and departments within the organisation, and it may be difficult to gain a shared understanding of what the culture is, because of differences in how various key managers perceive it.

Any serious appraisal of culture has to find the equivalent of a thermometer so that measurements can be taken. There is no one standard measuring instrument for culture, and generally the methods advocated are proprietary, although the principles behind many of them are more widely available. It is possible to take measurements of attitudes (in which case it is necessary to decide which attitudes would give a valid interpretation of culture) or of behaviour (but which behaviours are important?).

The method used here for illustration is by no means the only one available, and was used for many years by management consultants Harbridge House Inc. (acquired by Coopers & Lybrand in 1993). What was measured was climate, effectively a dimension of culture, which describes the way it feels to work inside the organisation. Climate was found to be largely caused by the management practices of the leaders (at various levels) within the organisation. The extensive research behind this concept found six aspects which were significant components of climate (Cannon, 1987):

- Structure – clarity of roles and responsibilities
- Standards – pressure to improve performance coupled with pride in doing a good job
- Responsibility – the feeling of being in charge of one's own job
- Recognition – the feeling of being rewarded for a job well done
- Support – the feeling of trust and mutual support
- Commitment – a sense of pride in belonging to the organisation.

Under each of these headings key management practices were defined. Measurements are taken using feedback instruments. At a minimum these are completed by the subordinates of each manager in the survey, and often in addition by peers, the manager of each manager, and possibly by customers and suppliers. All questionnaires are handled in confidence, with each manager receiving an aggregate report of his or her practices, without knowing what any one person has reported. These aggregate reports are confidential to the individual, and what the company receives is an overall report, which could be developed for each relevant organisational unit.

The advantages of this method are that differences in various areas of the organisation can be studied, a comparison can be made with what is a desirable profile for the climate, and because the assessment is based on how managers manage it becomes easier to develop strategies to change management behaviour. Change management behaviour in the critical areas, and you change the climate.

Bedingham (1999) describes another approach, the Organisation Culture Inventory (OCI). This uses 12 styles of behaviour as the basis for defining culture. He explains that the instrument can be used to identify a target culture, as well as to measure the curent culture. He states:

> Creating the target culture comes from an examination, by the senior management team, of the organisation's strategy, mission and values. They are then able to describe how things need to be done in the organisation in order to achieve the strategy with the highest level of effectiveness and efficiency and with the minimum amount of pain.

These are converted into a profile, based on the standardised items within the OCI instrument. These same items are used to survey the organisation to measure the current culture. The result is an ability to compare the culture of the organisation as a whole and by relevant sub-groups, with the target culture.

If there is someone in the organisation who is competent to assess culture, and has access to an appropriate instrument, there is no reason why this cannot be undertaken in-house. However, it is an area where lack of skill or knowledge may be dangerous, and it is one of the few areas discussed in this book where we should advise that serious consideration is given to using an external consultant.

Structure

The structure of an organisation can facilitate or restrict the development and execution of effective strategies: frequently there is a trade-off, in that the structure is beneficial in some aspects and harmful in others. An example is the structuring of the organisation into SBUs. This can facilitate the exploitation of market opportunities, but may make it harder for the maximum synergy to be gained from the development of technologies which are relevant to more than one SBU.

The first task is to collect information on how the organisation is structured. In most organisations this will already be defined, both in policy terms and in organisation charts. We say most organisations, because our experience includes quite large organisations that do not have this information readily available, although of course a de facto structure does exist.

Structure defines:

- the way the organisation positions itself towards its markets
- how it coordinates its activities
- where decisions are made
- responsibilities
- reporting lines.

Once the current structure has been established the appraisal should assess its appropriateness in the light of the organisation's vision, values and strategies. The following suggestions are made:

- Adapt Figure 6.2 to help determine which elements of the structure help, hinder or are neutral to the business needs.
- It may be useful to relate this exercise to specific elements of the vision etc., in line with the examples given earlier in this chapter for a strategic approach to HRM. This may be particularly necessary if significant changes in strategic emphasis have been taking place, such as a global expansion.
- Assess the role of the various elements of the head office organisation. How are these elements contributing to shareholder value? Do they duplicate what is going on elsewhere in the organisation?
- Determine how the structure aids or hinders the development of synergy between the various components of the organisation.
- What problems have been encountered in practice, which are caused by the structure?
- Are there too many layers of management in the structure?
- Is the structure compatible with the culture that the organisation requires?

APPENDIX 6.1

How Business-Driven is your HRM Activity? Score Sheet

BROAD INTERPRETATION
  Under 15: Not business driven
  16–30: A long way to go
  31–45: Still room to improve
  46–60: Business driven
  61–63: Excellent or wishful thinking!

DETAILED INTERPRETATION   Score

Total the score for questions 1–5   ☐   Central strategic role
  (maximum score 15)

Total the score for the remaining   ☐   HRM areas business driven
questions (maximum 48)

Use these scores to enter your position on the matrix

HAVE CENTRAL STRATEGIC ROLE

	(Score 10 or more) YES	(Score under 10) NO
(Score 36 or more) YES HRM AREAS ARE BUSINESS DRIVEN		
(Score under 36) NO		

The answers to this questionnaire will not reveal the whole truth about your organisation, but they may provide food for thought.

1. Having a key central strategic role is not enough to ensure that HRM is business driven.
2. Without a key central strategic role, HRM can only act in a reactive way and cannot easily help the organisation to foresee HRM issues that might change its vision and strategies.

If you are satisfied with your score, what do you have to do to maintain the business driven approach?
If you are not satisfied, what are the obstacles to improvement? How might you overcome them?

REFERENCES

Bedingham, K. 1999. The measurement of organisational culture, *Journal of Professional HRM*, 14, January.

Cannon, F. 1987. A note on organisational change, *Management Training Update*, July, Harbridge Consulting Group Ltd, London. Reproduced in Hussey, D. and Lowe P. (eds) 1990. *Key Issues in Management Training*, London, Kogan Page, p. 159.

Hussey, D. 1996. *Business Driven Human Resource Management*, Chichester, Wiley.

Kaplan, R. 1995. *Building a Management System to Implement Your Strategy: Strategic Management Survey*, London, Renaissance Solutions.

Leavitt, H. J. 1964. Applied organisation change in industry: structural, technical and human approaches, in Cooper W. W., Leavitt, H. J. and Shelly, B. (eds) *New Perspectives in Organisational Research,* New York, Wiley, pp. 55–71. An abridged version appears under the same title in Vroom V. R and Dec E. L. (eds) 1970. *Management and Motivation*, Harmondsworth, Penguin, pp. 363–75.

7

Evaluation of Information Systems

Any company analysis must include an investigation of the firm's internal and external information generating capabilities, analytical procedures for converting data into useful information, ways of disseminating this information to relevant departments, and the firm's practices for using information in decision making.

Any firm will as a minimum have an accounting system at the very core of the management information system (MIS). Needed for legal reasons in even the smallest of firms, this system should have evolved into something more comprehensive to provide management information, about, among other things, costs related to relevant activities and information that can be used in the subsequent adjustment of resource allocation.

Even in small firms it is observed that the accounting system created at the very outset of the firm's existence often does not evolve with the firm as it grows. This principle problem is similar to that of much larger enterprises, where the management information systems of yesteryear are ill equipped for the decision making of today and tomorrow.

It is therefore necessary for an evaluation of the firm's information system to consider not only the existing context, but also the evolving needs of the enterprise – something of a challenge with today's evolving computing and communication technology. How to transition the gap between the company's current information systems and new generations becomes a challenge of monumental proportions for executives (just ask any executive how recently they have attempted to install an enterprise resource planning system, such as SAP).

IT SYSTEMS IN MERGER AND ACQUISITION: A QUESTION OF DUE DILIGENCE

A report (KPMG, 1999) quotes Thomson Financial Securities Data (1999), which gives the value of annual global acquisitions as more than $2.2 trillion. The record of corporate success in M & A is not good. The same report by KPMG measured the impact on shareholder value of M & A initiatives across a sample of companies in Europe. The bad news was that, measured objectively in this way, only 17% of deals increased shareholder value, 30% left it unchanged, and 53% decreased it. Failure to consider IS/IT at an early stage is often a contributor to loss of value (there are other causes as well, of course).

A previous survey (KPMG, 1998) found that the IT systems of both organisations had been integrated by 37%, the acquired company's systems were discarded by 25%, and a completely new system for both companies was developed by 15%. Despite this, only 7% of organisations had allowed for a budget for restructuring IT.

A small proportion of respondents (12%) identified the IT strategy at the outset, but it was left principally to the stages of developing a post-merger plan and implementation (30% and 31%, respectively). Significantly, 14% did not have an IT plan at all.

Only 25% of respondents were able to say that they found no problems in dealing with the newly acquired company's systems. Slightly fewer than this did not know, and just over 50% found problems and obstacles.

These figures make the case for a careful appraisal of IT before the deal is signed. Obviously the need is greatest when the intention is to fully integrate the two organisations, but it is important in all situations. Although the real costs of processing information have fallen over the years, the size and complexity of organisations has increased, and the impact of new elements like e-commerce mean that the factors for consideration are numerous. The costs of developing new systems are significant, while failure to develop them means that the opportunities for synergy are reduced. The impact of IT on M & A success is considerable.

FROM STRATEGY TO INFORMATION FLOWS

Apart from checking that the organisation is fulfilling the legal requirements of information generation and handling, it is useful to let any MIS audit start by focusing on the firm's business strategy. As depicted in Figure 7.1, the information audit should aim to allow for maximum alignment between the company's business strategy and the information generating, processing, and decision impact of the MIS. In a research study of 124 companies, it was found that the highest performing firms had the best alignment between the distinctive competencies, dictated by the pursued strategy and the company's information systems. This follows the logic that managers implementing different strategies have different information needs; similarly, different information systems have different information generating capabilities. Thus, the more closely information is aligned with the desired strategy, the more likely managers will be to use the most appropriate levers in the formulation and implementation of the appropriate decisions (Jenster, 1985).

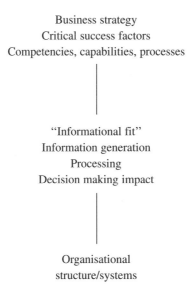

Business strategy
Critical success factors
Competencies, capabilities, processes

"Informational fit"
Information generation
Processing
Decision making impact

Organisational
structure/systems

Figure 7.1 Strategy–structure fit

The first requirement for the analysis is therefore a strategic audit of the firm and an assessment of goals and objectives (we have already met this need in previous chapters). The alignment of the MIS with the business strategy and goals of the firm must therefore be evaluated. In small and medium-sized firms, it is our experience that one rarely finds formal MIS plans, however. It is therefore necessary to extract whether or not the firm actually has a plan for the current and future information systems requirements. In addition, the various systems are rarely integrated (which can make transitions to more developed applications somewhat easier compared to highly integrated MIS structures).

In the past, MIS professionals have focused on tailoring the information systems requirements of the company to its business strategy. More recently, academics and other savants have questioned this adage, by arguing for more standardised solutions. The more of these that can be found to fit the firm's general needs, the more cost efficient and flexible the firm will be when upgrading or changing vendor for its information resources. This has recently been taken to new extremes with the advent of so-called application software providers, which sign-up companies to have standardised software run and operated not on the company's own computing system, but on large "server farms" where the connections to the firm are established via the Internet. Over the next five years, it is anticipated that 65–80% of standardised software for small and medium-sized companies will be changed over to application software providers. (However, there remains a need to seek the best fit possible between the various standardised solutions on offer and the business strategy.)

This is a natural consequence of the evolution in information technology. According to Semiconductor (1999), if you were to put 64 MB of DRAM in your PC today, you could do it for about $100 using one module containing 8 chips. If you had put the same amount of DRAM in your computer in 1974, it would have cost you more than $3,000,000 and you would have needed more than 130,000 chips to do it. To take it even further, if we extrapolate the trend in memory price and capacity from 1975 to 2000 and then add another 25 years, in 2025, we will pay $100 for 2,500 gigabytes of RAM. These technological developments not only create challenges in evaluating the current information systems of the firm, but they also add serious challenges to the assessment of the firm's marketing and channel strategy, its purchasing processes, outsourcing strategy and even the organisational structure and personnel practices, as depicted in Figure 7.2.

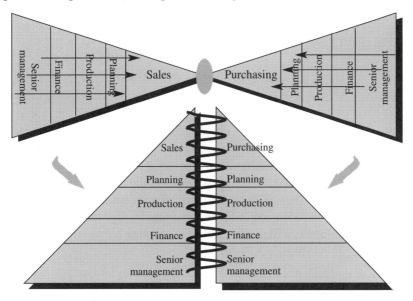

Figure 7.2 New technology leads to new types of business

The transition induced by the advent of new technologies, such as Internet protocol applications, broadband telecommunication technology etc., is leading to new ways of organising business transactions and markets. E-business ventures are not only displaying business models not known ten years ago, but also dictating rules of engagement not foreseen by the incumbents in industry after industry; for example:

- Car dealers: Auto-by-Tel, CarPoint
- Real estate brokers: Visual Properties
- Newspapers: CNet, Excite, Yahoo!, AOL
- Stock brokers: E*Trade, eSchwab, Ameritrade
- Insurance agents: Quicken Financial Services

In addition, we are seeing new firms anticipating efficiency and scale in ways which, only five years ago, were not predicted by most strategic plans. The point is that discussions about information systems are today not a question of merely reflecting on processes, procedures and data warehousing, but have now moved to be an integral part of strategic dialogue and design of the enterprise.

STARTER QUESTIONS FOR THINKING ABOUT THE MIS

When undertaking the appraisal of the MIS for strategic review purposes, it is useful to try to get a fix on what sorts of problems there may be. The questions below, used as a form of simple survey among managers at various levels, can help to identify the perception managers have of the MIS. By all means modify the questions to suit your own situation.

You will notice that although some of the questions ask managers about whether they are getting the information they need, there is also exploration of the timeliness of that information. Good information which always come too late to be useful may be as useless as having no information.

Questionnaire

These questions will help you obtain a broad feel for whether there are problems with the information system.

Possible answers, from "no competitive advantage for the firm" (1) to "excellent or significant competitive advantage for the firm" (4), are given below each question. They are examples derived from various firms. Use them as an aid in assessing the questions.

1. To what degree is the firm's administrative system organised to satisfy the internal as well as the external demands of a modern firm?

In light of your assessment, how do you evaluate its competitive impact on the organisation?

No competitive advantage		Significant competitive advantage	
1	2	3	4

Examples:
1. The administration is quite disorganised to the extent that it is hard to get required information for both internal and external needs.
2. The administration is satisfactorily organised in that it fulfils the legal demand for information. Internally, the administration is nearly exclusively organised to provide the firm's top management with the most necessary pieces of information.
3. Our administration interacts well with public authorities, vendors and customers, and through constant effort we try to improve its effectiveness and relevance to our needs for information.
4. We have a highly effective and efficient administrative system which provides the necessary and relevant information in a timely manner.

2. How effective is the firm's information and reporting system?

In light of your assessment, how do you evaluate its competitive impact on the organisation?

No competitive advantage		Significant competitive advantage	
1	2	3	4

Examples:
1. Not effective. Necessary information is unavailable to managers when they need it. Most frequently, top management makes decisions on a loose basis because they cannot get the necessary information.
2. It is informal in structure. The top management has the full general picture and can find the current information they need. There is no talk of a more formal system.
3. We try to uncover the required information, and all information is accessible for managers so they can use it if they wish.
4. Required information is discussed at regular intervals. Necessary new information is provided and the superfluous information is discarded; this ensures that the information is available to those who need it, when they need it.

3. To what extent is the firm's reporting system suitable for its information requirements?

In light of your assessment, how do you evaluate its competitive impact on the organisation?

No competitive advantage		Significant competitive advantage	
1	2	3	4

Examples:
1. We have no reports apart from the accounting department's annual report.
2. As long as everything is running normally, we don't do much reporting, but when something goes wrong, a report is made to management.
3. Besides short periodic accounts, management receives frequent production and sales reports.
4. Reporting takes place according to a firm plan and is essentially tied to budget follow-up. For instance, the reports address actual activity in relation to plans and also the development of budgetary consequences.

4. How much information is available on a daily basis?
In light of your assessment, how do you evaluate its competitive impact on the organisation?

No competitive advantage		Significant competitive advantage	
1	2	3	4

Examples:
1. None is available the day it is needed. It takes at least a day to pull together the information you need.
2. Not very much, because information is usually too old.
3. The daily management is based on existing plans; they are drawn up and altered on the basis of available and current information.
4. We have built up our organisation and information system such that information of current interest is used extensively in the daily management of our firm.

5. What are you doing to improve the administration?
In light of your assessment, how do you evaluate its competitive impact on the organisation?

No competitive advantage		Significant competitive advantage	
1	2	3	4

Examples:

1. The present plan is to continue to move very slowly in changing current methods.
2. We didn't change anything last year because it is expensive to alter the system. We did a few years ago and, on the whole, it was useful.
3. We always encourage employees to voice their suggestions for improvement. If their proposals are cost effective, we implement them.
4. Under the direction of a committee, we have an ongoing process to improve the firm. Tasks are routinely automated if the outcome simplifies administration and satisfies workers' demands.

It may be desirable to supplement this broad questionnaire with a more specific survey, which asked managers details of the internal and external information sources they use, the information they themselves generate, and their information and communication needs. Examples of survey questionnaires of this type can be found in, among others, Stanat (1990).

USING FIGURE 7.1

Although the answers to our questionnaire can be very helpful and will often pinpoint specific deficiencies, it would be wrong to assume that a top score means there are no problems. This is because the organisation may have made do with a deficient system for so long that the absence of key information is taken as an acceptable normality. In one consulting assignment the managing director of a subsidiary company had to provide one figure every day to the corporate chief executive: that for the previous day's sales. This was given so much importance in the organisation that neither the managing director nor his marketing director gave much thought to other information that would have been more useful. Although the system could print out a periodic analysis of sales by customer by product categories, this was not seen as important information and had never been requested. When the consulting assignment led to a demand for this information, it was found that one of the major products had a customer profile which was the opposite of what top management believed. Instead of having a leading position with major construction companies, the firm had a minimal position here, and most sales of this product were to small builders. The fall-off in total sales had been blamed on the recession prevailing at the time: the fact that the major customers were still buying other products from the company masked the changes, in the absence of any analysis by product. The problem was even more serious because lack of knowledge of the pattern of sales of this product had concealed a major strategic problem and a total shift in how the market was served. Had they been asked, the management at subsidiary and head office level would have said that the information received was what was needed. Although a more detailed survey would have identified the information each manager received, there would still have been no perception that anything critical was missing.

In Figure 6.1 we provided a view of the integrated organisation, and showed the inter-relationship or strategy, structure and other factors with information (see page 136). You may wish to refer back to this, as it is as relevant for IT as it is for HRM, the topic under which we introduced it. Figure 6.1 gives a worksheet for looking at the effect of the organisation's vision and strategy on HRM, using the integrated model. This could be applied to IT, with minor modification.

Figure 7.1 shows a sequence for auditing the MIS in closer detail, with the phases of the work grouped into three "sets".

Set 1

The three related elements in this set are business strategy, critical success factors, and competencies, capabilities and processes. Initially the audit can only be carried out against the existing strategy, but after the complete appraisal is finished, and new strategic decisions taken, it may be necessary to examine the situation to see if changes need to be made. This is when the integrated organisation model is most useful, because it helps ensure that all aspects of a new strategy are thought through. Critical success factors are the limited number of factors which if done well should enable the strategy to be implemented successfully. Chapter 9 deals with these in greater detail, including their use in determining competencies. Chapter 8 explores processes in some detail. For our purposes here we need only stress the links between the key processes, competencies and capabilities which enable the business strategy to be implemented. If we can define these, we have a basis to compare the information that is provided with that which is needed.

Set 2

The four elements in this set are informational fit, information generation, processing and the decision making impact. We have just touched on the first of these, which is the way the information we currently have fits with what is really needed. As we mentioned earlier, this is a question of timeliness as well as relevance, and it also covers frequency and format.

Information generation is about the way in which the required information is obtained. It is worth stressing here that not all important information is internally generated, or in a form that is suitable for a repetitive corporate-wide information system. So there are things to consider about how information like competitor data or market analyses is obtained and stored. Although IT may play a part in this in various ways, we should not overlook important information which may be held in filing cabinets and company libraries.

Processing covers not only the technical aspects of the equipment for collecting, collating, storing and distributing information, but also the degree of centralisation and decentralisation. When auditing an established system, the up-to-date (or otherwise) nature of the computers, applications software and networks is also important. There is also an integration issue of the hardware and software for MIS and that used for operational needs (for example word processing, email, and day to day management analysis and decision making).

We should also audit the security practices and assess the vulnerability of the organisation to hackers and virus attacks. Linked to this are the various internal policies and procedures which exist to reduce the risk of external raids on the system, and to protect the organisation against legal claims (for example, defamation actions arising from emails sent through the corporate system, even when these are unauthorised).

Decision making impact is an assessment of the value of the various elements of the MIS to the organisation.

Set 3

This set consists of organisational matters and structure/systems. Here we are back to our integrated organisation model. The effect of the MIS on the elements in this set may be because of the way information is obtained, or the way it is made available. In fact, as we have pointed out in the discussion on the integrated organisation, it is a two-way influence. If, for example, control information is produced in a way which does not match organisational responsibilities, the management of the affected units will be impaired in their role. So either responsibilities have to be changed to match the MIS, or the MIS has to adapt to the organisational needs.

FORMAL VERSUS INFORMAL INFORMATION FLOWS

As the analysis of the company's information system develops, the audit team will also be encouraged to examine the social structures of the firm to uncover the flows of vital informal information streams. Although the formal flows can be identified from an up-to-date organisation chart, interpreted in relation to the organisational style and the policies in place, much of the information flow is across informal groupings. Information rarely flows up and down within the confines of the little boxes and arrows of the formal chart, and most managers work closely with managers from other units, with whom there is a need to share information. This type of work-related informal grouping is vital to the effective management of the organisation.

However, informal groups go a stage further than this, and occur through the social interaction of people from different parts of the organisation: those, for example, who see each other regularly in the company restaurant, or in the lifts and passages, or who may be the smokers who can be found at various times clustering outside the doors of premises which have no smoking rules, or who have other opportunities for both planned and unplanned contact. Informal groups of this nature disseminate information, not always accurately, and may also be a source of new information.

The audit should examine the policies and procedures for communicating information to the whole organisation. The best way to reduce distortion and rumour is not to be over secretive, and to ensure that there are ways in which information about what the organisation is doing, its results, and to a degree its intentions are passed on to employees.

However, the other side of the coin is looking at the main informal sources of new information, to see which of these can be captured and disseminated more effectively. For example, competitor information systems frequently include ways of capturing and analysing information brought in by sales people and functional managers, who may pick up information from contact with customers, suppliers and competitors. At the other extreme there is information which in theory contributes to the collective knowledge of the organisation, but which in practice resides in the brains of various individuals, goes home in the evening with them, goes on holiday when they go on holiday, and leaves the organisation when they resign, retire or when their employment is terminated for other reasons.

MANAGEMENT OF KNOWLEDGE

This takes us nicely into another important and difficult part of the audit: knowledge management. In one sense this is a recent concept, growing out of the 1990s concept of the learning organisation. In another sense, it is as old as the hills, in that knowledge has always been important to organisations, and the modern problem is caused by the size and complexity of organisations, and in many cases a management view that people are disposable resources.

Mayo (1999) stresses the importance of the intellectual capital of the organisation. He divides this into three categories:

- Customer (external structural) capital (e.g. customer contracts, relationships, loyalty, satisfaction; market share; image; reputation; brands)
- Organisational (internal structural) capital (e.g. systems, methodologies, patents, know-how, data-bases, knowledge, culture)

- Human capital (e.g. individual competence and experience, judgement, wisdom; team competence; leadership and motivation).

To try to analyse and record all of this would result in more information than could possibly be used. To our personal knowledge some large organisations attempted to do this as far back as the 1970s, and possibly earlier, with questionnaires sent out to all managers in order to record their knowledge and skills. Although this might have worked in a few situations, such as enabling an organisation to locate quickly experts in a subject who also had a particular language competence, in general these broad attempts were never updated, resulted in information overload, and what we might also call information "underload": information that was really wanted had never been included in the questionnaires.

Mayo (1999) suggests controlling overload by concentrating on the components of knowledge management that relate to three questions:

- Is this component clearly linked to the achievement of a major strategy?
- How significant is this component in driving today's value?
- How significant is this component in driving tomorrow's value?

Knowledge management is partly an IT matter. However, it is also much more to do with how the whole organisation is managed, and how people are recruited, retained and developed. So among other things, it also relates to HRM. In auditing the intranet and database systems which are the IT component, it is also important to consider the HRM elements of knowledge management. The IT side may provide data capture, storage and dissemination methods, but does not determine the policies and procedures which recruit people with the right knowledge, hone and develop knowledge, and encourage people to share it.

The purpose of the appraisal is not to design a knowledge management system, but to examine what the organisation has, what it costs and how appropriate it is. When it has nothing, the facts are easy to record, although answering whether the organisation would benefit from such a system may be more difficult. Where there is such a system in place, there is more to audit.

First, the running costs should be identified. Although it may be tempting to want to record the development costs of the system being used, this is not really helpful information as the costs are sunk. It should be remembered that the costs incurred by the IT department are only one element: the other is the time people throughout the organisation spend inputting data into the system.

This should be compared with an estimate of the value gained, which is to do with how the system is used and what benefits flow from that use. Newell and Swan (1999) tell an interesting story of how a simple question can bring a revealing answer:

> This company has spent a considerable amount of money on developing an intranet to promote knowledge sharing. When members of the organisation were asked for an example of the useful knowledge that was on the intranet, the example given was the company bus timetable. This provides information on the time the company bus will be at one of three locations within the particular city. Given that 20 minutes is the maximum time between buses, and that this does not change from day to day, this is unlikely to really contribute to developing and using the intellectual capital within the organisation!

The final task is not just to mark the system as good or bad, but to indicate what, if anything. needs to be done about it.

NEW WAYS OF USING COMPUTER-BASED TECHNOLOGY

The terms "information technology" and "information systems" tend to misdirect our thinking about the new directions that we are moving into. The advent of affordable personal computers has transformed the way many people do their daily jobs. It is now unusual to go into any manager's office and not see a computer by the desk or somewhere in the background. But although the penetration of the PC has been fast, it has built on familiar ground. It changed how things are done, put greater power for effectiveness in the hands of many people at all levels, but in a way was a continuation of the things that had traditionally been done. Before word processing there was typing. Before spreadsheets there were calculators and analysis paper.

Certainly computers, email and voicemail have broken the pattern which says that people have to be concentrated in offices This has enabled large businesses to reduce office space by encouraging some home working, and has allowed self-employed people to have better communications and to offer large-organisation levels of quality in letters, reports and home-produced promotional materials.

These things have changed what is done, but have not been astonishing. We are now in a period when the new computer technologies are beginning to produce step changes in business. Instead of stepping off a rather slow escalator for something faster, we now have to work out ways of getting to the next floor when there is nothing tangible to slide on to. E-commerce is one of the big innovations, which is still largely in the question mark box, but with the queries gradually disappearing with the growing acceptance of things like Internet banking. While we would not suggest that any organisation should set up a dot-com operation just because it does not have one, we feel that the audit should look at the way the technology is changing, the potential implications for the organisation, and the mechanisms by which the organisation monitors the directions that the technologies are taking.

REFERENCES

Jenster, P. 1985. *Divisional Monitoring of Critical Success Factors During Strategy Implementation*, University of Pittsburgh, PA.

KPMG 1998. *Colouring in the Map*, Mergers and acquisitions in Europe research report, London, KPMG.

KPMG 1999. *Unlocking Shareholder Value: The Keys to Success*, Mergers and acquisitions global report, London, KPMG.

Mayo, A. 1999. Rebalancing the balance sheet – the contribution of human capital to growing value. *Journal of Professional HRM*, 16, July.

Newell, S. and Swan J. 1999. Knowledge management: what it is and what it should be, *Journal of Professional HRM*, 16, July.

Stanat, R. 1990. *The Intelligent Corporation*, New York, Amacon.

Semiconductor 1999. *DQ Monday Report*, no. 42.

8

Taking a Process View

In Chapter 1 we suggested that among the various ways of moving from a function-by-function analysis was the examination of processes. These may stretch across departments within a function, and/or across functions. A study of processes avoids the classic problem of thinking of the organisation as a series of watertight compartments, and falling into the trap of believing that optimising performance in each of the parts will automatically lead to the optimal performance of the whole organisation.

In this chapter we will look at processes in three ways, by exploring the idea of benchmarking, adding some remarks on business process re-engineering, and exploring the value chain approach.

BENCHMARKING

What Is Benchmarking?

Many organisations compare their performance ratios with those of their competitors, and this is a good thing to do. It can prevent complacency, allow a more accurate assessment of whether the results achieved show a strength or a weakness, and stimulate action. Many people call this benchmarking.

However, useful though this process is, it is not benchmarking.

It may be an essential first step to deciding to benchmark, but it is only a first step. So what is benchmarking?

Watson (1993, p. 3) quotes the definition given by the American Productivity and Quality Center:

> Benchmarking is a systematic and continuous measurement process; a process of continuously measuring and comparing an organization's business processes against business process leaders anywhere in the world to gain information which will help the organization take action to improve its performance.

This definition moves benchmarking a long way from ratio comparisons. It is very clearly about comparing processes, with a view to finding ways to improve. So the emphasis is not just on what the other organisation achieves, but how it does it. It does not take much pondering on this to realise that in order to benchmark against someone else's process, you have to understand your own.

Watson (1993, pp. 6–8) suggests that benchmarking has evolved to a fourth generation of the concept. He saw the first generation as the product level, with a main tool being reverse engineering. The idea was to study competitors' products. Xerox was the leading organisation in this field, and in much of the future development of benchmarking.

The second generation was competitive benchmarking, which made comparisons of the organisation's processes with those of competitors: "Xerox developed this capability after finding that the manufacturing cost of its products equalled the sales price of competitors' products" (Watson, 1993, p. 7). There are obvious difficulties in benchmarking processes of competitors, if one is to stay within the bounds of legal and ethical behaviour.

Watson's third generation was a logical development from the second. As many processes are applicable to a wide range of industries, there is much that can be learned from organisations which are not competitors. There are two advantages to moving this way. First, the best performance from a particular process may well be achieved by an organisation which is not a competitor; second, there are fewer legal and business limitations to cooperation between organisations which do not compete.

There is a link here to the concept of world class performance, which was discussed in Chapter 4. Once an organisation determines to compare its key processes with whoever is best in the world at each, it has moved a long way from just thinking about being as good as competitors.

The fourth generation is strategic benchmarking, which is also the title of Watson's book. This fits very well with modern concepts of strategic alliances, and is the exchange of information for benchmarking between organisations which are formally working together to achieve some strategic purpose. Because not all organisations have strategic alliance partners, this approach cannot be universal. Its advantage is that the close relationship makes it easier for organisations to collaborate to a much deeper extent.

We should add internal benchmarking to the types mentioned above. This can bring improvements in performance, although not necessarily taking the organisation to world class performance standards. It has the advantage that data is more easily available, and benchmarking is relatively simple to organise. In our experience the obstacle is a defensive attitude. This means that when a subsidiary in one country has a better performance in a particular area than a subsidiary in another, the "explanation" is spontaneous and given off the cuff. It focuses on the differences between circumstances rather than looking for commonalities. These differences are of course sometimes relevant, but not always, and large organisations in particular can gain much from the units in the group which are the leading performers in particular processes. The British Government may have learned this lesson, as it is now making efforts to identify best practice in various activities within the network of hospitals of the National Health Service.

The Steps in Benchmarking

Benchmarking requires considerable effort. Each stage in the benchmarking process may demand different skills.

1. *Identify areas for benchmarking.* Realisation that there is an area which would benefit from benchmarking can come from various sources. There may be an obvious problem with costs or the level of performance (for example, waste levels seem to be too high; customers are not fully satisfied with the way services are provided; productivity in a specific area does not seem to be improving). This may be enough to bring a

determination to do something about it. Similar conclusions may be reached through an analysis of competitors (Hussey and Jenster (1999) show how to undertake competitor analysis). Possibly an even more effective approach is participation in various ratio studies through which performance in specific areas of performance can be compared. Such studies are sometimes organised by trade associations, or on a syndicated basis by consultants.

2. *Understanding your own process.* The next step is to analyse and record the processes your organisation is following which lie behind your own particular performance. The reason we suggest doing this before looking for benchmarking partners is that better understanding on your part may make it easier to discuss a benchmarking arrangement with another organisation, and to be much more specific about what is wanted.

3. *Desk research to identify leading organisations.* It is not always obvious which organisations might be worth benchmarking against, and they can rarely be found without effort. Because the emphasis is on processes, many of which are common across a wide range of organisations, finding the right partner can be easier because there need be no competitive issues, but harder because the universe is so much greater. Desk research methods include examining published league tables of high performing companies, such as the annual survey in *Management Today*, journal and newspaper articles on specific companies, and personal contact with suppliers and customers.

4. *Seeking a benchmarking arrangement.* After you have produced a short list of organisations that are better than you in the particular aspect you want to investigate, the next task is to seek a benchmarking arrangement. Of course your first choice may not agree! Benchmarking arrangements are often reciprocal, although your partner may not want to study the same process. The terms of the benchmarking arrangement should be agreed, and the rules of engagement carefully defined. It will be necessary to act strictly within those rules.

5. *Examining the benchmarking partner's process.* You are now able to move to a detailed examination of *how* the other organisation achieves its results, which means defining its

process and studying it in detail. Sometimes the better performance may be because of something the organisation does which lies behind the process. For example, a superior performance in handling customer enquiries might be the result of careful selection and training which enable the process to be operated with greater effect.

6. *Spot the difference.* The next step is to compare your process with that of the benchmarking partner, to see just what it is that is different, and why the better results are achieved.

7. *What should your organisation do now?* Benchmarking should not just be making a slavish copy of what another organisation does. Among the reasons for doing more than this are the culture of your organisation, and the way the particular process studied interacts with other processes in your organisation. So there is a need to think carefully about the differences and how they should be adapted. Ideally you should also use the knowledge to inspire ways in which you can improve on what you have learnt, and so achieve an even better performance than your benchmarking partner.

What Role Does Benchmarking Have in the Corporate Appraisal?

Clearly, to undertake benchmarking takes time and organisation, and it would be difficult to fit external benchmarking within the time scale of the typical corporate appraisal. However, organisations which take benchmarking seriously have units set up to undertake it, which means that there is already a source of information, however incomplete, which may provide useful insight.

The first phase of benchmarking, identifying areas where performance needs improving, and comparison with the ratios from other organisations, is a valid and usually manageable activity of the corporate appraisal, which will help give a different insight into the assessments collected by other means.

Internal benchmarking should be considered as part of the appraisal process if there are appropriate benchmarking partners within the total organisation. It can be organised faster than external benchmarking, and, provided the processes are considered wisely, can be a manageable part of an appraisal exercise.

Both internal and external benchmarking are worth considering as a follow-up to an appraisal. This is to enable improvements
to be made in various operational areas which may have been
identified as having problems, and also means that when the
appraisal is revisited, there are additional elements that can be
brought within it.

The health warning is that benchmarking is not a substitute for
a strategy. Continuous improvement is an important aim, and the
organisation may fail if it neglects it, but improvement alone will
not guarantee success. Similarly, just copying what other organisations do, without adding any creative thinking of your own, will
not take you to the forefront of performance. Benchmarking has
to be a dynamic activity.

BUSINESS PROCESS RE-ENGINEERING (BPR)

We felt some diffidence in including BPR, as it is too complex a
concept to form part of the normal corporate appraisal. It is also
a widely misunderstood concept, frequently misapplied, which has
sent many babies down the drain with the bath water. The Bain
annual survey of tools and techniques (Rigby, 1999) implies that
BPR has entered the decline phase of its life cycle. When the survey started in 1993, BPR was used by 67% of respondents. It
reached a peak usage in the high 70s in 1995, and since then usage
has fallen every year, reaching 60% in 1998. But this is still a high
usage.

What made us decide to include a few words on it was that it
can be a logical follow-on from benchmarking, and if used effectively can enable fundamental rethinking of how an organisation
operates.

What BPR Is

BPR aims to identify those processes in the organisation which
may be considered core, and to make a new start by disaggregat-
ing what currently exists, and designing a different way to achieve
an improved result, preferably at lower cost. The idea is to design
the process without having all the baggage of the way things are
currently done. Although a process may have a technology

element, it is important not to confuse a core process with a core technology.

Johansson et al (1993), who wrote one of the first books on the topic, list three types of BPR: cost improvement, catching up with others, to effect a breakpoint. Their emphasis is on the third type: "A breakpoint is the achievement of excellence in one or more value metrics where the market place clearly recognises the advantage, and where the ensuing result is a disproportionate and sustained increase in the supplier's market share" (p. 113). We met their concept of value metrics in Chapter 4, Figure 4.1. By linking the definition of core processes to the value chain (which will be discussed later in this chapter) they see BPR as a way to move from the present to a desirable future state which gains competitive advantage.

Core Processes

Although BPR in its total concept is beyond the scope of the corporate appraisal, the identification of the core processes is not. In fact there is a strong affinity with the value chain, and the concepts of core competencies and core capabilities, which we will discuss later.

Johansson et al (1993, p. 57) state: "A process is a set of linked activities that take an input and transform it to create an output". And: "By thinking about businesses as processes rather than as functions, managers can focus on streamlining processes in order to create more value for less effort rather than focusing on reducing the size of functions in order to simply cut costs. Cost cuts will naturally occur as non-value adding activities are removed from the processes and as the processes increase in their level of effectiveness" (p. 58).

Organisations have thousands of processes, and identifying every one would be like one of those interminable tasks in the Hades of mythology. Even if identified and defined, we would be left with the problem of what to do with the information. Core processes are different. Normally a business may have between 5 and 10 of these, and because they are critical to the competitiveness of the organisation, there is valuing in identifying them, and charting each.

The core processes are those which have an impact on customers, so what processes are core can only be defined in the context of the market and customer needs and expectations. A good starting point for defining them is the value chain.

Problems with BPR

BPR is not easy to apply. The identification of the core processes can be difficult, but is a pushover compared to the task of developing something different to replace them. Coulsen-Thomas (1994) found in his research across Europe that most so-called BPR activities examined were process simplification rather than re-engineering, and were driven by a desire to reduce costs and not for longer term strategic benefits. He observed: "What is clear is that many of the BPR solutions being adopted are yielding cost benefits today at the price of inflexibility tomorrow. Thus paths and options are being limited and prescribed in order to 'speed things up' in ways that can reduce the scope for creative thinking and innovation".

If you ally the misunderstanding of what BPR is to the difficulties of doing it well, and the quick-fix mentalities of too many managers, the fall in popularity of the approach is easier to understand.

THE VALUE CHAIN

The value chain concept was originated by Porter (1985). He argued: "To diagnose competitive advantage, it is necessary to define a firm's value chain for competing in a particular industry" (p. 45). He also maintained that 'Competitive advantage cannot be understood by looking at a firm as a whole. It stems from the many discrete activities a firm performs in designing, producing, marketing, delivering, and supporting its product. Each of these activities can contribute to a firm's relative cost position and create a basis for differentiation" (p. 33). In other words, you have to work at a micro level to identify what is important.

Although the term is widely used by managers in general conversation, the Bain research (Rigby, 1999) showed that it was applied in only 26% of the sampled organisations. This could be interpreted as a signal of success for a method which was identified some 14 years previously, but it is clearly not at the top of the popularity list.

What is value analysis?

Porter envisages an organisation as having five generic primary areas:

1. *Inbound logistics.* This involves all the activities connected with the receipt, storage and handling of materials, components and supplies. In the case of a retailer this would be the finished goods for resale. Under this heading Porter (1985, p. 39) includes inventory control.
2. *Operations.* These are all the activities involved in converting inputs into their final form. It is easiest to visualise this by thinking of a manufacturing or processing business, but of course there are operations in service businesses. Think of an airline, a hotel and a hospital. After that it is easier to visualise operations in the context of other service businesses, like management consulting, banking or insurance.
3. *Outbound logistics.* This includes the physical distribution of the product, including order processing as well as the physical handling of the product.
4. *Marketing and sales.* Porter defines this as "Activities associated with providing the means by which buyers can purchase the product and inducing them to do so" (p. 40).
5. *Service.* This includes the service activities provided to increase the value of the product, such as after-sales service, spares availability or training the customer's employees.

Each and all of these is potentially capable of delivering unique value to the customer, which provided the economic equation is satisfactory, can create competitive advantage.

The primary activities do not cover the whole of an organisation. Porter sees four additional activities at the support level:

1. *Procurement.* Purchasing tends to be a mainly centralised activity, but with many exceptions. For example, the purchasing department may order most components and

materials, but not usually legal and similar professional services. What is purchased is affected by the managers from whom the purchase is made, and the quantities obtained will be influenced by the inventory control policies. However, the purchasing function has a great effect on the costs of inputs, and therefore on the value that can be passed on to customers. It affects every area of the organisation.

2. *Technology.* This affects the whole organisation. As we saw in Chapter 5, there is the technology of process as well as the technology of products and services. Functionally, technology may be centred on R&D and engineering departments, but in practical terms it influences everything the organisation does.

3. *Human resource management.* People are recruited, trained, promoted and paid, and every primary and support area employs people. The activity may be centralised or decentralised; it may be in the hands of specialist functions, or split between HR specialists and line managers. In some organisations the whole activity may fall to line managers. However it is organised, HR will affect every area of the organisation.

4. *Infrastructure of the firm.* The infrastructure activities in Porter's classification could be taken as whatever has not been discussed so far, but this would be to imply that the infrastructure has no effect on value. It implies as a minimum the functions of general management, finance and accounting, legal services and public affairs. How functions are divided between head offices and business operations has an effect on how they are able to contribute value.

Support activities may not be visible to the customer, but nevertheless can create or destroy value. For example, the comprehensive training given by an airline to its cabin staff may create value, not because the customer knows about the training, but through what he or she experiences, the behaviour of the in-flight staff. The accounting conventions may make some areas seem to be unprofitable, when in fact they are contributing to overall success. Performance targets and reward systems may drive behaviour in one direction or another, and not always in the way management wants.

The idea is that a chain of value exists inside every organisation, and understanding this and building on it is a way to build a strong competitive position. However, Porter's thinking goes beyond the boundaries of the firm, and argues that the industry company is only one of a series of links in a much larger chain which stretches from the raw materials to the ultimate buyer. Many of the value-creating opportunities lie at the interfaces between the organisations which make up this chain. Therefore there is considerable merit in working closely with suppliers, customers and through them the customers' customers, to seek areas of overall improvement. Collaborative work of this kind is, of course, a feature of modern approaches to quality management, and appears in much of the literature on business process re-engineering, and it is no longer considered stupid to give up an activity which is not performed as well as it could be, and to transfer it to a supplier.

How Is It Done?

Value is created, according to Johansson et al, (1993, p. 4), in four broad ways, alone or in combination: improved quality, service, reduced cost to customer and reduced cycle time. The starting point for an assessment of the value chain may be to establish what the *organisation* believes are the processes which deliver value to the customer, but by itself this may be dangerous and inadequate. It is the customer that is the key, and to make any sense of the value chain there is a need to establish what the customer is looking for. However, there are limitations to this, such as when the organisation is considering an innovation that has never been done before, and therefore customers may have no experience or even understanding of it.

Although Porter's framework may be helpful as a peg on which to hang various ways in which the organisation provides value, it has some drawbacks. It tends to mirror the organisation chart's labelling of functions, rather than the processes. JIT or MRP processes, for example, may link the inward logistic, operations, finished stock and procurement in a way that is not apparent from the way the functions are set out. But perhaps this could be a strength of the framework, if it led to the understanding that processes will overlap his headings, and that value may be created by this as much as by what goes on within each group of functions.

A second problem was hinted at in our introduction. Porter uses an arrow-shaped diagram to illustrate the value chain, and this has become world famous. His nine headings fit into this diagram. However, we have seen many so-called value chain reports which do little more than break down the organisation chart into sub-headings, which are then listed under the nine headings on an enlarged version of the arrow-shaped chart under each heading. Often, this gives no more information than could have been read off the organisation chart, does not indicate the processes that enable value to be created, and does not show the costs or benefits of what is done.

It is useful, as we said, to begin with an internal view of the processes which create value, and to separate these from the processes which are essential to serve a customer, but which are doing nothing special for that customer. In the first stages we may begin with what it is that we are providing the customer: for example, immediate access to technical advice; any product can be delivered next day; enabling the customer to reduce wastage rates; loan replacement immediately available if equipment breaks down. We can rate which of these things we think we are doing better than competitors, and which we believe give customers that extra element of value.

This part of value chain analysis is about self-inspection, but it will be meaningless unless it has customer inputs. Market surveys may yield some of this information, but greater depth may come from focus groups of current and potential customers. Such marketing research methods can also yield valuable information about the value chains of competitors. A focus on these formal ways of obtaining information should not obscure the important information that is gained when the organisation is always in close contact with its customers, enjoys good relations with them, and discusses their needs with them almost continuously. Unfortunately, comparatively few organisations have such a close relationship with their customers so that they are really in each other's confidence and, in any case, knowing a customer well may not help you understand why their competitors do not buy from you.

Remember that customers do not all obtain value from the same thing, or that value may not be for the same reason. For example, many small businesses deal with stationery suppliers that offer a good mail order service, one feature of which is next-day delivery. This gives potential benefits to customers, such as reducing the stock levels that have to be carried, and helping to avoid emergencies: none of these is particularly important to a business run mainly from home. The benefit to such businesses is the ability to know that the order will be delivered on a particular day, so that it is possible to ensure that someone is in the office to receive it. If this promise were unreliable, the supplier would be changed. For a larger organisation, which always has staff available to receive orders, the main value may be in obtaining the highest volume discounts, and having the benefit of being able to reduce stocks of stationery supplies to reduce the money tied up. The benefit from the offering is thus quite different for different customer situations.

The information obtained has to be specific. Generalised comments from customers like 'good service' are not specific enough. What is it about this service which is seen as good, and what is the benefit that the customer perceives?

When both the internal and external information has been put together, it is possible to sort out what is giving the customer value, and to move to the processes which enable that to be achieved.

The example in Box 8.1 makes two important points. The first is that the customers see the outcome, not all the elements of the process that creates that outcome. The second is the need to look at the costs of the processes which bring a customer benefit. Management consulting firms measure the time their employees spend on different activities, and these systems make it easier to look at the costs of what is done. And in the example given there are no fixed assets exclusively dedicated to providing this particular value.

Unfortunately this is not true of the majority of organisations, where little record is kept of how much time is spent in indirect areas of activity, and assets are distributed within functions rather than processes. To make real sense of value chain analysis, it is necessary to look at the costs of providing the benefits to customers, and the fixed and working capital that enables the benefit to be provided. Chapter 2 looked at the accounting implications of the corporate appraisal in some detail, and will give some pointers to the problems that need to be overcome to provide this

Box 8.1   Processes behind a customer benefit

A management consultancy offered tailored management education and training. A requirement of many organisations was often to cascade the programme down the organisation, as part of an organisational change programme. It was found that extra value could be provided to organisations which operated in more than one European country, by running sessions of the programme in the languages appropriate to each country of operations.

There were numerous ways in which the service could have been provided, each with different cost implications. The elements of the process which were put together included adding language capability to the profiles for new recruits, training programmes to enhance the language skills of those employees who already had a language capability, methods to identify and recruit strategic alliance partners in several major European countries, ways to work with them to ensure that they had an understanding of client needs, and that their work was to the standard the client expected, processes to translate, desktop publish and proofread the teaching materials developed for the course, and procurement of any purchased material in the appropriate language. It required close relationships with suppliers and the alliance partners.

To provide this service involved linking all of the components of the Porter value chain model.

They also had to be costed, and the value to the business as well as to the customer established. Some costs, like the language training, were part of the extra general overhead costs the firm had to bear. Others were related to specific projects, and were considered at the time of bidding.

information. But it is not easy, and in a large organisation can be very difficult indeed.

What Do We Do with the Analysis?

The analysis described so far gives a snapshot of the current value chain of the organisation. It may have been enhanced by an examination of the value chain of the whole industry. This may have been made even more useful if an attempt is also made to understand the value chains of key competitors, to the degree that it is possible to do this from outside. This information gives a platform for a number of strategic considerations, such as:

- Is it possible to modify a process to provide the same benefit to customers at lower cost?
- Can we change a process economically so that it delivers greater value to customers?
- Would it be sensible to negotiate with suppliers, so that a process in the value chain is either passed back to them, or brought on board by us, in order to provide greater overall value?
- Are there areas where we do not provide a value to customers that they can obtain from competitors, or will require in the future?

The purpose of the corporate appraisal is not to answer these questions, although the options may be identified as part of the analysis. It is to see that the importance of the questions is understood, and in a form which can be given proper attention when strategies are formulated.

REFERENCES

Coulsen-Thomas, C. J. 1994. Business process re-engineering and strategic change, *Strategic Change*, **5**(3).

Hussey, D. E. and Jenster, P. V. 1999. *Competitor Intelligence: Turning Analysis into Success*, Chichester, Wiley.

Johansson, H. J., McHugh, P., Pendlebury, A. J. and Wheeler, W. A. 1993. *Business Process Reengineering*, Chichester, Wiley.

Porter, M. E. 1985. *Competitive Advantage*, New York, Free Press.

Rigby, D. 1999. *Management Tools and Techniques*, Boston, MA, Bain & Co. (copy of presentation dated 19 April).

Watson, G. H. 1993. *Strategic Benchmarking*, New York, Wiley.

9

Core Competencies and Related Methods

Core competencies and its relations, critical success factors and core capabilities, are among those methods which stretch across the whole organisation. Apart from the usefulness of the approaches themselves, as a way of thinking about strategy, they also have value in the integrated view which they provide. But they are not easy concepts to use.

In corporate appraisal, there is merit in identifying what the organisation possesses that is core or critical, both as a foundation for corporate endeavour, and to ensure that these attributes are maintained and developed. This makes it possible to analyse the gap between what the organisation has and what it needs.

There is a real difference between these methods and the more traditional approaches that were discussed in earlier chapters. It is possible to analyse the sources of profit, the risks from reliance on too few customers, and many other such matters without very much awareness of the vision of the organisation, or knowledge of the view it holds of the future. When we come to critical success factors or core competencies, we move into new territory.

We can look backwards and say this is what has been core or critical to this organisation in the past, or that we have suffered because we lacked a particular attribute possessed by competitors. Indeed, most examples we have seen in books on core competencies have given their examples through this use of hindsight, and we have yet to see well-documented work which demonstrates that such core competencies were predetermined by far-sighted managers, based on their perception of what the future might be. But looking backwards can provide lessons, and will establish a platform of where the organisation stands today.

However, identifying what critical success factors or core competencies are needed for the future can only be done if those undertaking the appraisal have a clear sense of what the organisation believes is the vision for the future. This may be available in some organisations, in which case it can be used to assess what is needed and the gap with what exists. Where the view of the future is unclear, or if the current view is suspect, the forward-looking part of the process becomes part of the strategic decision process and moves outside the boundaries of the corporate appraisal.

In describing three different, but related, concepts in this chapter, we are not urging any organisation to use them all, nor would we press any organisation to use any that they did not see as relevant to their problem.

CRITICAL SUCCESS FACTORS (CSFs)

The critical success factors approach is well established, and has been particularly useful in helping top managements define their management information needs. CSFs are "the limited number of areas in which results, if they are satisfactory, will ensure successful competitive performance for the organisation" (Rockart, 1979).

They relate to the basic internal or external conditions for the firm's strategy (e.g. customer acceptance, competitive moves), or those competencies or resources (e.g. human, financial) it must attain.

Jenster (1984) expanded this notion into a more comprehensive and strategic concept, suggesting that the definition and monitoring of CSFs differs for various strategy types. His study of 128 firms in mature manufacturing industries found that the firms which had a higher return on equity:

1. formally identified their CSFs,
2. used these factors to monitor their progress in the implementation of strategic changes,

3. benefited from formally integrated reporting and information systems.

Miller (1984) found that CSFs, when formally identified, implicitly communicate the top management's priorities and thereby direct organisational efforts in the desired direction. The desired direction is attained through the motivation of the organisation's employees, by providing a framework against which they can make sense of priorities, assumptions and environmental conditions, so that they are able to contribute better to the execution of corporate plans.

For example, consider a company which views the introduction of new products as one of its CSFs. Beyond communicating that top management views the organisation's future as hinging upon being a product innovator, this clearly conveys to individuals where their most significant contribution can be made. Most members of management are strongly motivated to excel in relation to the expectations of corporate leadership. They will adapt to meet those expectations provided that top management's wishes are clearly and consistently communicated. Effective leadership necessitates the clear definition of success factors, the ideal organisational performance in relation to them, and the explicit communication of these factors to all appropriate levels of management in a structured manner.

In addition to providing a bridge between the firm's objectives and management's strategy, the isolation of critical factors also provides a vehicle for the design of an effective system of performance measurement and control. This way, the design of CSFs becomes more than just identifying the areas which "must go right", but assumes a powerful strategic role in which the specific efforts of top management and the employees are joined and aligned in a manner consistent with the firm's vision.

In summary, the factors identified as essential to the organisation's success serve as the primary integrating mechanism between management's long-range goals and the channelling of resources and executive attention. Explicit recognition and use of such CSFs provides, therefore, a planning process/system through which strategy formulation can be made operational and controlled within the firm.

1. Determine the Elements which Affect Success

The first step in determining CSFs is to audit the forces which are relevant to the firm's present and future position. Strategic areas may include:

- *General environment.* Factors which influence the firm and over which it has no control. Included here may be issues such as general socio-demographic trends, interest rates and exchange rate fluctuations.
- *Industry characteristics.* Features of the firm's industry and related industries. In general, it appears that each industry has a set of common dimensions to which individual firms need to adhere. For example, supermarket chains will have one set of dynamic factors and banks another.
- *Competitive forces.* Postures of competitors, suppliers, customers and potential new entrants, as well as those elements which firms following similar strategies in related industries need to be alert to. These may include certain quality standards, product mix, cost control etc.
- *Company-specific characteristics.* Factors derived from the unique aspects of a particular firm's competitive position (i.e. its strengths and weaknesses as well as opportunities and threats), traits of the management team, and/or time elements.
- *Personal values of key players.* The demand, wishes, needs and capabilities of key players, executives and other personnel must be examined. For example, the personal preferences of the major stockholders should not be neglected.
- *Resource availability.* Availability of financial, as well as physical and human resources, will have an impact on the strategic success.

These strategic characteristics may form the basis for defining the firm's sensitivity to the influences or changes along the various dimensions. Figure 9.1 shows how the firm's sensitivity can be examined using a weighting scheme where 1 equals no effect, and 10 implies substantial or critical impact. The impact grid can also be used in the design/review and integration of a firm's strategic plans, as well as to assess reversibility of resource commitments. Moreover, this evaluation is used to create the list of potential

		Government issues (specific)	Competitor X (specific action)	Exchange rate etc.	etc.
FUNCTIONS	Marketing				
	Personnel				
	Production				
PROJECTS	Project 1				
	Project 2				
PRODUCTS	Product 1				
	Product 2				
GOALS	Goal 1				
	Goal 2				

Figure 9.1 Assessing a firm's vulnerability to the environment: using an impact grid

elements from which management selects the firm's 5 to 10 CSFs.

The dimensions may also be used to develop alternative result scenarios and for the identification, achievement and evaluation of management's objectives, as well as in the subsequent transformation of ideas into action. (See, for example, Grant and King, 1983.)

Some of the identified factors affected by the various elements are *strategic* in nature, in that they relate directly to the way senior personnel interpret situations and carry out plans. Other success factors are *operational* and not necessarily directly useful to the tasks and activities of key personnel. Although they are important to the way lower personnel define and integrate particular tasks, they may receive management attention on a less frequent, ad hoc or by-exception basis.

2. Review the Current Strategic Plan

The next step is to look at the information from the current strategic plan, if one exists, or to deduce the vision and strategy from the organisation's actions (and from the other approaches to the appraisal which have already been discussed) if no such plan exists. Later it may be necessary to repeat this action if new strategies are made following the appraisal. Essentially what we are doing here is to establish a baseline to record the current situation. The information we extract from the plan should give the present perception of the answers to questions such as:

- What type of firm do we want the organisation to be?
- What type of activities do we want to engage in?
- What markets do we want to pursue?

Although these questions sound simple and straightforward, answering them can be a long and tedious affair. Validation of the answers by panels of experienced managers will help to ensure that the appraisal is not wandering in the wrong direction.

3. Step 3. Identify the Current Critical Success Factors

CSFs are the limited number of factors important to strategic success. They are the limited number of areas which must be

---

Box 9.1: Iowa Farmatics Inc.

Bill Sobek, founder of Iowa Farmatics Inc. (IFI) a distributor and manufacturer of fertiliser spreading equipment, was proposing to withdraw from day-to-day management of the firm. The last 15 years had been marked by steady increases in sales, averaging 23%. The success of the firm over the years had rested on a philosophy based on the primacy of customer service. Since the period for fertilising fields is short, a disabled spreader can cost a customer a considerable amount of money. Although the firm initially was a distributor and assembler of equipment, management realised that it had to ensure a quick response to a customer's needs for spare parts, so the firm had branched out into the manufacturing and extensive stocking of spare parts. In order to fully satisfy customer needs, the firm also began designing and manufacturing customised liquid sprayers. Unlike the standardised dry spreaders, these liquid spreaders are made to customer specification. Because of the unique nature of liquid spreaders, these units take considerable amounts of time to design and manufacture.

Although most producers of farm machinery were hurting in 1984, the firm was straining capacity and planning for future growth became essential. The prospects for expanding sales of liquid sprayers into states outside the present market area looked very favourable. Bill Sobek desired growth for the firm, but recognised the need for any growth to be controlled. Additionally, he desired that even with future growth of the firm, his personal involvement would be significantly reduced. It was clear that the future growth strategy required an improved monitoring system and management structure.

The impact grid shown in Table 9.1, exemplifies the relationships between developments in some of the CSFs and elements of Sobek's strategy for IFI.

---

monitored to ensure successful execution of the firm's strategic programmes. These factors can be used to guide and motivate key employees to perform in the desired manner, and in a way which will ensure successful performance throughout the strategy.

The use of these factors in discussions and planning within the firm will clearly and succinctly communicate critical elements of

Table 9.1   An impact grid for Iowa Farmatics Inc.

CSF	Introduction of liquid spreader by connection	Disruption of parts supply	Securing distributors in new markets	Decentralisation of management	Expansion of facilities
Marketing:					
Distribution	10	2	10	1	4
Promotion	10	8	2	1	1
Personnel:					
Design	10	2	1	1	5
Management	8	6	1	10	8
Production	8	4	1	1	8
Production:					
Assembly dry spreaders	1	10	1	1	10
Design liquid spreaders	10	1	1	1	10
Manufacture spare parts	1	10	6	1	10
Projects:					
Plant construction	7	1	6	1	10
Products:					
Dry spreaders	1	1	2	1	8
Liquid spreaders	10	1	8	1	8
Goals:					
Controlled growth	5	1	7	1	10
Reduced time commitment/ CEO	1	2	3	10	2
Customer service	1	10	3	3	7

Key: 1 = Little or no impact; 10 = substantial or critical impact.

the strategy to members of the organisation. More importantly, the CSFs direct the attention of key managers to focus on the basic premises of the firm's strategy. The selection of proper strategic dimensions is essential, inasmuch as they will serve as motivation for those whose performance is being measured. Thus, the CSFs must:

- reflect success of the defined strategy,
- represent the foundation of this strategy,
- be able to motivate and align the managers as well as other employees,
- be very specific and/or measurable.

A manufacturer of cutting tools has as its major strategic theme "Shipping of orders within 24 hours". The board of directors identified timeliness of shipments and industry market share as two of their CSFs.

A diversified organisation will have a family of CSFs, as the requirements of the centre and each SBU will be different. On the other hand, a global single business organisation may have a common core of CSFs which are applicable to subsidiaries in all countries, although they may need to be supplemented by others which reflect the different local market situation.

4. Measure the Degree to which the Organisation Fulfils the Current CSFs

The fact that a CSF has been identified does not mean that the organisation is able to meet it. The next step is to audit performance against each of the CSFs. Ideally this should be on the basis of objective criteria, which is easier if the CSFs have been used as the basis of strategic performance indicators.

Strategic performance indicators (SPIs) should be used to measure the short-term progress toward the long-term objectives. The SPIs are the indicators specifically used to measure and monitor key individuals' short-term progress toward achieving good performance along a critical dimension. SPIs provide motivational information which must be explicit enough to allow managers to understand how their actions influence strategic success, even though they may not have a full understanding of the underlying strategy.

SPIs must strive to satisfy six specifications. They should be:

- *Operational.* They must focus on action and provide information which can be used for control.
- *Indicative of desired performance.* Indicators must be measured against a desired level of performance.
- *Acceptable to subordinates.* Subordinates should have significant input into determination of the indicators during the design/review process.
- *Reliable.* Most phenomena cannot be measured with precision, but can be described only within a range or as a degree

of magnitude. It is up to the steering committee to think through what kind of measurement is appropriate to the factor it is meant to measure.

- *Timely.* This does not necessarily imply rapid reporting. The time dimension of controls should correspond to the "time span" of the event.
- *Simple.* Complicated strategic performance measurement systems often do not work. They confuse the organisation's members, and direct attention towards the mechanics and methods of control, rather that towards the targeted performance results.

After being selected, the indicators should be analysed in terms of the information required to measure their achievement. Performance indicators will generally require information from a wide variety of different sources, both internal and external, in order to enable management to monitor progress in the different functional areas of the organisation.

Where SPIs of this type do not already exist, it will be necessary to use what data is available. Where hard data is totally lacking, one method that can be used is to get groups of key managers together, to rate performance against each CSF on a scale of 1 to 10. Although judgements of this type may be helpful, remember that they may also be tainted.

5. Reassess the CSFs If Vision or Strategy Changes

The CFSs only have validity in relation to a specific situation. Any change in the vision for the organisation, or the strategy, should trigger a re-examination of the CSFs. This may not, strictly speaking, be a part of the corporate appraisal, but is an essential step to remember.

CORE COMPETENCIES

As a popular strategic approach, core competencies came to the fore with the publication of a *Harvard Business Review* article (Prahalad and Hamel, 1990). Among their later publications was a much acclaimed, but somewhat evangelical, book (Hamel and Prahalad, 1994). In fact, the originators of the idea, in so far as it is ever possible to track a business concept to its starting point, were Learned et al (1965): "A central idea was distinctive competence – the concept that every firm has its own uniqueness which is crucial to developing its strategy Andrews/Christensen/Learned were the originators of the notion of core competencies that was rediscovered in 1990" (Porter, 1994, p. 247).

It may be of passing interest that management consultants Bain & Co. (Rigby, 1999) found in their 1998 annual survey of management tools and techniques that core competencies was ninth in terms of popularity (63% of their sample of companies were using it). In 1993, when they began this annual survey, the figure was 52%, reaching a peak of over 70% in 1996. Of course the figures must be interpreted in relation to the sample, and cannot be extrapolated to the universe of all companies, but the trends are significant.

What are Core Competencies?

> "A competence is a bundle of skills and technologies that enables a company to provide a particular benefit to customers. At Sony that benefit is 'pocketability,' and the core competence is miniaturisation. At Federal Express the benefit is on-time delivery, and the core competence, at a very high level, is logistics management." (Hamel and Prahalad, 1994)
>
> "In the long run, competitiveness derives from an ability to build, at lower costs and more speedily than competitors, the core competencies that spawn unanticipated products. The real sources of advantage are to be found in management's ability to consolidate corporate-wide technologies and production skills into competencies that empower individual businesses to adapt quickly to changing opportunities." (Prahalad and Hamel, 1990, p. 81)

From these quotations, we can see a competency as a bundle of skills and technologies which can be used for the benefit of the organisation. Identification of these bundles builds naturally on the audit of the technologies (see Chapter 5), but competencies are more than technological know-how: they include the skills built up across the organisation that enable the firm to provide a product or service which customers want, and which builds into a defensible competitive position.

Prahalad and Hamel (1990) use an analogy of a competence tree when thinking of the diversified company, which has many similarities with the technology tree looked at in Chapter 5 (Figure 5.1). The main roots, which feed the tree and give it stability against storms, are the core competencies: there are usually between 5 and 15 of these (we might suggest that the minor roots are those competencies which, although not core in the particular sense used here, are still required to enable the organisation to function). The trunk of the tree is made up of the core products. The branches are the different businesses that have grown to exploit the core products, and the leaves, flowers and fruit are the end products, many of which could not be foreseen when the core competencies were developed.

There are warnings hidden in this analogy. The roots have to continue to grow and develop, and expand. A tree that grows top heavy will fall. Second, leaves, flowers and fruits mature and fall off, therefore there has to be a continual process of renewal if the tree is to survive. We will assume that our tree is not deciduous!

But what makes a competency core? In order to qualify, Hamel and Prahalad (1994, pp. 223–32), argue that a core competency must:

- give access (or potential access) to a wide variety of markets,
- deliver a clear benefit to the customer (or more accurately, a benefit that the customer perceives),
- be hard for competitors to copy, so that it provides a clear basis for differentiation.
  A core competence is *not*, therefore:
- a single skill,
- a competence that all competitors have,
- a product,
- Something possessed by only one small area of the organisation.

Identifying Core Competencies: The Concept

The corporate appraisal task is to answer two questions:
- What are the competencies of this organisation?
- What are the current core competencies?

This foundation would make it easier to think about a further three questions in the strategic thinking phase which should follow the appraisal:

- What *should* the core competencies be, in order for us to create the future for the organisation that the strategic thinking requires?
- Which existing core competencies do we need to nurture and grow?
- How do we acquire any new competencies and enhance the existing ones?

It would, of course, be possible to start the appraisal by defining the core competencies that are needed, but we would still have to establish the answers to our first two questions, before we could develop a strategy to plug any gaps. To plug a gap, you need to know where the hole is!

Defining technologies is no easy task, but it looks simple compared to defining competencies. This is because we are talking about bundles of skills. Skills can be defined in various ways, and of course there are choices about how they are bundled. And if you get over these hurdles there is always the nagging concern that you have missed the skill which is really the "ingredient X" that turns the rest from the mundane to the spectacular.

Hamel (1994, p. 16) says:

> There are probably hundreds of different ways to categorise core competencies. We have found it useful to distinguish among three broad types: *market-access competencies* (management of brand development, sales and marketing, distribution and logistics, technical support, etc. – all those skills which help put a firm in close proximity with its customers); *integrity-related competencies* (competencies like quality, cycle time management, just-in-time inventory management and so on which allow a company to do things more quickly, flexibly, or with a higher degree of reliability than competitors); and *functionality-related competencies* (skills which enable the company to invest its services or products with unique functionality, which invest the product with distinctive customer benefits, rather than merely making it incrementally better).

The technological skills would appear to fit in his second and third categories.

There is nothing wrong in inventing your own classification. This is not a situation where there is only one right answer, and at present most of the published articles on the application of core competencies have been by academics, and not much has been written about how organisations and consultants have solved these problems.

Hinterhuber et al (1996) suggest a number of steps in the identification of core competencies, which we have built on, adding to them some ideas from Klein and Hiscocks (1994). What is described below thus draws from the views of both authorities, plus some of our own experiences. It is not meant to reflect the full views of any particular authority, and if you want to look at these you will need to go to the original sources. The separation of the steps into appraisal and strategic tasks is ours, to fit the needs of this book.

- The appraisal task:
  - determining current competencies
  - assessing the relative strengths of the competencies
  - identifying those which deliver value to current customers.

- The strategic task:
  - establishing which are needed for the longer term
  - examining the portfolio of competencies.

The Appraisal Task: A Method

Determining Current Competencies

At this stage we are trying to assess all the competencies of the organisation, many of which will not prove to be core. This is where a classification like that suggested by Hamel is helpful, to try to get some order into what can otherwise appear to be a daunting task. Four starting points are suggested. It is recommended that all of them be used, as the whole truth is unlikely to emerge from any one of them.

1. What can be interpreted from the organisation's structure (for example, if the organisation has a telephone sales operation, it is likely to have some competencies in this area). At this stage it may not be possible to define these precisely, but we can at least note them for further consideration.

2. Interviews with key people inside the organisation. Who is key will vary with the organisation, but a good rule is to cast the net wide, as important competencies may be buried inside departments of the organisation, where they are invisible to top management. This part of the process is likely to work better if the interviews are structured.
3. Competencies which are obvious from an examination of the activities, products and services of the organisation. Often the intangible elements are taken for granted within the organisation, although the competencies required to achieve them may be among the most important for the organisation.
4. What can be learned from customers and suppliers, both from market research reports, and from discussions and focus group interviews.

At this stage the organisation will have a long "laundry list", which will probably contain individual skills that need to be grouped into competencies, and will certainly include many competencies which are neither strategic nor core. Before moving on, it is sensible to try to validate this list, possibly through focus group discussions with key managers. Even though as a validation method this has drawbacks, it does mean that there is involvement of others, both in assessing the facts and making judgements on them.

Assessing the Relative Strengths of the Competencies

The internal perception of the extent to which a competence is possessed may not be the reality. We can make what is meant here somewhat clearer by using an individual competence with which everyone will be familiar: writing. Everyone who uses this book has a technical ability to read and write. However, our individual competencies at writing will vary with the purpose, and if there were an objective way of scoring how good we all were there would certainly be differences.

• To write an occasional academic article requires knowledge of vocabulary and grammar (including the correct use of the apostrophe!), technical knowledge of the subject and an ability to organise thoughts. There is usually no real time pressure on the author, and many go through several drafts before they are satisfied, and have to make further changes after peer review. Yet if we think about articles of this type we know that some are more interesting to read than others, and not all have the same high quality of thought. For many occasional authors like this, the task does not come easily.

- To write a book on, say, a management subject requires mastery of more aspects of the subject than is needed for the single article, and the ability to hold to a clear objective, and to coordinate many different topics. An author of such a book will find it very hard going if writing is a struggle, and if he or she is working under a publisher's contract there is a deadline to be met. And from your own reading you know that you could rate the overall competency of the author by using a simple classification like clarity, readability, relevance and practicality. You would not consider all authors with the competence to produce a book to have equal strengths in that competence.

- A journalist has to add other skills, among which is the ability to write quickly, to a predefined length and to a tight deadline.

- A novelist requires many of the skills of the management book author, plus creativity and insight into what makes people tick. And for most novels not even the authors would claim to have the same level of competence as a literary giant (and not all need it for the market for which they are writing).

Although it is possible for any one person to have all four competencies, it is unusual. We have never met such a paragon.

Using this analogy, we can see why we need to spend time trying to plumb the depths of the corporate competencies we have identified. Are we strong, average or mediocre, and how appropriate are the strengths of the competencies for the objectives we have to fulfil?

Sometimes a closer correlation between truth and beliefs can be achieved through further internal assessment, performed by a panel of managers from within the organisation who have knowledge of customers and competitors. Scoring the organisation against each main competitor can sometimes help assess the strength relative to competitors. External expert knowledge may be used to perform a similar function. The most objective method is benchmarking, against direct competitors, against other firms which are high performers in one or more areas of competence, and internally across the organisation to assess the extent to which the competence is truly shared.

By definition, any competence which is common to all in an industry, and which every competitor is good at, cannot be a core competence (although it may still be important).

Identifying those Competencies that Deliver Value to the Customers

A competence should deliver value to at least a significant segment of the market. The next stage is therefore to examine what each of the competencies we have identified does for the customer. Johnson and Scholes (1999, pp. 161–5) suggest that this part of the analysis should begin by asking customers what is important to them, which gives primary reasons for success. Management should next consider the secondary reasons for success: what lies behind the things that the customers value. So if one of the customers' reasons was "good service", the secondary definitions might include "flexibility". The hardest task is to move below this to a third set of reasons – in this example, what the organisation does to provide flexibility.

Hinterhuber et al (1996) recommend identifying "the articulated, and if possible non-articulated customer wishes concerning product characteristics and product-related services". With this information, and the CSFs discussed earlier in this chapter, they suggest that it is possible to move on a two-phase evaluation chain to identify what is important, and to show visually the relative strength of each element analysed. The first matrix they propose enables each CSF to be compared with the performance characteristics the customers are seeking. Symbols are used to indicate the organisation's strength (or otherwise) in each of the cells in the matrix. The second matrix compares the same performance characteristics with the competencies needed to support them, using a similar system of symbols. Both matrices include weighting and scoring, one use of which is to aid the positioning of each competence in a portfolio of core competencies.

Both of these methods have strong links with the value chain discussed in Chapter 8, and if this has been analysed effectively its results can be coordinated with the competency analysis.

It would be possible to establish the historic core competencies that support the present position, from the analysis so far, and the appraisal itself should end at this point. In practice some thought should also be given to the next steps, which move into strategy. For the sake of completeness, these are mentioned below.

Establishing which Competencies Are Needed for the Longer Term

If an aim is to use core competencies to change the industries in which an organisation operates, it follows that some attempt should be made to think beyond the current range of products and services, and to explore what may be core in a more future-oriented manner. Klein and Hiscocks (1994) offer one method for doing this, although this is built on an analysis of skills rather than competencies. They call it the opportunity matrix, a method which requires the use of an appropriate computer database. Skills are listed and scored, and entered as one axis in the database. Possible diversification and potential future products are then listed, and scored for the level of skill needed. A five-point scale is used, varying from "skill not required" to "world class capability essential".

The database may be programmed to identify opportunities which match skills, and which could represent opportunities for the organisation.

However, there is a strong argument for a more visionary approach, perhaps looking at a number of scenarios of how the organisation might change its market, and working back to the skills needed to achieve this.

Skills still need to be clustered into competencies. However, the approach could also be used to analyse current products and services, and the resultant matrix used as a basis on which they may be grouped into competencies. The assessment of all this evidence can help to determine which competencies are indeed core.

Examining the Portfolio of Competencies

Hinterhuber et al (1996) use the scores from their correlation chain to position the organisation's competencies. The matrix is reproduced in Figure 9.2, and positions could be plotted judgmentally, provided there is some evidence to support the contentions.

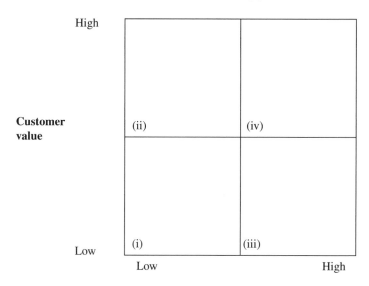

Relative competitive strength

Figure 9.2   The portfolio of core competencies. (Source: H. H. Hinterhuber, S. A. Friedrich, G. Handlbauer and U. Stubec, The company as a cognitive system of core competencies and strategic business units, *Strategic Change*, **5**(4), 1966. © John Wiley & Sons, Limited. Reproduced with permission)

The three most interesting positions are quadrants ii, iii and iv. Quadrant ii may indicate areas of weakness which the organisation should either correct, or render unimportant by changing its activities. Quadrant iv contains the core competencies, which require management if the organisation is to be able to sustain and develop its competence. Quadrant iii may provide opportunities to use some of these competencies to develop products which the customer would value. The danger of this quadrant is that these competencies may include those needed for the future rather than the present, and that a more dynamic assessment might decide that some of them are really core.

Although the portfolio examination of competencies has a lot of appeal, and indeed is following suggestions made by Hamel and Prahalad, there is one weakness. The fact that a competence has high customer value and is an area of high corporate ability misses out one key dimension: uniqueness. This could be solved when competencies are listed on the chart, by showing with a symbol against each the degree to which the organisation shares the competence with competitors. The quadrant would be renamed critical and core competencies.

CORE CAPABILITIES

A lot has been made in the literature of the core competency approach. However, there is a school of thought which likes the basic principle, but criticises the definition of competencies.

Stalk, Evans and Shulman (1992) argue that these are inadequate as a basis on which to build competitive advantage, as the foundation is narrow and technical. What is needed is to add to this the bundles of processes which enable the organisation to be successful at using those technological strengths, such as the way in which the organisation is able to continuously innovate, or the particular approach to customer service which enables them to keep the core competence ahead of competitors. In other words, it's not just what you have, but how you use it which makes the difference.

They define a capability as "a set of business processes strategically understood". The way they are defined is very much as described for competencies, and core capabilities are no easier to define than these.

Leonard-Barton (1992) uses a different definition of core capability, which she describes as a knowledge set to which there are four dimensions. Two are the knowledge and skills:

- of employees
- within technical systems.

The other two are concerned with the creation of knowledge through:

- the enabling management systems
- the values and norms.

If you prefer the capabilities approach to competencies, by all means use it.

REFERENCES

Grant, J. H. and King, W. R. 1983. *Topics of Strategic Planning,* Boston, MA, Little, Brown.

Hamel, G. 1994. The concept of core competence, in Hamel, G. and Heene, A. (eds) *Competence Based Competition,* Chichester, Wiley.

Hamel, G. and Prahalad, C. K. 1994. *Competing for the Future,* Boston, MA, Harvard Business School Press (page references are to the 1996 paperback edition, which contains extra preface material).

Hinterhuber, H. H., Friedrich, S. A., Handlbauer, G. and Stubec, U. 1996. The company as a cognitive system of core competences and strategic business units, *Strategic Change,* **5**(4).

Jenster, P. 1984. Divisional monitoring of critical success factors during strategy implementation, Doctoral dissertation, University of Pittsburgh, PA.

Johnson, G. and Scholes, K. 1999. *Exploring Corporate Strategy,* 5th edn, London, Prentice Hall.

Klein, J. A. and Hiscocks, P. G. 1994. Competence-based competition: a toolkit, in Hamel, G. and Heene, A. (eds) *Competence Based Competition,* Chichester, Wiley.

Learned, E. P., Christensen, C. R., Andrews, K. R. and Guth, W. D. 1965. *Business Policy: Text and Cases,* Homewood, IL, Irwin.

Leonard-Barton, D. 1992. Core capabilities and core rigidities: a paradox in managing new product development, *Strategic Management Journal,* **13**, 111–25.

Miller, V. 1984. Decision-oriented information, *Datamation,* January.

Porter, M. E. 1994. Competitive strategy revisited: a view from the 1990s, in Duffy, P. B. (ed.) *The Relevance of a Decade,* Boston, MA, Harvard Business School Press.

Prahalad C. K. and Hamel, G. 1990. The core competence of the corporation, *Harvard Business Review,* May/June.

Rigby, D. 1999. *Management Tools and Techniques,* Boston, MA, Bain & Co. (copy of presentation dated 19 April).

Rockart, J. F. 1979. Chief executives define their own data needs, *Harvard Business Review,* March/April.

Stalk. G., Evans, P. and Shulman, L. 1992. Competing on capabilities: the new rules of corporate strategy, *Harvard Business Review,* March/April.

10
Industry Analysis

THE IMPORTANCE OF INDUSTRY ANALYSIS

Figure 1.3 included industry analysis as one of the key elements of the corporate appraisal. This can be thought of as the first stage in competitor analysis, the understanding of the arena in which the organisation operates. Basically, industry analysis is a study of the forces within the industry which affect profitability. The line of thinking we have followed came from Porter (1980), although it has been modified as a result of our experiences in applying the concept. In this chapter we concentrate on industry analysis as a tool of the corporate appraisal. Hussey and Jenster (1999) shows how to progress from this to in-depth competitor analysis.

Strategic thinking is a creative, innovative process. Sensible strategies should be based on a thorough understanding of the industries in which the firm operates. Creativity unsupported by analysis is likely to lead to poor strategies; analysis unsupported by creative thinking is likely to lead to a copycat strategy.

We can visualise the industry as being made up of eight centres of competitive forces affecting profitability, which operate within the context of the business environment (Figure 10.1). This is three more than in the famous Porter five-forces model, although we should add that only one of these is fundamentally new: the others clarify certain aspects of the Porter concepts. The analytical process is described in this chapter, and is supported by a

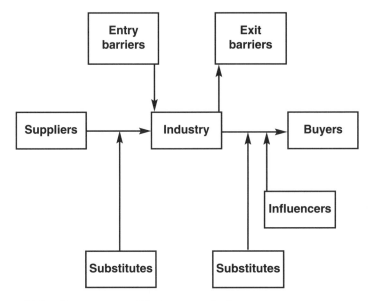

Figure 10.1   Components of industry analysis

questionnaire which can be used to facilitate the work. The creative thinking is what you as managers must bring as you work through the various stages of analysis in your own organisation.

DEVELOP A BLOCK DIAGRAM OF YOUR INDUSTRY

A useful first stage in industry analysis is the drawing of a block diagram which gives a framework for thinking about the industry, and helps to move from the broad concepts of Figure 10.1 to the specific situation in a real industry. For example, *suppliers* is a very general heading, and it is more useful to think in terms of more specific groupings of suppliers. It may also be that, in the industry being analysed, it is sensible to consider different stages in the supply chain, and to represent these in the diagram.

Similarly, few industries have only one type of buyer, and a more typical flow might be through a chain of distribution. A fast moving grocery products company is likely to reach its final consumer by selling to different types of wholesalers and retailers. A company making industrial components might sell to an original equipment manufacturer, which sells on its product to industrial users. It may sell direct to those final customers, or reach them through dealers and wholesalers in order to offer spares. There may also be a reconditioning sector, which has a requirement for the components. Mirroring this reality is an important step to understanding (the term *intermediaries* might be used to indicate the organisations that stand between the industry and the ultimate customer).

The industry itself may not be homogeneous. The lift industry, for example, has at least two activities, manufacture and installation of lifts, and servicing and repair. Some firms do both, but many others only operate in the service and repair side. Representing these essential differences on the block diagram is important, because the forces of competition may not be the same for all.

There are also what can be termed contractual specifiers and influencers, and if these exist in the industry under analysis they should be reflected in the block diagram. An example is the general practitioner or consultant who is not a distributor of ethical pharmaceuticals, but who determines what the patient obtains from the pharmacist. Specifications for sewage treatment plant may be laid down by a consulting engineer, whose role may shut out some competitors, or provide opportunities for others. The *contractual influencers* are one of the additions made to the original Porter concept.

Why is this important? First, this thinking about the outline structure of the industry will make it easier to apply the principles of industry analysis to the particular situation. Second, it will give a basis for an approach called industry charting, which is an analytical and communication tool. Third, industry charting can be used in a dynamic way, to help think through how the industry might change.

But remember, the block diagram and subsequent analysis should give a picture of the whole industry, and not merely reflect what a particular company in the industry actually does. The fact that your company does not deal directly with consumers, for example, is no reason to exclude this option if others in the industry do operate in this way.

An example of an outline block diagram is shown in Figure 10.2. This, of course, is industry specific, and is included to illustrate the idea.

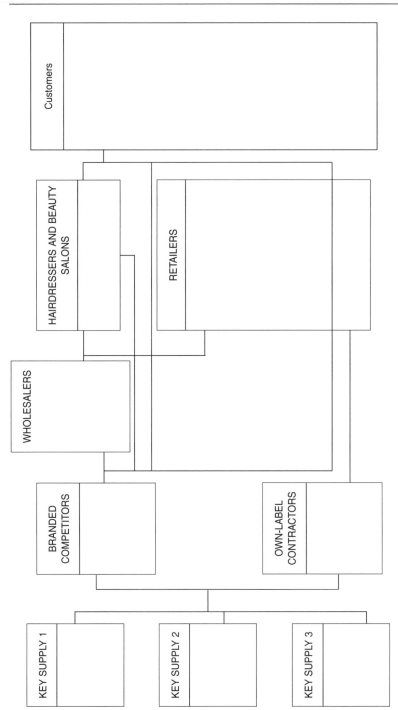

Figure 10.2 Outline chart for toiletry product such as hair care

UNDERSTANDING THE INDUSTRY FORCES

Industry analysis is about understanding the forces which shape the profitability of all the organisations in the industry. We will look at these under the headings of Figure 10.1. However at the outset we should stress that advantages may be neutralised by disadvantages elsewhere, and that we need to take a balanced view using the whole model to reach sound conclusions.

Buyer and Intermediary Power

There are two reasons for studying the structure of the industry through the chain to the ultimate consumer. The first is to ensure that the whole of the present structure is known, as this may reveal new strategic options, including the all-important one of changing the "rules of the game" by finding another way to get the product to the ultimate consumer.

A second reason is to determine the relative influence over profits exercised by the various stages in the chain, and the way power is likely to shift in the future. It is not necessarily the industry itself which determines its own margins and profitability; sometimes the greater power is in the hands of the buyers. Factors which influence the relative location of this power and influence include:

- *Relative size.* If the industry includes firms that are considerably larger than their customers, sheer weight of resources may put them in the dominant position. The converse may apply when the buying organisations are the larger. This is not a universal truth, as other factors may outweigh size in importance. For example, in the UK grocery products are largely controlled by supermarket chains, which not only have most of the retail outlets, but also have developed own-label products that they can adjust in volume and price if the brand manufacturers do not toe the line. In this way they may determine the profitability of manufacturers, whose organisations may be considerably larger than those of the supermarkets.
- *Dependencies.* Bargaining strength may lie with the least

dependent of the two parties. This is a composite of the number of industry firms contrasted with the number of buying firms (what flexibility does each have?), and the importance of the product to the profits of each party.

- *Profitability of the buying industry.* The industry firms are likely to be in a healthier position when they are selling to a profitable industry. Where buyers are unprofitable or have low profits, there is likely to be stronger resistance against price increases. This resistance will increase when the buyer is facing an elastic demand curve, and cannot easily pass on its extra costs.
- *Experience of buyers.* Buyers purchasing from a mature industry are likely to have more experience than those dealing with a new industry. Thus, the more mature the industry, the weaker its bargaining position may become (subject, of course, to other factors). Where the buying industry is also mature, there may be a tendency for the degree of product differentiation to fall, making it more difficult for the industry to sustain high margins.
- *Threat of integration.* The industry firm that patently has the capability and strength to integrate into its buying industry possesses a key bargaining point. If the buying industry thwarts its profit aims, it has the potential to remove the blockage. The opposite applies when the buying industry can offer a credible threat of backwards integration. In either case the credibility of the threat is enhanced when both parties are aware that such a move would be economically viable. Do not forget that the actions of *your* customers may be affected by the power of *their* customers.

The key factor in successfully analysing the intermediaries and customers in a particular industry is segmenting them into groups and distinguishing them either by the reason they buy or how they buy. Criteria for segmenting customer groups include the following:

- Industry or market segment
- Product application
- Geographic location
- Size of purchase

- Frequency of purchase.

A key task is to define the main groups for each intermediary and to classify the customer groups by buying characteristics, and to analyse each of these groups in terms of the relative power they exercise against companies in your industry and the implications of that power for you and your competitors, and for the success of their own businesses.

"Contractual Influencers"

This term covers those who have a contractual role in the buying process, although this may not always be obvious to the industry. We previously gave the example of the general practitioner or medical consultant who prescribes an ethical pharmaceutical, which the patient then obtains from a pharmacist (this industry is complicated in the UK by the role the National Health Service plays in paying for prescriptions, and exercising some influence on what doctors may prescribe). If the doctor knows nothing about the drug, it will not be prescribed and therefore a sale is lost, despite the fact that the doctor is not a stockist of the drug. Similar examples occur in the construction industry, where an architect may specify, for instance, a lift, and that specification may exclude some lift companies from bidding. Another example is plant and machinery, where the buyer may rely on specifications drawn up by a consulting engineer.

The term does not include informal and non-contractual influencers, such as the neighbour who recommends a particular brand of lawn mower, the magazine article which draws attention to a slimming pill, or the teenager's peer group who strongly influence his or her choice of clothes. These types of influence are important for marketing purposes, but are not part of the structure of the industry.

Contractual influencers, on the other hand, are part of the industry. It would be impossible to make sense of the ethical pharmaceutical industry without including the role of the medical profession.

Do contractual influencers exist in the industry you are studying and, if so, who are they?

Suppliers

It is traditional for an industry to believe that it holds the edge over both its buyers and its suppliers, a statement that patently cannot always be true since the industry itself is a buyer to its supplier. Relations with the supplying industry are not always seen as a matter of strategic importance. In reality the analysis of suppliers is the converse of the analysis of buyers. The factors to consider are therefore the same: industry or market segment, product application, geographic location, size of purchase and frequency of purchase. If you doubt this, consider the change in the personal computer industry. Initially it was the manufacturers of the hardware which were in the position of power in the overall industry. Over the past 15 years or so this power has moved into the hands of two of the supplying companies, Intel, which provides most of the world's chips, and Microsoft, whose domination of the operating system and software puts them in a dominant position to dictate what happens to the hardware manufacturers. Would you rather own shares in IBM, Apple or Microsoft?

Suppliers exercise power in an industry in a number of ways: by lowering the quality of goods for a given purchase price, by tightening payment and service terms, and so on. To the extent that suppliers in general, or particular supplier groups, exercise significant power, industry costs increase, profitability diminishes, and the industry competitors may lose control over the future direction of new product developments.

As is the situation between the industry and the buyers, there are countervailing sources of power that the industry can exert on suppliers. The actual balance of power between the industry and particular suppliers is a result of considering the net result of all the factors.

An early step in industry analysis is to cluster suppliers to your company and your competitors into meaningful groups, according to the most significant characteristics of supplier behaviour (e.g. size, type of product, distribution channels). You should then analyse those groups to identify the power they exert on the industry and what that means for a company participating in the industry.

Entry Barriers

The entry barriers will affect the profitability of an industry and the way in which competitors behave. If it is easy for new firms to come into the market competition may be fiercer, as organisations have to battle against known and unknown competitors.

Entry barriers can only be interpreted in relation to the attractiveness of the industry. Relatively low barriers will deter firms from entering low-profit/low-growth industries. The barriers may have to be very high to keep a new entrant out of a highly attractive industry.

Examples of entry barriers which *raise the costs* of a new entrant are:

- Economies of scale or the experience curve factor may raise the capital costs of entry to a very high level (e.g. electronic calculators).
- Highly differentiated products may require extensive advertising support before a newcomer can break in (e.g. household detergents). This may raise costs to prohibitive levels.
- The nature of distribution may require entry at a high level of output (e.g. supermarkets will not stock brands which are slow moving and have low market shares).

Other entry barriers may create a *legal restriction* to entry, or in some way *deny access* to a critical part of the market.

- Patents.
- Legal controls (e.g. auditors, television broadcasting companies).
- Control of distribution outlets (e.g. the British film industry until recently).

Where entry barriers are very low the industry may become fragmented and competition fierce, with new competitors regularly coming into the market. Industry profitability is to a large extent dependent on market imperfections, and one element of corporate strategy might be to find ways of raising the entry barriers.

It should be noted that there are four types of possible new entrants, and the barriers will not have the same effect against all of them.

1. Competitors that are already in the industry, but not in the country being studied.
2. Those in related areas, such as a bank which has acted as an insurance broker, and now wishes to move into the insurance industry.
3. Firms which are new, but which have been set up by people who have operated in the industry as employees.
4. Firms which are totally new to the industry.

Exit Barriers

Exit barriers are the factors which tie a firm to the industry and make it difficult or impossible for it to leave. These conditions are relevant when firms would like to leave because of low earnings and poor prospects, and because of the nature of the industry there are few organisations willing to acquire the business at an acceptable price. If the industry is successful, there are usually potential acquirers who make exit possible. Where the barriers occur, firms will hang on, trading as best they can, and depressing profits in the industry.

Exit barriers may be the need to write off high-value specialised assets for which there is no buyer. Examples are petrochemicals, steel works, oil refineries and mines. Any firm may be tied to its industry through particular contracts, or legal requirements which make it costly to meet severance payments to employees.

There may also be government pressure on the firm to stay in the business. In businesses of low capital intensity, and low entry barriers, small firms may remain in the business because the owners may prefer to take lower earnings instead of facing unemployment if they close down.

In certain countries, exchange control regulations may make it impossible for a company to repatriate any capital sum realised on the sale or closure of a business.

Substitutes

The availability of substitutes may have a dramatic effect on the prospects for an industry, and will unleash a further set of competitive relationships. Emergence of a new substitute may bring new firms with different cost structures into the competitive arena. A substitute will often increase the power of the buyer and reduce the power of the seller. The emergence of potential new substitutes is therefore a possibility that should be studied for each industry.

Where the number of existing substitutes is large, the possibility that the industry has been ill defined should be considered. It may be that a production view has been taken rather than a marketing view. In any event, the substitute industry should be studied as rigorously as the firm's own industry.

It should be noted that substitutes may occur as an option for the buyers, instead of taking the products of the industry firms. They can also occur between the industry firms and their suppliers, giving them more options and reducing supplier power. This is why we show them in two positions in Figure 10.1.

Industry Firms (Competitors)

It is normal for analysts to examine such factors as market shares and to pay some attention to the different positioning of each firm in the marketplace. Industry analysis tries to identify all the factors which affect the intensity of competitive behaviour. The competitiveness of the industry is not revealed by brand shares alone, although these are important. Competitive behaviour is also influenced by many other factors, including:

- *Growth rates of the industry.* Competitive behaviour tends to be less aggressive if industry growth rates are relatively high, because each firm can increase its sales without necessarily increasing its market share. This statement is considerably modified by the position on the life cycle curve. In a new industry high growth rates may bring in new competitors, which will tend to lead to aggressive behaviour. In almost all industries, a fall in the growth rate will tend to intensify competition. Often it is the change that causes new patterns, rather than the growth rate itself. Other things being equal, one would expect to find more aggressive behaviour in an industry whose annual growth rate has fallen suddenly from 10% to 3% than in an industry whose growth has stabilised at 3%.

- *General level of profits.*   Lack of profits among the industry (or significant firms in the industry) will tend to make competitive behaviour less predictable. Where profits are high for all, there may be a measure of tolerance of competitors. A change to lower profits may trigger a more aggressive attitude.

- *Level of fixed costs.*   Where investment is large and highly specialised, and fixed costs are a relatively high proportion of total costs, competitors tend to "hang on", selling at less than full costs, when the market slumps or there is over-capacity for some other reason. Shipping, oil refinery and petrochemicals all provide examples where competitive behaviour may lead to low profits or losses over a very long period of time, because the alternative is plant closure when assets cannot be realised.

- *Economies of scale/experience curve.*   Competitive behaviour is likely to be more aggressive when there are clear advantages to being big. This may happen when cost levels are dependent on high volumes, or when the experience curve effect means that progressively higher volumes will lead to progressively lower costs. Lower costs mean prices can be reduced, which in turn means that even higher volumes can be gained. In a growth market, where demand is elastic and the product subject to mass production (e.g. motor cycles, calculating machines, electronic components) the experience curve effect can bring dominance to the firm that gets far enough ahead. Competitive behaviour is likely to be very aggressive during this period.

- *Degree of differentiation.*   Market imperfections give a degree of protection to individual firms and reduce the impact of competition. Thus it is reasonable to expect the fiercest competition when all firms are offering products of commodity status, and the most peaceful behaviour when each firm offers such a highly differentiated product that it is almost unique.

- *Number of firms and market shares.*   A fragmented industry, with no one firm having a significant market share, tends to be more competitive than one which has a clear market leader that is in a dominant position. To some degree, these tendencies may be modified by the position on the product life cycle. It is unwise to assume that mature markets will all have gone through the shakeout period. Some are highly fragmented because the economic circumstances do not favour large firms (many service industries).

- *New entrant.* In long-established industries, firms often reach an unspoken form of accommodation with each other, softening the aggressiveness of competition. This will often change with the entry of a new firm which either does not know or chooses to ignore these implicit "rules" (for example, the emergence in the UK of the insurance company Direct Line, which over a decade or so has caused many competitors to change their strategies). A similar effect may occur if one of the companies appoints a new chief executive from outside the industry.
- *Nature of product.* A perishable product (e.g. airline tickets, fresh produce) is likely to be more susceptible to random price cutting than one which can be stored easily and cheaply.

PLOTTING STRATEGIC GROUPS

The analysis of the industry requires much detailed knowledge about the competitors. Understanding may be improved if we can cluster competitors into groups that have similar strategic characteristics. This may be essential in an industry where there are hundreds of competitors and it is impractical to study every one of them in detail. It may be desirable when the numbers are manageable, but it is helpful to get a fix on who is competing and where. Porter developed the idea of "strategic groups", which could be plotted on a diagram to show the variations in competitive activity. One value of this is that it may show up which are the real competitors to a particular company, and which are in the same industry, but are not really a threat.

Porter suggested a matrix with specialisation (narrow to full line) on one axis, and vertical integration (high to assembler) on the other. However, this is illustrative, and what he advocates is a matrix which shows the way in which the firms are similar to other firms in the competitive strategy they are following. The two sides of the matrix might in another industry be quality brand image and mix of channels. The groups are illustrated by circles which diagrammatically represent the collective market share of the firms in the group, and the names of the firms are written in each circle. The example in Figure 10.3 shows how the matrix was adapted for a particular industry.

A QUESTIONNAIRE TO HELP CAPTURE THE INFORMATION

The forgoing points have been put into a questionnaire form (see Appendix 10.1) to help you undertake industry analysis in

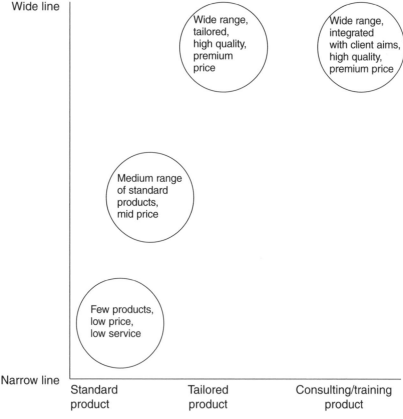

Figure 10.3 Strategic groupings: a hypothetical example from the training industry. The terms low and high quality are relative to each other, and do not imply that one is "better" than another. © Harbridge Consulting Group Ltd, used with permission

your own organisation. It is possible to make a useful analysis with the aid of this. However, we have found it useful to supplement this with one further analytical approach, the development of industry charts, which provide a helpful way of recording the detailed information that should lie behind the answers to the questions.

CHARTING THE INDUSTRY

The charting approach described here has been used in many companies and industries. It develops from the block diagram of the industry, which is used as an outline onto which all the relevant facts about the industry are noted. The points we have gone through so far should be supported by hard facts about the industry, and the charts record that data in a way that enables us to see it all together and helps us to understand the full situation.

The industry charting approach in a real situation is usually done on A3 paper, with one page for the map and another for drawing together the implications of the analysis. It is sometimes necessary to use part of the second sheet as a note pad for information which does not easily fit on the main map, but at the end of the exercise the aim should be to have everything that matters about the industry structure on a couple of sheets of paper. This aim may change when an organisation spans more than one industry, or in a global industry when it is necessary to look at the industry on a world as well as a country-by-country basis.

Of course it is possible to interpret an industry without drawing an industry chart, but the two main advantages of this method are that the exercise helps ensure that the right questions are asked, and the resultant chart communicates a great deal of information in a compressed way to other persons. Strategies to respond to what is discovered rarely emanate from only the analyst, and information has to be shared with, and the issues fully understood by, other key managers. The charting approach helps do this, and also provides a framework for keeping information up to date.

Another benefit found from this approach is that it reveals where information is lacking, and often shows up other problems.

It is not uncommon for different parts of an organisation to be using different figures for the market or market shares, and this approach makes these differences very clear. Our experience is that the method often shows that a piece of information that the organisation has relied on in the past is inaccurate, occasionally dangerously so. Market size, for example, may be calculated from a variety of sources, not all of which are as complete or as accurate as they might be. It is rarely easy to take market information from several overlapping sources, without exposing some areas of doubt. Any mechanism that shows that if "fact" A is correct, "fact" B has to be untrue is potentially very helpful, and may reveal that assumptions that have been used in the past are unreliable.

The charting approach becomes an early stage in competitor analysis, and if each competitor is profiled, can become the basis for developing scenarios of how an industry could change, and who might be likely to initiate changes.

Figure 10.4 provides a summary of the type of information which should be included on an industry chart.

THE INDUSTRY AND THE BUSINESS ENVIRONMENT

The past, present and future of any industry is affected by the forces of the business environment. Technological development has, for example, been a driving force in the merging of what used to be the separate industries of typewriters and computers, and, more recently, in extending the "new" industry to telecommunications and video.

Figure 10.5 provides a classification for thinking about the trends in the environment. The connections between all the points remind us that a change in one factor may affect all or any of the other factors. Positioning the industry in the centre stresses the importance of these external changes, and that they should not be neglected. We should also recognise that an industry may be a driver of changes to the environment: technology, in particular, is strongly influenced by how businesses try to exploit it.

Although there is much that will affect a whole industry, a word of warning should be given. It is wrong to believe that every

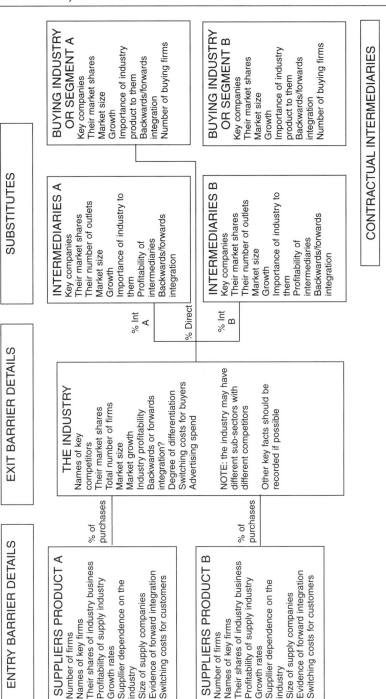

Figure 10.4 Data required for an industry map (generalised view)

ENTRY BARRIER DETAILS

EXIT BARRIER DETAILS

SUBSTITUTES

CONTRACTUAL INTERMEDIARIES

SUPPLIERS PRODUCT A
Number of firms
Names of key firms
Their shares of industry business
Profitability of supply industry
Growth rates
Supplier dependence on the industry
Size of supply companies
Evidence of forward integration
Switching costs for customers

SUPPLIERS PRODUCT B
Number of firms
Names of key firms
Their shares of industry business
Profitability of supply industry
Growth rates
Supplier dependence on the industry
Size of supply companies
Evidence of forward integration
Switching costs for customers

% of purchases

% of purchases

THE INDUSTRY
Names of key competitors
Their market shares
Total number of firms
Market size
Market growth
Industry profitability
Backwards or forwards integration?
Degree of differentiation
Switching costs for buyers
Advertising spend

NOTE: the industry may have different sub-sectors with different competitors

Other key facts should be recorded if possible

% Int A

% Direct

% Int B

INTERMEDIARIES A
Key companies
Their market shares
Their number of outlets
Market size
Growth
Importance of industry to them
Profitability of intermediaries
Backwards/forwards integration

INTERMEDIARIES B
Key companies
Their market shares
Their number of outlets
Market size
Growth
Importance of industry to them
Profitability of intermediaries
Backwards/forwards integration

BUYING INDUSTRY OR SEGMENT A
Key companies
Their market shares
Market size
Growth
Importance of industry product to them
Backwards/forwards integration
Number of buying firms

BUYING INDUSTRY OR SEGMENT B
Key companies
Their market shares
Market size
Growth
Importance of industry product to them
Backwards/forwards integration
Number of buying firms

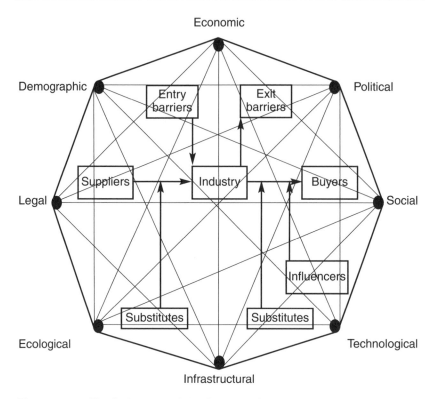

Figure 10.5   The Industry and the Business Environment

Table 10.1   The industry and the business environment: checklist

What factors are affecting the industry?	What are their implications?
Political	
Demographic	
Economic	
Legal	
Technological	
Infrastructure	
Ecological	
Social	

organisation in an industry is affected to the same extent by a change in the environment. So although a general view is helpful, we should accept that it has limitations.

The checklist in Table 10.1 can be used to put some flesh on the bones of the figure. It uses the same broad classifications as the figure, but provides space for them to be expanded into sub-factors. Equally important is the space provided to record the implications of these factors.

CHANGING THE INDUSTRY

Industry analysis gives a snapshot of the competitive arena at a given point in time. This is useful, but we should not allow the thinking to stop there. There are four broad types of strategy which may be followed:

1. *Continuing the same activities within the same industry structure.* This leads to strategies that try to improve performance, such as cost reduction, or ways of creating greater value for customers.
2. *Continuing the same activities, but changing the structure of the industry.* Such strategies might include acquiring competitors, backwards or forwards integration, strategic alliances, or developing new ways of getting the product to the customers
3. *Novel activities within the same industry structure.* For example, by developing new products or add-on services, or finding new niches and ways to segment the market.
4. *Changing the activities and the structure.* These are strategies which try to change the fundamental nature of the industry. They are the hardest to get right. This thinking about changing the industry has a good fit with the core competencies concept, which we met in an earlier chapter.

We are not arguing that the appraisal is the place to undertake fundamental strategic thinking, but it is appropriate to identify the options to the degree that this is possible. Industry analysis can be used as a dynamic tool to help do this, although in practice it is more often restricted to taking a snapshot at a particular point in time, leading to strategies like those listed in points 1 and 2.

APPENDIX 10.1

INDUSTRY ANALYSIS QUESTIONNAIRE*

This questionnaire was designed to facilitate analysis of an industry. It should be modified to fit the characteristics of the industry being studied. It has been found useful as a way of coordinating industry analysis with portfolio analysis, as the information collected can be used for both purposes.

The questionnaire follows concepts originally developed by Porter (1980). It has been used in many practical situations.

1. DEFINITION OF INDUSTRY

1.1 How would you define the industry in which you operate (by product and services)?

1.2 What is your definition of the relevant geographical scope of your industry? (You may find it important to analyse more than one geographical area, grouping regions with similar product life cycles, competitors or government policies.)

1.3 Is your activity directed at a definable market segment or segments? What are these?

1.4 What is the approximate size of the market(s)?

1.5 What is the range of profits for your industry (in terms of ROCE)? are they:

Above average for all British* industry ☐

Average ☐

Below average for all British* industry ☐

*Amend according to relevant geographical area.

1.6 How stable are the profits in your industry?

	Year to year	Within a year
Very stable	☐	☐
Stable	☐	☐
Unstable	☐	☐

2. COMPETITION

2.1   As the number of competitors increases, or as they become more equal in size and power there is a tendency for grow ing contention in the industry.

2.1.1 List the competitors in the industry by major segment (as defined) (including your firm) with approximate market shares and position description (defined below):

Competitor   Market share   Position   description*

*Use the description which best fits each firm:

Leader: a company which by virtue of its market position is likely to be followed by others in pricing.

Major: the position where no one firm is a leader, but a number of approximately equal dominance.

Minor

Negligible

(*Note*: these definitions are based on those used in the Directional Policy Matrix, a portfolio analysis tool originally developed by Shell Chemicals.)

2.1.2 Which word best describes the type of competition in your industry?

Friendly ☐   Gentlemanly ☐   Polite ☐

Bitter ☐   Warlike ☐   Fierce ☐

Cut-throat ☐

2.2   Contention increases as growth rates slow.

2.2.1 Which phase of the life cycle characterises your industry and your products?

	Industry	Your products
Introduction	☐	☐
Take-off	☐	☐
Slow down	☐	☐
Maturity	☐	☐
Decline	☐	☐

2.2.2 What rate of annual market growth (in volume terms) occurs in your industry?

Last five years (%):
Forecast next five years (%):

2.3   Rivalry increases where fixed costs are high, efficient incre-ments to capacity are large, or external factors lead to recur-ring or chronic excess capacity.

2.3.1 What is the approximate percentage of fixed costs to total costs in your industry?

2.3.2 What is the lead time required to increase capacity?

2.3.3 What is your estimate of current utilisation of capacity? (Normal shifts)

Your industry as a whole:
Your firm:

2.3.4 Are periods of chronic excess capacity a characteristic of your industry?

2.3.5 Are margins maintained when capacity exceeds demand?

2.4.   Competition increases when the product is perishable or difficult or costly to store. (*Note*: an airline ticket, a consultancy service and a banana are examples of very dif-ferent perishable products.)

2.4.1 Does your industry fall under these categories?

Perishable ☐

Difficult to store ☐

Costly to store ☐

2.5 Contention increases the more standardised the product and the less differentiated it is in the eyes of the buyer, reaching a peak as it nears commodity status.

2.5.1 How do the buyers view the products in the industry?

Standardised/interchangeable ☐

Substitutes ☐

Differentiated ☐

Requiring a major change (e.g. engineering, formulation or manufacturing process) if products changed ☐

2.5.2 Does pricing behaviour in the industry suggest that the industry regards its products as standardised? (Note: these questions may need to be considered separately for different market segments).

2.6 Competition becomes more unpredictable as firms in the industry develop different "personalities" or when recent entrants have different historical origins and ignore the "norms" of industry behaviour.

2.6.1 How would you describe the firms in your industry?

Club or fraternity (homogeneous interests) ☐

Tend to act according to unwritten "rules" ☐

Little common interest ☐

Irrational in behaviour ☐

2.6.2 Are the firms in the industry long established, or have there been recent entrants to the industry whose values and objectives appear to be different? (*Note*: A similar change may occur when a new chief executive is appointed.)

2.6.3 Are there one or more "mavericks" in the industry which regularly upset the industry?

3. SUPPLIERS

3.1 (a) Industry profits may be reduced when the bargaining power of the suppliers of the major items increases. This will happen as a supplier industry becomes less competitive.

(b) The bargaining power of suppliers tends to reduce if the purchasing industry is highly concentrated.

3.1.1 What is the ratio of suppliers to industry firms for each of the most important supplies?

3.1.2 To what extent are the most important supplies:

Standardised/interchangeable ☐

Substitutes ☐

Differentiated ☐

Tied to the industry through particular ☐
processes, plant etc. (e.g. if the firm changed,
its supplier would it have to modify its product,
manufacturing process etc?)

3.2 (a) Suppliers will tend to try to influence the growth of the purchasing industry when it accounts for a large proportion of the total output of the supplying industry.

(b) The availability of competing substitute products will tend to reduce the power of suppliers and increase purchasing industry profitability.

3.2.1 To what extent are the supplier industries dependent on the sales of your industries?

3.3 Suppliers may increase their bargaining power if they can demonstrate a credible threat to integrate forward.

3.3.1 List any suppliers which have integrated forwards in the industry. (*Note*: backwards integration is covered in Question 3.4)

3.3.2 How does profitability in your industry compare with that in your suppliers' industries? (If higher, the threat of integration is increased, since the suppliers will tend to judge the investment opportunity against present returns. *Note*: this is not the only factor they will consider – opportunity cost of capital is also important.)

Rates of return:
  Very much higher ☐

  Higher ☐

  The same ☐

  A little lower ☐

  Considerably lower ☐

3.3.3 Is the volume of business in the hands of any one supplier sufficient to justify their operation in your industry? (That is, sales volume in relation to efficient scale of operations).

3.3.4 Could the supplier obtain any economies by integrating?

3.3.5 Are there any barriers to integration?

3.3.6 Does the industry act as a barrier to thwart suppliers' technical innovations and new products?

3.4   On the other hand the purchasing industry can reduce the power of the suppliers if it can offer a credible threat to integrate backwards.

3.4.1 List any firms in the industry which have integrated backwards.

3.4.2 Are the entry barriers to backward integration high or low?

4. BUYERS

4.1   The ability to increase prices is reduced when the buying industry has a low value added.

4.1.1 How significant is the value added at each stage in the industry?

e.g.

	Very high	High	Medium low	Very low
Supplier				
Industry				
Buyer				

4.2 (a) The power of the buyers is higher the more it is domi-
          nated by powerful customers, the fewer the number of
          buying firms, and the greater their percentage pur-
          chases from the industry.
     (b) The power of the buyer decreases as the industry
          becomes more concentrated.

4.2.1 What is the percentage of industry firms to buying firms?

4.2.2 Is the market dominated by a small group of powerful cus-
      tomers?

4.2.3 What percentage of sales goes to each of the various cate-
      gories of buyer:

Category	Industry	Your firm

4.3 The power of buyers is reduced by a credible threat of for-
     ward integration by the industry: it is increased by a credible
     threat of backwards integration by the buyers.

4.3.1 List any firms in the industry which have integrated forward.

4.3.2 List any buyers which have integrated backwards.

4.3.3 Are there any significant economic advantages in integra-
      tion?

4.3.4 Does the volume of business justify the buyer considering
      operation in the industry (i.e. sales volume in relation to effi-
      cient scale of operations)? Or vice versa?

Backwards by buyer _____

Forwards by industry _____

4.3.5 How does profitability of the buyer firms compare with that
      of the industry?

Higher   ☐

Same   ☐

Lower   ☐

4.4 As buyers become more experienced, normally as a market matures, they may exercise more influence over the profitability of suppliers.

4.4.1 What proportion of business (by each main category of buyers) is by competitive tender?

☐ %

4.4.2 How effective are the buyers in imposing their standards on you and your competitors?

4.4.3 What is the nature of the buying decision process in the main categories of buyers?

4.4.4 Please describe the nature and importance of firms which may influence the buying decision, but which are not themselves buyers.

5. NEW ENTRIES: EXITS

Some of the factors which make an industry attractive to new entrants have already been covered: profitability, growth, degree of competition etc. In addition there might be added a lack of entry and exit barriers.

5.1 Entry barriers make it more difficult for an outsider to get into the industry.

5.1.1 Are economies of scale important in your industry, sufficient to ensure that new entrants have to make/set up a significant capacity at high capital cost in order to compete?

5.1.2 Would vertical integration provide significant additional economies?

5.1.3 List any absolute cost advantages possessed by your firm and each of the major competitors.

Advantage	Competitor (Name)
Patents on products or processes	
Control of proprietary technology	
Control of raw materials	
Availability of low-cost capital	
Experience	
Ownership of effective depreciated assets	

5.1.4 To what degree does each of the major competitors (including your firm) have a barrier of brand loyalty (product differentiation)?

5.1.5 Does success in the industry require access to tied distribution networks (e.g. dealers in the motor car industry)?

Yes ☐   No ☐

Could a new entrant secure these?

Yes ☐   No ☐

5.1.6 How would firms in the industry react to a new entrant?

5.1.7 Do any of the following exit barriers exist in the industry?

Specialised, durable assets which have little resale value ☐

High fixed costs associated with exit ☐

Interrelatedness with other businesses ☐

REFERENCES

Hussey, D. and Jenster P. 1999. *Competitor Intelligence: Turning Analysis into Success*, Chichester, Wiley.

Porter, M. E. 1980. *Competitive Strategy: Techniques for Analysing Industries and Competitors*, New York, Free Press.

11

Conclusions: Finding the Real Strengths and Weaknesses

The systematic approach we have outlined will result in the uncovering of four types of facts about the organisation:

- There are those that indicate strengths and weaknesses which have a strategic importance. Such weaknesses include lagging behind in a key technology, relying for most of the profits on products in declining markets with no successful new products to take their place, or having a portfolio of SBUs all of which require more cash to develop their potential than the organisation can generate. Such strengths might be a true leadership position in a key technology, and preferred supplier status with customers for 60% of sales.
- It is probable that there will be matters identified which have immediate operational significance, such as a cost saving opportunity or a change in the promotional material to emphasise a particular aspect of the product or service which gives value to customers.
- There will also be some supporting information which is useful in identifying the absence of a weakness, and which may need to be used when strategies are considered, but is not otherwise helpful. Of course in some situations the absence of a weakness can be a strength, but in many other situations it is no more than giving the ability to play the competitive game.
- The fourth category is all the information which has yielded

no findings of any significance. This includes the blind alleys that have been explored, and also various facts uncovered which have no obvious importance.

A book has to be written in sequential chapters, which implies a chain relationship between the various elements of the appraisal, with item neatly following item. Of course reality is not like this at all, and the key elements have a sort of spider's web relationship, with a tangle of crossed lines and a pattern of mutual dependency. We have heard it called a can of worms, but although this may describe with some accuracy the feeling induced through having to pull together numerous facts from the various parts of the appraisal, it is erroneous because each worm in a can is independent of every other worm. We are trying to imply that in any organisation what is found from one element of the appraisal is unlikely to be totally independent of what is found in other elements.

Something needs to be done to draw the whole appraisal together, and to concentrate on the things that matter. How this task is tackled will depend on the purpose of the appraisal. If it was undertaken as part of a due diligence report in an acquisition situation, there are four groups of things that should be clear at the end:

- Evidence that aids a decision about whether to proceed with the acquisition.
- Identifying serious weaknesses and the implications of these should the organisation make the acquisition.
- Highlighting where strategic decisions would be needed in order to obtain synergy between the organisations.
- Providing information which enables decisions to be made on how the two organisations should be merged operationally.

This would be a somewhat different conclusion to the appraisal than if it had been undertaken as part of a strategic review. It is the strategic review use that will be examined in more detail.

INVOLVING MANAGERS

In our first chapter we were critical of the way SWOT is used in many organisations. This does not mean that we undervalue the knowledge and insight managers have into their businesses. The issue is how to tap into this in a sensible way. The appraisal itself may have been undertaken by a single person, but is more likely to be a team effort. Or there may have been several teams to look at different aspects, whose work has been planned and coordinated from one central point. It is possible that management consultants have undertaken all or part of the appraisal, or that outsiders have been involved in some way with the internal teams. To some degree various managers will have played a part in getting the information together. But this will not necessarily mean that managers have had any opportunity to see the conclusions or to discuss them in a collective way.

Although it may occasionally be inappropriate, in most situations it is important to widen the involvement of managers across the organisation in drawing out the strengths and weaknesses, and the implications of these. One way to do this is to organise focus groups at various levels, with the membership of each being people with appropriate knowledge and experience. The agenda would be modified to the scope of contribution that those attending are able to make. Each group meeting should be based on those facts from the appraisal which are relevant to the group attending.

Instead of asking people to think of strengths and weaknesses, we suggest that the meeting approach the subject more obliquely, and for each group of related findings follow a sequence something like this:

1. Here are some facts which seem to us to be important.
2. What implications do these have for the organisation?
3. How important is each grouping of findings to the organisation?
4. What are the causal factors for each state of affairs?
5. What actions do we need to take to correct things we do not like, or to build on things that we do like?

The equilibrium analysis approach discussed in Chapter 1 is particularly helpful when discussing item 4. What this approach should do is to make people aware of things they may not have considered. For example, people may be feeling quite satisfied with the performance of the organisation based on year on year comparisons, but would not have this feeling if they were shown that the rest of the industry was doing much better.

In addition, there is the chance to gain extra background and insight. One thing that frequently happens in the way SWOT is often used is that the same fact is identified as both a strength and a weakness, which is hardly logical. Many of us were brought up on traditional legends and adventure stories, and in this context it is easy to see how the helplessness of the maiden rescued from the dragon by the gallant knight could be the factor that increases her attractiveness to him and leads to the "happy ever after" ending. But was the helplessness ever a weakness? With this stereotype character, it is this which is the strength, as our damsel's aim in life is to gain a gallant husband. Of course, it would have been unfortunate if she had been roasted and eaten by the dragon, but this would be a mischance rather than a fundamental weakness! We might reach a different conclusion if a real-life modern woman were unable to deal with her personal dragons, but again our answer would depend on her aims and ambitions.

The mix of underlying hard facts and management insight, related to an understanding of what the organisation is trying to achieve, should prevent the simultaneous classification of something as both a strength and a weakness. "Our 90% market share is a strength, but it is also a weakness because we cannot defend it against new entrants who might be attracted to the market." Does this sort of statement mean that you should remove the weakness by reducing market share? The real issue we want to get at is that "Our present rate of profitability is potentially vulnerable, because it depends on an unsustainable 90% market share". Looking at it in this way takes us into a number of different actions we might consider, as it takes us to the heart of the issue. We can even make estimates of how profits would be affected by various reductions in market share to help clarify our thinking. The insight of managers who are helped to see the facts in an appropriate way can lead to a very different understanding of what is the real issue.

The minimum result that might come out, which can still be useful, is that managers do not see as critical something which the team believes is very important. This is useful information because an issue which is ignored does not go away.

There are some cautions over the involvement process. Managers have vested interests in the future of their own activities, or in resisting what might be seen as a criticism of past decisions. It is not just that careers may depend on how something is seen, but that subconsciously we want to defend something in which we have invested our hearts and minds. There may be rationalisation of the status quo, the introduction of unsupported "facts", or attempts to play down a particular fact. The motivation is not necessarily obstructive, and may come from a heartfelt belief. So when you involve managers in this way, you need some skill to separate fact from erroneous belief and wishful thinking.

CREATING A PICTURE FROM THE PIECES

By this stage there is a dossier of the things that have been discovered, plus the results from the various focus group meetings. The appraisal team should put all of this together in a report, so that the facts and the interpretations are readily available. However, if this is all that is done, top management is passed the whole task of making sense of what has been found. This would not be particularly helpful, so there is a need to pull out from all this the information that the team believes is relevant, and the supporting key facts. This is the second most important result of the appraisal: the most important result will be the strategic decisions which are taken in the light of the findings.

We will first give some indications of how the findings might be written up, if we were undertaking a corporate appraisal of a business. Later we will look at some of the special requirements if we were sitting at the top of a diversified multi-SBU company. With some adaptation on your part, we hope that this will enable you to think about the position in your own organisation.

CORPORATE APPRAISAL OF A BUSINESS

You may have a very thick file as a result of your appraisal, now made thicker by the outcome of the various meetings. While this should be available to top management, it should be used to *support* the conclusions of the appraisal, and not to *be* those conclusions. The suggestion here falls into two parts: an analysis of what seem to be the important facts, and some key figures which enable a clear picture of the organisation to be seen. How this report is put together will depend on the organisation. It can be prepared and presented as a report to top management, and this is what is most likely to happen if management consultants are used. However, it may be more effective if the chief executive is involved in going through the information with the team, so that his or her insight is gained, and that ownership of the report is established where it should be, right at the top.

A Summary of the Strategic Issues

The threads of the appraisal may be drawn together in the form of a series of factual statements about the organisation, together with the strategic implications and some of the possible strategic options that might be investigated. There are of course numerous ways in which this document can be written, and it is not something that we should be dogmatic about. However, it is important that the statements *are* written, since in most companies there are likely to be areas of dispute (in fact, it is almost possible to say dogmatically that if everyone agrees with the report, the job has not been done properly), and emotions will be involved. It is much easier to make an objective decision if all the evidence is fully documented.

The reports may not always be pleasant. Few people enjoy trying to convince their chief executive that an area of the company which is dear to his or her heart is not right for the organisation, or of similar unpopular measures. But this sort of study must be approached with integrity, for without a genuine attempt at honest appraisal the whole exercise may become a meaningless gesture.

The final report should show clearly the strong and weak points of the organisation. It should assess the vulnerability of the internal factors to external changes, and should establish what we like to call the organisation's "risk balance" (which, put simply, is the number of baskets it has to keep its eggs in!).

Our example in Box 11.1 is somewhat simpler than a real situation (for most organisations this is a gross understatement). Too complex an example would add more to length than elucidation. Our aim is to illustrate that only the key findings need appear in the summary, and that each key finding should be based on evidence which must be recorded and available if required to justify the statements (cross-references could be included to the pages in the dossier). Simple lists, however accurate and insightful, only do part of the job, and we recommend adding a column to show the strategic implications. It would be possible to go one step further and suggest various strategic options that might be considered.

Box 11.1 One method of summarising the key points from an appraisal

Part 1: Weaknesses/limiting factors

Factor	Strategic implications	Possible options
1. The service division (half of total sales) provides 40% of profit before corporate overheads and tax, but its market is declining at 10% per year. Market share has been constant for the last 5 years at 30%.	This important department will be in a critical position in a year or so. There are few opportunities to reduce costs in line with sales, without also impairing the level of service which supports our market share. We are at crisis point.	• Add new areas of service activity • Redefine the service needs of the market • Alliance with another organisation • Divest
2. Three customers contribute 80% of the sales of the service division.	This reduces our administrative costs, but increases our vulnerability.	
3. We lag behind our competitors in introducing modern service technology.	Is it wise to invest heavily in a declining business?	• Divest • Acquire competitor with the new technology • Invest to bring up to date
4. The product division has six products which provide the remaining 50% of sales. This division contributes 60% to profit before corporate overheads and tax. However, the management reports hide the fact that three products (10% of sales) are in loss or make no contribution. Three products (40% of sales) contribute all the profits of this division and subsidise the other three products.	The poor performers are pulling down overall performance, and reducing the funds that could be used for developing the profitable products. However, just to drop the unprofitable products without reducing costs would lose the small contribution that they make.	• Slow withdrawal of poor performers to coincide with a planned expansion of the good products • Drop the poor performers but obtain contract work to recover the space costs etc. that would remain in the business • Find new range of products from in-house development or alliance with overseas organisation

continued

Factor	Strategic implications	Possible options
5. We spend £2 million per year on management education and development. About half of this is focused on training that is loosely related to our strategy, but attendance is on a voluntary basis, and few of those who need the training ever attend.	Training is not directed at those who need it. Policy must be changed to force those designated to attend training events. The results of training should be measured.	• Reduce the number of training events to cater only for those with the specific need • Redirect the cash saved into other essential training • Redirect the cash saved into new product development
6. The remaining half of training expenditure is misdirected. Money spent here could usefully be used to address the many critical aspects of training needed if we are to achieve our corporate strategy.	One reason we are slipping in so many areas is that we have many long-service people who have not been kept up to date with new concepts of management and new technological developments. This includes our most senior people.	• Develop programmes which have a defined strategic aim, and use them to help implement the necessary strategic changes that we have to tackle
7. There is no obvious successor to the chief executive, who is already aged 65.	Lack of succession planning could plunge the company into crisis.	• Recruitment • Seek merger with an organisation with strong top management
8. Three of our executive directors are due to retire in the next three years. There are no obvious successors.	An expansion of the problem seen in 7 above	• As above
9. Three years ago we were leaders in the pneumatics technology on which our three successful products are based. We have now fallen behind competitors, and are no longer state of the art.	Unless addressed this will lead to a decline in our market position	• Strategic alliance to give access to new technology • License technology • Crash effort to develop own technology • Acquire a company which has what we need

Factor	Strategic implications	Possible options
10. Our ability to develop innovative new products has declined. we have launched none in the last three years, and have none in development.	This is partly due to our lagging in technology, and partly to our culture. The internal culture and the HRM policies which reinforce it discourage risk taking and new ideas. Failure to address this will lead to our ultimate decline	• A complete sea change in our control and reward systems, and in the importance placed on innovation (Acquisition or alliance will not help us innovate unless we change ourselves too)

Part 2: Strengths/enabling factors

Factor	Strategic implications	Possible options
1. The value chain analyses shows that we are giving value to customers in the areas of quality and responsiveness to their needs. This applies to both divisions. The value is perceived as important by competitors.	Although this is a good position to build on, and is reinforced by our brand shares, we should not be complacent. As shown above, there are areas where we are not as good.	• A careful study of the value chain analysis to identify how to build on this, to build an even stronger market position
2. Our manufacturing operation is in the top quartile of the industry for its performance ratios.	These may be difficult to maintain without extra effort, if our volumes decline. They provide a springboard to do even better.	• Benchmarking process to become world class
3. A good industrial relations climate.	This has been achieved through the management policies of the company, and by keeping all employees informed about the state of the organisation.	• Continue to work on this. It will facilitate change, but must not be neglected in times of crisis
4. The company is sound financially, and has the ability to raise significant funds for expansion.	No reasonable strategy would be restricted through lack of capital.	
5. Patent protection on most of the critical components of our products.	This enables us to offer certain benefits which cannot be copied by competitors.	• This gives us great strength if we want to follow a strategic alliance strategy

Box 11.2 Relating products to resource utilisation

Products		Sales			Profit contribution				Market	
Name	Life cycle	£ Million	Growth	% Sales	£ Million	% Sales	% Total	Share	Relative share	Growth
1 Serv Dept	Decline	50	−10%	50	12	24	40	20%	0.75	−10%
2 A	Growth	10	4%	10	4	40	16	35%	1.5	12%
3 B	Growth	20	5%	20	7	35	28	20%	0.6	10%
4 C	Growth	10	10%	10	3	30	12	15%	0.6	9%
5 D	Mature	3	1%	3	0	0	0	2%	0.15	2%
6 E	Decline	1	0	1	0	0	0	6%	0.25	0
7 F	Decline	6	−15%	6	−1	−17	−4	3%	0.2	−25%

Products		Financial assets		Factory		Human resources			Management
Name	Life cycle	Fixed	Current	Capacity	%	% R&D	% Sales	%	Quality
1 Serv Dept	Decline	20%	50%	80%	5%	0	20	40	Good
2 A	Growth					30			
3 B	Growth	50%	25%	60%	60%	30	60	20	Good
4 C	Growth					10			
5 D	Mature					15			
6 E	Decline	30%	25%	25%	35%	5	20	40	Some problems
7 F	Decline					10			

Notes
Sales growth: forecast for next year   Sales %: base is £100m sales for last 12 months
Profit contribution to HO costs and profit (after all direct overheads)
    % Sales: contribution margin   % Total: percentage of total corporate contribution
Relative share: relative to market share of the market leader
Factory capacity: percentage of dedicated available capacity used   Factory %: of total corporate capacity
The information headings can be adjusted to suit the needs of the particular organisation.
In this sort of organisation it would be useful to include an ROI chart as part of the report.

Schedules of Key Information

Pieces of information uncovered in the appraisal may be interesting in themselves, but often have more value if they can be related to each other. Summarising a lot of information about each product in a table, such as the classification of the product, its annual sales and profit contribution, market shares, expected growth rates of the market, the various types of resources needed to obtain this (assets, percentage of factory capacity, working capital, percentage of sales force time devoted to this product, and whatever else is relevant) can give a clearer view of the issues than a series of functional analyses. The headings suggested are indicative, and it is important not to let each table get so large that the wood is concealed among the trees. In Chapter 2 we introduced Figure 2.3 as a blank chart for recording this sort of information. To complete our example we have filled in what this table might look like for the fictitious company whose position was summarised in Box 11.2.

CORPORATE APPRAISAL OF A MULTI-BUSINESS ORGANISATION

At the business level the requirements would be much as above. The diversified organisation, divided into a number of SBUs, has an additional requirement. At corporate level the interest is certainly on total corporate performance and the role of each SBU in contributing to this. However, at this level it is unlikely to need to know all the detail that appears in Boxes 11.1 and 11.2. There is a need to understand the businesses, but corporate-level strategy requires a somewhat different way of seeing the information.

Tabular Presentations

Arraying information in a tabular format is always helpful in comparing the different parts of a multi-business organisation. At the centre there is a specific concern about the overall finances of the whole organisation, and the ability to finance the growth of SBUs. In fact it was the inability of conglomerates to be able to support

From the Consulting Experience of David Hussey

In case our example seems to cover things that management would already have known about, here are some snippets from my experience.

- *Diversified service organisation.* This company had several unrelated businesses. One of these had two distinct activities in the same industry, one in the consumer market and the other business to business. There were different critical skills factors for each, with no overlap of facilities or personnel. The consumer side was in a highly competitive situation, and its results were poor. The business to business side was fast growing and profitable. Results of the two activities were amalgamated and together made the overall business accept-able, but not inspiring. Effectively the growth area was being held back to prop up the weak side. Part of our report sug-gested that the two activities should be untangled, and the growth area backed. Within a year or so the organisation sold the consumer activity. Over the next decade it divested most other business units, and built up its global position in the business to business market, which is now its main activity.
- *Asian life Insurance Co.* Sales analysis revealed many things that management did not know about this organisation. One analysis related information about age and occupation to the national statistics, from which it was possible to see that most new policies were on the lives of young clerical workers. There was little penetration of the management/professional segment, nor of age groups of 30 and upwards. As a result of this, a number of changes were made, and in a follow-up assignment some three years later I was shown statistics that revealed a much greater penetration of the previously neglected segments which had been identified in the analysis as offering the best potential.
- *Management consultancy.* When I took over as managing director of the UK operations of a US firm, it would have been possible to rationalise the gap between costs and revenues as being down to changed economic conditions. The previ-ous year had been a record for the firm in terms of revenue and profits. My appraisal showed that there was more to the situation than this. The strengths of the firm included good

client references, quality people and a strong capability in the development of management education and training programmes which were highly tailored to help solve real client problems. The US parent was the pioneer organisation in this field, and held a pre-eminent position, and there had been many past successful assignments in this area by the UK company. However, more recently the emphasis in the UK had been on consultancy rather than management education. The limiting factors included the fact that at the time I took over assignments had come to an end with most clients, there was little information about the market and competitors, and the UK firm was known only to its clients. Short-term cost problems had to be addressed, but we also changed the strategy. One element was to set out to gain 70–75% of our business in the development and delivery of management training and education programmes. Not only did this build on strength, but the nature of this type of work solved another problem.

Contracts with large organisations normally meant working to a plan that spanned several years, and although the formal contract did not stretch this far, the intention to continue did. Assignments in this field therefore removed much of the problem of planning for a forward workload. The remaining 25–30% of our revenue we wanted to come from management consultancy, and over the next few years we built a business that was able to integrate a knowledge transfer style of consultancy, in areas like strategic management, with the subjects offered on the training side, and with the change facilitation capability of the approaches to course design. We also addressed the issues of market information and promotion.

Although the strategy was related to opportunities as we saw them, it was also driven by a careful corporate appraisal. If there had been no clients wanting the service, it would, of course, have failed. But fundamentally it built on strengths, and by so doing corrected or avoided some of the limiting factors. It also built a business that offered a great deal of job satisfaction to employees.

all the needs of healthy growth businesses which was one reason why, beginning some 20 years ago, there was a move to float off many businesses, and reduce to a core of businesses that could be supported. A further pressure when organisations did not realise the issue themselves was the spate of takeover bids where the aim was to release value by breaking up the organisation. Clearly it is a corporate weakness for a conglomerate not to be able to provide the finance that its businesses need.

Portfolio Analysis

A second approach which is useful, although less fashionable than it once was, is portfolio analysis. This approach is very helpful in enabling a view to be gained of all SBUs in the organisation, or sometimes all products. Our view is to avoid the prescriptive labels attached to some portfolio charts which imply a strategy, and instead to use the chart to help think of the relative value of each area plotted to the organisation, and its likely future cash using or cash generating potential. We have touched on portfolio analysis in previous chapters, both the business portfolio and others for comparing competencies and technologies. It is also possible to add an exploration of relative risks to a portfolio chart. Hussey (1998) provides a description of the basic approach and the enhanced method showing risks, and provides full scoring rules. Segev (1995a, b, 1997) are also recommended, and compare various methods. The 1995 books are related. They give detailed scoring rules for several different portfolio approaches, and have the added value of software with the second book to facilitate use on the computer. For SBU comparisons we would normally use a method which has market prospects on one axis and competitive position on the other, but not the simplistic Boston Consulting pioneer matrix. For comparison of products it might be better to use one of the methods which uses life cycle stages and competitive position as the two axes. The decision should be based on what gives most insight into the company, and what facilitates communication of the findings to others. Once SBUs are plotted the matrix can be used to show a different perspective of the organisation. By adding the totals of the key financial figures of all the businesses entered in a particular cell of the matrix, it is possible to show the sources of earnings by matrix position, together with the amount of assets attributable to those businesses, and the positive or negative cash flows of each. It is also possible to make the analysis more dynamic, by indicating likely movements in the matrix position of each SBU.

Sources of Shareholder Value

The question of whether and how value is added through being part of a corporate family was addressed by Porter (1987), and it is his thinking which is largely followed here. Some additional insight was provided by Buzzell and Gale (1987), who drew their conclusions from the PIMS database.

The appraisals at business level can be used to help assess whether the corporate whole is adding or reducing shareholder value by its ownership of various SBUs. This requires grafting additional knowledge of the organisation on to various elements of the basic analysis. If value is not created by membership of the whole, the position of any or all of the businesses may be weakened, and the total business may become a takeover target. The stock market frequently values diversified organisations at less than the sum of their parts. Obviously there is a strength if shareholder value is added, a possibly fatal weakness if it is not, and an opportunity if the situation could be improved. There are at least five aspects of the creation of shareholder value that should be considered:

1. *How the centre manages.* Goold, Campbell and Alexander (1994) argue that value can be created or destroyed depending on how the parent manages. There are no black and white answers, as the skill lies in fitting the parenting style to the particular circumstances of the businesses. There is value in examining the appropriateness of the corporate planning, decision making, and control processes and systems in relation to the nature of each of the businesses.
2. *Shared resources/activities.* Map how the different businesses add value by sharing resources and activities. For example, common physical distribution facilities may give a cost and service advantage to all the businesses in the portfolio. If there

are no benefits from this aspect, is this because sharing is not possible, or because it would have a negative impact on results?

3. *Spill-over benefits like R&D.* Are businesses benefiting from inventions and technologies developed in other parts of the group (see Chapter 5). Is there a mechanism to allow such sharing to happen? Does this mechanism work well?

4. *Shared knowledge and skills.* What synergy is gained from shared knowledge: for example of markets, common customers and suppliers? Is there any transfer of skills between businesses?

5. *Shared image.* What is gained or lost from common brands and the overall image?

CONCLUSION

Corporate appraisal is complex, but we hope that we have also shown that it is important and essential. It is indeed the foundation of strategy, and the only sure way of identifying and understanding the capability of the organisation. The decisions that can emerge from it may be far reaching.

It should lead to different perceptions, and it is not enough to make it a one-time exercise. In fact the experience of the first occasion may lead to setting up systems for collecting information that was not available at the start, but which will lead to different insights in the future. This was the case with two of the organisations described earlier in the chapter, and of course with many others in our experience.

There are limitations. Organisations are dynamic, moving and evolving. An analysis of the type discussed here cannot be stretched over too long a period before conclusions are reached, because if this happens the first pieces of the puzzle may no longer be connected to the last pieces. Therefore, in practice there is need to compromise, and to concentrate on what seems to be the most important. But all this is an argument for ensuring that the appraisal is undertaken regularly.

The findings from the analysis become the foundations for strategic thinking. They may not themselves be enough to make sound strategic decisions and we would argue that there is much more to strategy than this. But we would draw an analogy with a building. A building is something different from its foundations, and it is this difference which brings admiration or dissatisfaction. But if it has no foundations it may be physically impossible to build it, and if by chance it is built on faulty foundations it has a high chance of falling down. Foundations matter.

REFERENCES

Buzzell, R. D. and Gale, B. T. 1987. *The PIMS Principles*, New York, Free Press.

Goold, M, Campbell, A. and Alexander, M. 1994. *Corporate Level Strategy: Creating Value in the Multi Business Company*, New York, Wiley.

Hussey, D. 1998. *Strategic Management: From Theory to Implementation*, 4th edn, Oxford, Butterworth-Heinemann.

Porter, M. E. 1987. From competitive advantage to corporate strategy, *Harvard Business Review*, May/June.

Segev, E. 1995a. *Corporate Strategy: Portfolio Models*, London, International Thomson/Boyd & Fraser.

Segev, E. 1995b. *Navigating by Compass*, London, International Thomson/Boyd & Fraser.

Segev, E. 1997. *Business Unit Strategy*, Chichester, Wiley.

Index